WRITERS IN WONDERLAND

WRITERS IN WONDERLAND:
Keeping Your Words Legal

Kathryn Page Camp

KP/PK Publishing

Munster, Indiana

Neither the publisher nor the author is your lawyer, and this book is not a substitute for individualized legal advice.

Printed in the United States of America.

Library of Congress Control Number: 2013906786

ISBN: 978-0-9892504-1-2

KP/PK Publishing
PO Box 3477
Munster, Indiana 46321

Cover Illustrations and Parts I, II, IV, V, VI and Appendix Illustrations by John Tenniel.

Part III Illustration by Henry Holliday.

DEDICATION

In memory of Dad Camp, who used to introduce me as "my daughter-in-law the liar—I mean the lawyer." I miss his strange sense of humor.

Table of Contents

Foreword

As a lawyer who is also a writer, the issues addressed in this book have fascinated me for a long time. Through the years other writers have asked me legal questions that I was happy to answer or, in many cases, to research and then answer. Encouragement from my fellow writers became the motivation for *Writers in Wonderland*.

There are other legal-themed writing books on the market, but they aren't always easy for non-lawyers to understand. And those that manage to limit the legalese are often boring. This book is unique among the competition because it entertains while teaching.

I wrote *Writers in Wonderland* for writers rather than lawyers, so I avoided legal terminology as much as possible. Unfortunately, the law has its own language, and some words have no good substitute. Try replacing "copyright" or "defamation" with a single word, or even a short phrase, and you will see the problem.

Still, I have tried to simplify the discussion while remaining true to basic legal principles. Lawyers may wince when I talk about renting out a copyright rather than assigning it, but the rental analogy is a good one and helps explain this complicated idea to non-lawyers. So if your lawyer uses different terms, think of this book as a paraphrase rather than a word-for-word translation.

Lawyers may also question why I spelled out most of the words in the case names. The citing convention uses abbreviations for practically every common word in existence, and some are not easily understood by people who don't make their living in the legal profession. I did, however, use the official format for the rest of each citation.

The material in this book is, by necessity, selective. If I were to discuss every case and cover every issue of interest to writers, the results would fill a library. Instead, I attempted to focus on the matters that arise most often or have the greatest impact. I also chose cases that are both informative and entertaining.

I did extensive legal research and am confident that the information in this book is accurate, but I cannot guarantee it. The law is constantly changing, and a case that is good authority today may be overturned tomorrow. Also, most legal issues covered in this book depend on state laws, and those laws vary. I have tried to keep the discussion fundamental enough to steer clear of state law differences (or to point them out when I must address them). If you have specific concerns, however, you should contact a lawyer familiar with the law in that state or subject matter.

You would not ask your family doctor to perform heart surgery, and you should not ask a lawyer who does wills and divorces to answer your tax or intellectual property (e.g., copyright, trademark) questions. Those are separate legal specialties. The resources section at the back of this book provides information on finding a lawyer with the right background.

This book is written for writers who live, work, or publish in the United States. Some principles may be similar in other countries, but the discussion is limited to U.S. law.

Fair uses of the material in this book are encouraged, and permission for other non-commercial uses will be liberally granted. The Lewis Carroll quotations and the illustrations by John Tenniel (cover, Parts I, II, IV, V, VI, and Appendices) and Henry Holiday (Part III) are in the public domain, and my use of them in this book does not change their character. See Chapter 5 for discussions of fair use and the public domain.

The language and punctuation in the Lewis Carroll quotes may seem awkward to a Twenty-First Century American, but I left it mostly untouched. There is one exception: I used the American quoting conventions to avoid confusion. This means that quotations are enclosed in double quote marks unless they involve a quote within a quote, which is enclosed in single quote marks. It also means that commas and periods are located inside the quote marks even if they are not part of the quoted materials.

The appendices include the complete text of Lewis Carroll poems that are quoted piecemeal or simply referred to in the body of the book. The poems are: "The Hunting of the Snark," "The Voice of the Lobster," "The Walrus and the Carpenter," and "You are Old, Father William."

I checked at least three different sources for each poem and Lewis Carroll quote. If there was a difference, I went with the most frequent usage.

Since this book draws heavily on Lewis Carroll's works, I included a biography in Appendix XII. The appendix also includes biographies for John Tenniel and Henry Holiday.

I cannot possibly thank everyone who helped, supported, and encouraged me as I wrote this book, but a few deserve special mention. Thanks to my husband, Roland, for supporting and encouraging me through the entire process. Thanks to my on-line critique partner, Celeste Charlene, for her painstaking critiques and to Carole King for her editing help. Critiquing thanks also go to the Highland Writers' Group, particularly leaders Gordon and Heather Stamper, Kenneth Alexander, Eldridge Brown, Cynthia Echterling, Janine Harrison, Michael Poore, Helena Qi, Nancy Stamper, and Richard Welty.

Kathryn Page Camp

Part I

How Doth the Little Crocodile
(Avoiding Lawyers)

CHAPTER ONE
Crocodiles and Fishes
(Introduction)

How doth the little crocodile
Improve his shining tail,
And pour the waters of the Nile
On every golden scale!

How cheerfully he seems to grin
How neatly spreads his claws,
And welcomes little fishes in,
With gently smiling jaws!

Lewis Carroll, "How Doth the Little Crocodile"
From *Alice in Wonderland*

Many writers see the law as a Lewis Carroll Wonderland—inside out and totally illogical. These writers would rather write than worry about legal issues. But the reality is that writers who ignore the law are the ones who are actually living in Wonderland. They blissfully swim through the crocodile's jaws into a stomach filled with defamation lawsuits, plagiarism scandals, and IRS proceedings. These situations turn writers into bait for fee-starved litigators.

Unfortunately, the courts don't always agree on the law, and sometimes very similar facts have opposite outcomes. In those cases, the best advice is to assume you would lose, so find another way to make your point.

That isn't as hard as it sounds.

Many novice writers—and even some seasoned ones—beg for lawsuits by combining laziness and ignorance of the law. Imagine you had a petite college roommate named Mandy Elfanzo who was also a champion boxer. Mandy spoke in a soft voice and wore her blond hair in a bob. So now you write your first novel, and your main character is Amanda Elendo, a petite, blond college student with a soft voice. The plot has this deceptively innocent girl picking up men at boxing matches and having sex with them. How many of your old college friends will identify the protagonist as Mandy? And will any of them wonder if she slept around with the men she met at her matches? If the connection is this easy to make, Mandy might sue you for defamation.

"I don't care," you say. "It's fiction, so she'll lose."

Wrong.

On the other hand, what if you name your protagonist Sarah Denison, make her twenty-five and dark-haired, and give her an office job during the day? Then when the deceptively innocent girl meets men and has sex with them, people wouldn't be likely to associate her with Mandy.

Or what about making the character a wimpy-looking man who is a light-weight boxing champion? Or . . . The possibilities are endless and will probably produce a better story than if you try to build it too closely around people you know.

There are times when a writer will choose to risk a lawsuit. Think about all those unauthorized biographies of living people. Still, knowing the law can make litigation less likely even then. Wouldn't you rather take a calculated risk than find yourself swimming through the jaws of a crocodile you didn't even see?

Failure to understand the copyright laws is another source of expensive lawsuits. Many of the high profile cases were filed by individuals claiming famous writers stole their ideas. But ideas can't be copyrighted, and all that the plaintiffs got was public scorn and bills for legal fees.

That leads to another reason you need to understand the law. Litigation is expensive, and the parties rarely recover their attorneys' fees even when they win. So it is usually better to avoid a lawsuit in the first place. Victory isn't sweet if your lawyer is the only one who benefits.

It isn't just defamation and copyright that could hurt you. What if you don't understand the terms of your book contract? Did you know you became an indentured servant when you signed that option clause?

Then there are those tricky tax questions. Can you deduct writing expenses when preparing your income tax forms? Do you have to pay employment taxes on your earnings?

This book will answer these questions and others that apply to writers.

In *Alice in Wonderland*, Alice found herself as a witness in the King and Queen of Hearts' court. The courtroom procedures seemed nonsensical. The queen even called for the sentence before there had been a verdict.

Earlier, Alice had learned about Father William, a lawyer who strengthened his jaws by arguing each case with his wife. Would Alice have stayed out of court if she had consulted with him first?

Of course not. The story is fantasy, after all, and the book is set in Wonderland.

For writers, however, Wonderland itself is avoidable. All it takes is a little knowledge of the law.

Reading this book will not save you from an occasional visit to Father William's law office. But it will make it less likely that you will end up in the King and Queen of Hearts' courtroom.

And isn't that worth it?

Part II

Down the Rabbit Hole
(Copyrights)

CHAPTER TWO
A Mad Tea-Party
(Copyright Background)

> "Take some more tea," the March Hare said to Alice, very earnestly.
>
> "I've had nothing yet," Alice replied in an offended tone, "so I can't take more."
>
> "You mean you can't take *less*," said the Hatter: "it's very easy to take *more* than nothing."
>
> Lewis Carroll, *Alice in Wonderland*

Lewis Carroll was a master at using words literally to change their meaning, as in the passage above. A second-class imitator who is writing a book about legal issues for writers might rework the passage this way:

> "Have a copyright," the March Hare said to Alice, very earnestly.
>
> "I've written nothing yet," Alice replied in an offended tone, "so I can't have a right to it."
>
> "You mean you can't have a *write*," said the Hatter: "it's very easy to have a *right* to nothing."

Reality is nearly as confusing. Shouldn't it be "copywrite" because it is about what people write? Or is "copyright" the better term because it deals with legal rights? The latter spelling is correct: a copyright is the right to control the copying of what you write or draw or record.

Even so, it isn't an inalienable right or even one you've earned.

Copyright isn't a reward: it's a bribe. It isn't wages for an author or artist's finished work: it's motivation to start working in the first place.

Article I, Section 8 of the United States Constitution gives Congress the power "To promote the Progress of Science and useful Arts, by securing for limited Times to Authors and Inventors the exclusive Right to their respective Writings and Discoveries."

Writing is a "useful Art." Yes, even when the writer creates garbage. Since no one knows who the next William Shakespeare is until she's written something, the rules must encourage everyone equally.

Patents, Copyrights, and Trademarks

So what does the Constitution mean by "sciences and useful arts"? The modern terminology is "intellectual property," and there are three main types: patents, copyrights, and trademarks.

A patent is the right to prohibit others from manufacturing, using, or selling your invention. Actually, it's much more complicated than that, but this simplified definition is sufficient for most purposes. While many people think in terms of physical things like machinery or medicine, the government also gives patents on new methods and processes.

Broadly defined, a trademark is a word or symbol or a combination of the two that identifies goods produced by a particular manufacturer (e.g., Nike) or services from a particular provider (e.g., FedEx). Once consumers recognize the mark, competitors may not use it on similar goods or services without the owner's consent. There are very few restrictions on a writer's use of trademarks, but a later chapter will discuss the consequences of referring to trademarked goods in a manuscript.

Copyright, on the other hand, has a huge impact on writers. In simple terms, copyright is the right to control the copying, modification, publication, performance, and public display of a creative work. For writers, it protects the original arrangement of words. This includes protection against paraphrases that are close enough to the original work for people to recognize. Copyright does not, however, protect against similar works and word arrangements that the second author came up with independently.

The history of copyright dates back to the development of the printing press, and its original use was for the written word, so spelling it "copywrite" would make sense. Over the years, however, copyright expanded to include drawings and paintings and photographs and television programs and You-Tube videos and Internet websites. As Chapter 5 explains, however, it does not allow the copyright owner to prohibit all uses of his or her creative works.

Most of our rights and responsibilities as U.S. citizens are governed by state law. So why does the Constitution elevate intellectual property rights to the federal level? Because they reach across state lines.

The Supreme Court has addressed these rights numerous times, and you may be surprised at the Court's view. Here is its description of copyright law as summarized in *Twentieth Century Music Corp. v. Aiken.* (The quote is found at 422 U.S. 151, 156 (1975), and the footnotes are omitted.)

> The immediate effect of our copyright law is to secure a fair return for an "author's" creative labor. But the ultimate aim is, by this incentive, to stimulate artistic creativity for the general public good.

In other words, a writer doesn't receive the copyright because he deserves it. He gets it as an incentive to keep writing. It's all about the public good.

But is the incentive necessary? Writing is a disease, and many writers simply can't help themselves. While the same can be said of some scientists and inventors, the extra incentive provided by Article I,

Section 8 is responsible for many important discoveries. So it is easier to explain how Section 8 works by using patents as the example.

Pharmaceutical companies developed many of today's successful medicines. These companies spent millions of dollars on research and development, and they tested many unsuccessful products before they found a successful one. If the drug companies didn't expect to recoup the millions spent on research and development, they'd probably be in a different business. And civilization might still be waiting for medicines we now take for granted.

Drug patents don't guarantee financial profits, but they take away the largest source of potential losses—competition from drug manufacturers who didn't spend any money to develop the drug but now would get a free ride. Patents are designed to provide the incentive to spend time and money developing drugs and other inventions that improve our lives, and they do this by giving an inventor a limited period during which it has almost exclusive rights to its invention.

Not all medical researchers need the motivation that Congress provides in the patent laws. Nor are all authors motivated by the benefits they receive from owning a copyright. But some are.

Although the founding fathers thought that copyrights were important enough to give Congress authority over them, the Constitution does not dictate how Congress should provide copyright protection. By using the words "for a limited time," the Constitution prohibits Congress from giving authors perpetual rights to their works, but it places no other restrictions on Congress' judgment. Congress, and Congress alone, decides how long copyright protection should last and what rights it conveys.

Copyright vs. Plagiarism

Unlike copyright, there are no federal laws regulating plagiarism. But don't the two terms mean the same thing?

No.

You plagiarize when you use someone else's material—either verbatim or by significant paraphrase—without giving the real author credit. It doesn't matter whether the material is under copyright protection: you can plagiarize works by William Shakespeare as easily as works by Stephen King. On the other hand, you can violate a copyright even if you give the author credit. If you really mess up, you can be guilty of both plagiarism and copyright violations.

A recent plagiarism controversy involved Harvard sophomore Kaavya Viswanathan and her book, _How Opal Mehta Got Kissed, Got Wild and Got a Life_. Shortly after Little Brown and Company published the novel, the _Harvard Crimson_ reported a number of similarities between passages from _Opal Mehta_ and passages in novels by Megan McCafferty. Viswanathan admitted that she was a fan of McCafferty's works and may have "accidentally" borrowed some passages, and the publisher decided to pull _Opal Mehta_ off the shelves while Viswanathan revised the book. When further allegations arose claiming that she had also borrowed passages from books by several other authors, the publisher withdrew the book from the market permanently and cancelled its contract for a second novel.

Was Viswanathan a cold-blooded plagiarist, an immature teenager whose teachers taught her it was okay to paraphrase encyclopedia entries for school reports, or an unwitting victim of her own memory? And did she plagiarize? The following table contains just a few of the disputed passages. Read them and reach your own conclusions.

Opal Mehta	*Sloppy Firsts* and *Second Helpings* by Megan McCafferty
Priscilla was my age and lived two blocks away. For the first fifteen years of my life, those were the only qualifications I needed in a best friend. We had first bonded over our mutual fascination with the abacus in a playgroup for gifted kids. But that was before freshman year, when Priscilla's glasses came off, and the first in a long string of boyfriends got on.—pg. 14	Bridget is my age and lives across the street. For the first twelve years of my life, these qualifications were all I needed in a best friend. But that was before Bridget's braces came off and her boyfriend Burke got on, before Hope and I met in our seventh-grade honors class.—*Sloppy Firsts*, pg. 7
The other HBz acted like they couldn't be more bored. They sat down at a table, lazily skimmed heavy copies of Italian *Vogue*, popped pieces of Orbit, and reapplied layers of lip gloss. Jennifer, who used to be a bit on the heavy side, had dramatically slimmed down, no doubt through some combination of starvation and cosmetic surgery. Her lost pounds hadn't completely disappeared, though; whatever extra pounds she'd shed from her hips had ended up in her bra. Jennifer's hair, which I remembered as dishwater brown and riotously curl, had been bleached Clairol 252: Never Seen in Nature Blonde. It was also so straight it looked washed, pressed and starched.—pg. 48	Throughout this conversation, Manda acted like she couldn't have been more bored. She lazily skimmed her new paperback copy of *Reviving Ophelia*—she must have read the old one down to shreds. She just stood there, popping another piece of Doublemint, or reapplying her lip gloss, or slapping her ever-present pack of Virginia Slims against her palm. [...] Her hair—usually dishwater brown and wavy—had been straightened and bleached the color of sweet corn since the last time I saw her... Just when I thought she had maxed out on hooter hugeness, it seemed that whatever poundage Sara had lost over the summer had turned up in Manda's bra.—*Second Helpings*, pg. 69

Opal Mehta	*Can You Keep a Secret?* by Sophie Kinsella
"And I'll tell everyone that in eighth grade you used to wear a 'My Little Pony' sweatshirt to school every day," I continued. Priscilla gasped. "I didn't!" she said, her face purpling again. "You did! I even have pictures," I said. "And I'll make it public that you named your dog Pythagoras..." Priscilla opened her mouth and gave a few soundless gulps. "And that you couldn't get a date to the freshman fall dance, so you had to take your cousin..." "Okay, fine!" she said in complete consternation. "Fine! I promise I'll do whatever you want. I'll talk to the club manager. Just please don't mention the sweatshirt. Please."—pg. 282	"*And* we'll tell everyone you got your Donna Karan coat from a discount warehouse shop." Jemina gasps. "I didn't!" she says, color suffusing her cheeks. "You did! I saw the carrier bag," I chime in. "*And* we'll make it public that your pearls are cultured, not real..." Jemina claps a hand over her mouth. "...and you never really cook the food at your dinner parties..." "...and that photo of you meeting Prince William is faked..." "...and we'll tell every single man you ever date from now on that all you're after is a rock on your finger!" Lissy finishes. I shoot a grateful glance at her. "OK!" says Jemina, practically in tears. "OK! I promise I'll forget all about it. I promise! Just please don't mention the discount warehouse shop. Please. Can I go now?"—pg. 350

Opal Mehta	*The Princess Diaries* by Meg Cabot
Every inch of me had been cut, filed, steamed, exfoliated, polished, painted, or moisturized. I didn't look a thing like Opal Mehta. Opal Mehta didn't own five pairs of shoes so expensive they could have been traded in for a small sailboat. She didn't wear makeup or Manolo Blahniks or Chanel sunglasses or Habitual jeans or La Perla bras. She never owned enough cashmere to make her concerned for the future of the Kazakhstani mountain goat population. I was turning into someone else.—pg. 59	There isn't a single inch of me that hasn't been pinched, cut, filed, painted, sloughed, blown dry, or moisturized. [...] Because I don't look a thing like Mia Thermopolis. Mia Thermopolis never had fingernails. Mia Thermopolis never had blond highlights. Mia Thermopolis never wore makeup or Gucci shoes or Chanel skirts or Christian Dior bras, which by the way don't even come in 32A, which is my size. I don't even know who I am anymore. It certainly isn't Mia Thermopolis. *She's turning me into someone else.*—pg. 12

Opal Mehta	"The Mail Coach," from *Haroun and the Sea of Stories* by Salman Rushdie
(Scribbled on posters) If from drink you get your thrill, take precaution, write your will. All the dangerous drug abusers end up safe as total losers.	(Road signs) If from speed you get your thrill, take precaution, make your will. All the dangerous overtakers end up safe at the undertaker's.

Plagiarism of uncopyrighted works does not violate the law. As the U.S. Supreme Court has stated, "once the patent or copyright monopoly has expired, the public may use the invention or work at will and without attribution." (*Datstar Corp. v. 20th Century Fox Film Corp.*, 539 U.S. 23, 33-34 (2003))

You may, but should you?

If you pass Shakespeare's words off as your own, he won't sue you, but your reputation as a writer will suffer. If you rely on quotes from Stephen King's books to make yours marketable, he may sue you for copyright infringement even if you tell the world that they are his words. And if you paraphrase freely and don't give him the credit, you may end up with both a copyright lawsuit and a reputation for stealing from others—a situation guaranteed to end your writing career.

It's easy to avoid plagiarizing: just give the author credit. And if you don't know who the author is, attribute it to "author unknown." Because if you try and pass someone else's words off as your own, you may be halfway across the swamp before you notice you are walking on quicksand.

CHAPTER THREE

Painting White Roses Red

(Obtaining a Copyright)

> A large rose-tree stood near the entrance of the garden: the roses growing on it were white, but there were three gardeners at it, busily painting them red.

> Lewis Carroll, *Alice in Wonderland*

The gardeners were afraid they would lose their heads if the Queen of Hearts discovered they had planted the wrong color roses. So they painted the flowers red to hide their mistake. Could they have copyrighted their handiwork? That depends on Wonderland's laws.

Change the setting to modern-day America. If a contemporary judge found that painting white flowers red had some minimal originality, the painted roses would be entitled to copyright protection. That's because Section 102(a) of the 1976 Copyright Act provides copyright protection to "original works of authorship fixed in any tangible medium of expression . . . from which they can be perceived, reproduced, or otherwise communicated." (17 U.S.C. § 102(a))

But what exactly does that mean?

Copyrighting Your Material

Obtaining a copyright is as easy as getting the material out of your head and putting it down on paper or a computer drive. The minute you put it in tangible form, it is copyrighted.

"Wait," you say, "don't I have to register it with the government?" Only if you created it before January 1, 1978. The 1976 Copyright Act, which made significant changes to copyright law, does not require registration for more recent works.

What Can Be Copyrighted?

Still, not everything gets a copyright. The material must be an original work of authorship.

The statute doesn't define "original," but the courts give the word a two-prong definition, and both prongs must be present. First, the writer/artist/composer must put individual effort into the work beyond merely copying it. Second, the material must add something to what people think of naturally. To put it another way, the material must have a small amount (and it can be very small) of creativity.

Since most people wouldn't think to paint white roses red, the gardeners' art may well be entitled to copyright protection. But what about other material?

Between the statute and the court cases, the law is well-settled that you cannot copyright the following:

- Titles, names, short phrases, and slogans (but see Chapter 16 on trademarks);

- Ideas, such as the general concept for an article or novel;

- Facts;

- Material composed entirely of information that is common property and contains no original elements (e.g., phone books); and

- Procedures, methods, systems, processes, discoveries, or devices.

Practically everything else that contains a germ of creativity and is put in tangible form (written down, typed into a computer, drawn on canvas, and so on) is copyrightable. This includes fiction, non-fiction, visual arts, and music. It also includes blog posts and works that are not intended for public dissemination, such as personal letters.

So why does a writer care about the elements that can't be copyrighted? Two reasons. First, you can use them without worrying about infringing someone else's copyright. Second, a number of writers have wasted time and money—and sometimes reputation—suing for infringement of uncopyrightable material. If you know the difference, you won't be among them.

The distinction between copyrightable and uncopyrightable material can be slight, and the courts are charged with drawing the line in individual cases.

1. Titles, names, short phrases, and slogans

Copyright protects the way you put words together but does not protect the words themselves. The fewer words you use, the greater the chances that someone else will come up with them, too. Names are a good example.

When Bernard Clare discovered that his name was the title of a book, he sued and lost. Mark Twain used the name "Eschol Sellers" in the first printing of *The Gilded Age*, and an individual he knew nothing about appeared and threatened to sue. While the allegation in these instances was defamation rather than copyright infringement, the two situations show that it is almost impossible to find a name that is completely unique and unused. This is why copyright protection does not apply to titles, names, short phrases, and slogans.

On the other hand, titles, names, short phrases, and slogans can be trademarked under the right circumstances. Trademarks are discussed in Chapter 16.

2. Ideas

Ideas and concepts cannot be copyrighted, either. That's because "what has been will be again, what has been done will be done again; there is nothing new under the sun." (Ecclesiastes 1:9, NIV) *West Side Story* is just another version of Shakespeare's *Romeo and Juliet*. It's also the same story that was played out in the feud between the Hatfields and the McCoys, the Native American legends of maidens leaping to their deaths because their parents banned their lovers, and a million real-life scenarios. There is nothing original about these plots.

Did *Jurassic Park* infringe on a series of children's books set in a man-made animal park for dinosaurs? In *Williams v. Crichton,* the court held that the idea of a theme park or zoo with live dinosaurs was not copyrightable. Nor is the story of a trial to determine whether Judas Iscariot will spend eternity in heaven or in hell. (See *Porto v. Guirgis.*)

Similarly, you can't copyright elements (called *scènes à faire*) that arise naturally from an unprotectable idea. Zoos usually have animal nurseries and uniformed workers, and complexes populated by dangerous creatures may well have electrified fences. And wouldn't you expect Caiaphas, Pontius Pilot, and Peter to testify at Judas' trial? Because these circumstances are often part of the larger idea, they are not protected.

Historical figures cannot be copyrighted, but what about purely fictional characters? Are they merely ideas, too? Courts often quote Judge Learned Hand from a 1930 case:

> If *Twelfth Night* were copyrighted, it is quite possible that a second comer might so closely imitate Sir Toby Belch or Malvolio as to infringe, but it would not be enough that for one of his characters he cast a riotous knight who kept wassail to the discomfort of the household, or a vain and foppish steward who became amorous of his mistress. These would be no more than Shakespeare's "ideas" in the play, as little capable of monopoly as Einstein's Doctrine of Relativity, or Darwin's theory of the Origin of Species. It follows that the less developed the characters, the less they can be copyrighted; that is the penalty an author must bear for marking them too indistinctly.

Nichols v. Universal Pictures Corp., 45 F.2d 119, 121 (2nd Cir. 1930) Judge Hand concluded that the characters in the plaintiff's play were too indistinct to create a copyright.

A boy with black hair and glasses is a generic character. (See *Scholastic, Inc. v. Stouffer.*) Add a lightning-shaped scar on his forehead, and you have Harry Potter.

Even when a character is distinctively drawn, however, the extent of copyright protection is not clear. In a 1954 case, Warner Brothers purchased the production rights to *The Maltese Falcon* by Dashiell Hammett. Detective Sam Spade was the main character in that movie. So when Hammett used Sam Spade in radio broadcasts, Warner Brothers sued. This case was primarily a contract matter, not a copyright one, and the Ninth Circuit Court of Appeals held that Warner Brothers' contract did not include exclusive rights to the characters. Still, the opinion stated:

> It is conceivable that the character really constitutes the story being told, but if the character is only the chessman in the game of telling the story he is not within the area of protection afforded by the copyright.
>
> . . .
>
> We conclude that even if the Owners assigned their complete rights in the copyright to the *Falcon*, such assignment did not prevent the author from using the characters used therein, in other stories. The characters were vehicles for the story told, and the vehicles did not go with the sale of the story.

Warner Bros. Pictures, Inc. v. Columbia Broadcasting System, Inc., 216 F.2d 945, 950 (9th Cir. 1954)

The Ninth Circuit recognized that a line must be drawn somewhere, but it concluded that Sam Spade was on the wrong side of the line because he was merely a vehicle for telling the story. So what does it take to move a character over to the copyrightable side of the line? The cases do not answer that question.

But all is not lost. Although character names cannot be copyrighted and the character itself may or may not be copyrightable, the words used to describe that character are.

3. Facts

There is no copyright in facts. As the U.S. Supreme Court has stated: "[F]acts do not owe their origin to an act of authorship. The distinction is one between creation and discovery: the first person to find and report a particular fact has not created the fact; he or she has merely discovered its existence." (*Feist Publications, Inc. v. Rural Telephone Service Co.*, 499 U.S. 340, 347 (1991)) Since facts are not original works of authorship, they cannot be copyrighted.

The courts have found the following to be uncopyrightable facts: telephone numbers, names, addresses, information on the current status of basketball games, recipe ingredients, quotes from third-party interviews, and historical events. Although facts cannot be copyrighted, however, the choice of words used to describe them can be.

Consider the plagiarism chart in Chapter 2 comparing *Opal Mehta* to other works of fiction. None of those quotes were copied directly from the books at issue. Instead, all of the quotes were taken from news articles. So does the chart violate the journalists' copyrights in their articles? No. Although the commentary in the articles is copyrighted, the journalists did not create the quoted material but simply used the quotes as facts, as in "*Opal Mehta* says A and the other book says B." So the journalists do not own a copyright in those quotes.

4. Material composed entirely of information that is common property and contains no original elements

As noted above, material can be copyrighted only if it is original. Telephone books, for example, take uncopyrightable elements (names, telephone numbers, addresses) and organize them based on logic rather than on creativity. Anyone producing a phone book would use the same format. After all, how useful would a white pages directory be if it was not arranged alphabetically? Or yellow pages that were not arranged by business category? These elements are not protected even if one person does all the work gathering and organizing the information and the other simply copies it. It may seem unfair, but the test is originality rather than effort.

Does this mean you will never get a copyright in a compilation of facts? The test is whether the material contains any original elements. Although you can't get a copyright in the actual facts, there are some parts of the compilation that may qualify for protection. Added text, for example. Even the selection and arrangement of facts may be protected if it contains some minimal level of creativity. So being a compilation of facts does not necessarily doom the work.

Cookbooks are a good example of compilations that are a mixture of protected and unprotected elements. Recipes are usually unprotected and the arrangement is also unprotected if it merely divides the recipes by logical categories, such as snacks, soups, salads, main courses, and desserts. On the other hand, text describing the use of a particular recipe and photographs of the various dishes may be protectable. Where this mixture occurs, the compilation as a whole is copyrighted, although the individual elements retain their status as copyrightable or uncopyrightable.

The same is true for pocket organizers. Many elements, such as blank forms and non-textual utilitarian aspects (e.g., binder pockets) are unprotectable. Instruction text is protectable. The selection, coordination and arrangement of the material may also be protectable if it contains minimal creativity. Since some of the material is subject to copyright, the compilation as a whole can be copyrighted, but the copyright does not transform the individual elements.

5. Procedures, methods, systems, processes, discoveries, or devices

Think about sweepstakes rules and instructions for preparing a recipe. There are only so many ways to tell someone to write their name and address on a sheet of paper and mail it in. Or to instruct a cook to mix ingredients together and bake them in a 350 degree oven. If that information could be copyrighted, sweepstakes and Internet recipe sites would all be at risk.

Inventions and similar devices are covered under patent law rather than copyright law, so they cannot be copyrighted, either. On the other hand, descriptions, explanations, and illustrations of those devices can be copyrighted if they meet the standard for minimal creativity.

Useful articles cannot be copyrighted, but the design elements incorporated into them can be if—and only if—these elements are not necessary to the article's function. A statuette used as the base of a lamp can be copyrighted, as can the ornamentation on a belt buckle. But the ribbon design of a bicycle rack cannot be copyrighted when the steel ribbon is the very thing that holds the bicycles in place.

What Does Copyright Protect?

U.S. copyright law gives an author the following exclusive rights:

- To reproduce the copyrighted work,
- To prepare works derived from the copyrighted work,
- To distribute copies by sale or other means,
- To perform the work publicly,
- To display the work publicly, and
- For sound recordings, to perform the work digitally.

The term "exclusive rights" is misleading because the law allows certain fair uses, which will be discussed in detail in Chapter 5. Absent a fair use, however, these rights belong exclusively to the copyright holder.

1. Reproducing the copyrighted work

This is simply the right to make copies of the work and includes the right to quote or paraphrase significant portions. If you are the copyright holder, the reproduction rights are yours to keep, assign (rent out), sell, or give away. If someone else makes copies without permission or a fair use, that person has violated your copyright.

2. Preparing works derived from the copyrighted work

The copyright law defines a derivative work as one that is "based upon one or more preexisting works, such as a translation, musical arrangement, dramatization, fictionalization, motion picture version, sound recording, art reproduction, abridgment, condensation, or any other form in which a work may be recast, transformed, or adapted." (17 U.S.C. § 101)

The copyright holder has the exclusive right to create derivative works or to authorize someone else to do so. A derivative work is separate from the original and receives its own copyright.

Movies based on novels are common examples of derivative works. So are children's books taken from movies, as when The Walt Disney Company hires someone to create a picture book with the same story line and cartoon images as its version of *Cinderella* or *The Lady and the Tramp*. Photographs can be derivatives of their subjects, meaning that a picture of a sculpture can be an infringement of the sculptor's exclusive right to prepare derivative works. An edited version of a television production is a derivative work, as are revised song lyrics.

So can a non-fiction work based on fiction be a derivative work? *Welcome to Twin Peaks: a Complete Guide to Who's Who and What's What* was an unauthorized description of the television show "Twin Peaks." Although it purported to be a guide to the show, it was essentially an elaborate recounting of the plot rather than a commentary. Because of that, the 2nd Circuit Court of Appeals characterized the book as an abridgment, which is included in the list of derivative works.

A district court took a different approach to an encyclopedia, or lexicon, based on the *Harry Potter* books. There, the judge refused to classify the lexicon as a derivative work. "By condensing, synthesizing, and reorganizing the preexisting material in an A-to-Z reference guide, the Lexicon does not recast the material in another medium to retell the story of Harry Potter, but instead gives the copyrighted material another purpose." (*Warner Bros. Entertainment Inc. v. RDR Books*, 575 F.Supp.2d 513, 539 (S.D.N.Y. 2008)) The difference appears to be that *Welcome to Twin Peaks* was essentially a summary that could replace the need to see the show, while the *Harry Potter* lexicon supplemented the books.

As will become evident in future chapters, however, the second work does not have to be a derivative in order to infringe the original work's copyright. In fact, the judge held that the lexicon infringed the *Harry Potter* copyrights for other reasons.

3. Distributing copies by sale or other means

The copyright holder's exclusive right to distribute copies should be self-explanatory, but it is still misunderstood. Some teachers seem to believe that distributing material for classroom use is always permitted, but they are wrong. As discussed in Chapter 5, the fair use doctrine allows limited copying and distribution under certain circumstances. Even in an educational setting, however, wholesale copying and distribution of significant portions of copyrighted material violate the copyright holder's exclusive rights.

4. Performing the work publicly, displaying the work publicly, and performing the work digitally

These rights should also be self-explanatory. The copyright holder's permission is required before putting on a public performance of a play or ballet, showing a movie to a large group of people, or displaying a piece of art in a public place. The copyright holder has the right to control the digital performance of the copyrighted material as well as the in-person performance.

The statute defines a public performance or display as one "at a place open to the public or at any place where a substantial number of persons outside of a normal circle of a family and its social acquaintances is gathered." (17 U.S.C. § 101) The definition also includes transmissions that members of the public are capable of receiving at different times or places. So if you put copyrighted material on your website or blog, you had better have permission.

Copyright Registration

Since the copyright exists from the moment the work is put into tangible form, why spend the time and money to register it?

First, registration provides a record that you created the material. Registering your work isn't foolproof, though. If you claim that someone stole it, that person could still show that he or she created the material independently.

Although registration may discourage people who intend to steal your work, it is unlikely to stop someone who uses your work out of ignorance. The easiest way to solve that problem is free: just add a copyright notice. You don't have to register the material or even publish it to do that.

The biggest benefits of registration don't arise until you sue someone for infringement, but then they can be huge. If the work was created and first published in the U.S. and you want to sue for copyright infringement in a U.S. court, you can't even file a lawsuit until you have registered the copyright.

So, you say, I'll save my money until someone infringes the copyright, and then I'll register it before suing." There is no time limit on when you can register a copyright, so you could do it that way. But here is the advantage of not waiting: as discussed in Chapter 4, if you register the copyright before the infringement occurs (or no later than three months after publication), you have a greater number of legal remedies.

One other advantage of registration is international. If your work is registered, you can record the registration with the U.S. Customs Service and receive some protection against infringing copies that are smuggled into the U.S. from other countries. And most authors would love to be popular enough to deal with that concern.

The copyright in a collective work, such as a newspaper or magazine, only applies to the work as a whole and not to its individual components. Unless done as a work for hire or under a contract that assigns the copyright to the publisher, the authors retain the copyrights for their articles. This means that the authors are responsible for filing separate registrations for those articles.

Derivative works also require their own registrations. The copyright owner of a derivative work must register it before suing for infringement of the derivative work, and this is true even if the same person owns the copyright in both. Registering the original work is not enough.

This is not a how-to book, nor is it a primer on registration. If you want to know more about registering a copyright, the United States Copyright Office has a number of helpful publications that are available at www.copyright.gov.

When you publish a book or distribute it widely, you should register it. For smaller pieces like blog posts and for books still seeking a publisher, weigh the time and expense involved against the likelihood that someone will steal your material and the potential damage from such a theft. Only you can decide where the scales tip.

Joint Authorship

Do all three gardeners get equal credit for their creation? Or, to put it in other terms, if two or more people are involved in creating a work, are they all authors?

Not necessarily.

The 1976 Copyright Act defines a joint work as one "prepared by two or more authors with the intention that their contributions be merged into inseparable or interdependent parts of a unitary whole." (17 U.S.C. §101) A play or novel is often a unitary whole, since you cannot split it up easily without destroying its worth. On the other hand, lyrics and music are separable, so the lyricist and the composer own separate copyrights in their contributions rather than a joint one in the entire song.

Each joint author has an undivided interest in the entire work. Both authors have to consent to a contract that gives a publisher the exclusive right to publish the book. But either author can rent out the publishing rights on a non-exclusive basis, and no consent is required as long as the other author receives his or her share of the proceeds. These principles apply to all exclusive rights that come with copyright ownership.

The mere fact that two or more people have contributed to a unified work does not make them joint authors. The courts have recognized two additional requirements for joint authorship. First, the person claiming joint authorship must have made a copyrightable contribution. Factual research, for example, is not copyrightable, so a person who provides extensive factual research is not a joint author.

Second, both contributors must intend it to be a joint work, and this intent must exist at the time the work is created. When the New York Theatre Workshop (NYTW) agreed to produce Jonathan Larson's musical *Rent*, the workshop director urged Larson to hire help with the storyline and narrative structure of the script. After some initial resistance, Larson agreed to let NYTW hire Lynn Thomson as a "dramaturge," and she spent significant time with Larson working on the script.

The court did not have to decide whether Thomson's contributions were copyrightable since the evidence showed that Larson never intended Thomson to be a coauthor. Larson was billed as the only author on each version of the script; he retained sole approval right over any changes; and he entered into the NYTW contract on his own without any reference to Thomson. Based on this information, the court decided that Larson was the sole author of *Rent*.

"That isn't fair," you cry. "If I put time and effort into a work, I should share in the copyright." If that's the payment you require for your contribution, get it in writing. The author may assign you some of his or her exclusive rights. More likely, however, the author will share royalties or simply pay you a lump sum for your work. If you don't like the compensation arrangements, you don't have to take on the project.

Work for Hire

Unfortunately for the gardeners, the rose tree was probably a work for hire rather than a joint work. As a work for hire, they would have no ownership interest in the copyright.

Federal law gives the copyright to the author. In most cases, that's the person who wrote the manuscript. But the definition of "author" changes if the material is what copyright law calls a "work made for hire."

So what is a work for hire? The statute creates two categories. The first is simply "a work prepared by an employee within the scope of his or her employment." (17 U.S.C. § 101) If you are a staff journalist writing articles for the newspaper that employs you, those articles are works-for-hire. You may be the writer, but your employer is the author for copyright purposes. And since the Queen of Hearts employed the gardeners to work with her roses, they are not the authors of their creation.

The line gets blurry when the writer is working on his or her own time but using the employer's equipment, facilities, or resources, or when the project is related to the work the writer does for the employer. If a college professor writes her memoir on school premises or if publication is a requirement for continued employment, that memoir could be a work for hire. In those situations, the writer should try to get the employer to agree—in writing—that the work is not within the scope of the writer's employment.

How you label your relationship doesn't matter. If you are billed as a "freelance correspondent" or an "independent contractor" but are required to work a certain number of hours every week and are paid for vacations and sick days, you are probably an employee rather than an independent contractor. It isn't always easy to draw the line, but the more you look like a traditional employee, the more likely it is that the writing you do as part of the relationship is a work for hire.

You don't have to be an employee to create a work for hire, however. That's because there is a second category for certain commissioned works.

To determine if a work fits into this second category, ask yourself the following three questions. If you answer "yes" to all of them, it is a work for hire and the person who commissioned it is the author. If even one answer is "no," as the writer you are also the author.

(1) Was the work specially ordered or commissioned? In other words, did someone ask you to write it? If you did the work on assignment, it may be a work for hire. If you wrote it on your own initiative and followed a normal submission process, it is not.

(2) Was it created "for use as a contribution to a collective work, as a part of a motion picture or other audiovisual work, as a translation, as a supplementary work, as a compilation, as an instructional text, as a test, as answer material for a test, or as an atlas"? Magazines and newspapers are collective works. A novel is not a collective work, but a single book containing four novellas is.

(3) Have the parties signed a written agreement calling it a work for hire or a work made for hire?

If the material is a work for hire (either because you are an employee or because you answered all three questions in the affirmative), does that mean you can't use it? The answer depends on your agreement with the legal author. Your employer may let you republish the material for certain purposes or under certain conditions, but ALWAYS get it in writing. The same is true for a commissioned work. See what you can negotiate, and put it in writing.

Should you enter into a work-for-hire arrangement? Weigh what you get out of it against what you give up, and then make your own call.

Now you know what can be copyrighted and who owns the copyright. But what happens if someone violates your copyright? The next chapter answers that question.

CHAPTER FOUR
Fighting the Serpent
(Copyright Litigation)

As there seemed to be no chance of getting her hands up to her head, she tried to get her head down to them, and was delighted to find that her neck would bend about easily in any direction, like a serpent. She had just succeeded in curving it down into a graceful zigzag, and was going to dive in among the leaves, which she found to be nothing but the tops of the trees under which she had been wandering, when a sharp hiss made her draw back in a hurry: a large pigeon had flown into her face, and was beating her violently with its wings.

"Serpent!" screamed the Pigeon.

"I'm *not* a serpent!" said Alice indignantly. "Let me alone!"

Lewis Carroll, *Alice in Wonderland*

When two works are similar, how do you know whether a serpent or an innocent bystander wrote the newer work? And if there really is a serpent in your path, what can you do about it?

Did Someone Copy?

"Copy" is an important part of the term "copyright." A copyright gives the owner the right to prevent others from copying the work—with some exceptions discussed in the next chapter—but it does not prevent others from coming up with the same information independently. To win a lawsuit for copyright infringement, the person who claims that his copyright was infringed has to prove both (1) that he or she owns a copyright in the work that was allegedly infringed and (2) that the other person copied it.

The first element is usually easy to prove. The second is not.

For simplicity, this book refers to the person who claims that her copyright was violated as the "plaintiff" and the person who is accused of the violation as the "defendant." Those are the roles that the parties most often play in a lawsuit, and using them makes the discussion easier to follow. In real life, however, the person who is claiming a copyright violation can be the defendant and the person who is accused of the violation can be the plaintiff.

Similarly, this book refers to the work that has allegedly been stolen from as the "original" work and the one that supposedly stole from it as the "infringing" work. These labels aren't always accurate in real life cases, but they make the discussion easier to follow.

So how do you know whether one work was copied from another? There are two types of evidence: direct evidence and circumstantial evidence. For copyright cases, the most common type of direct evidence is where the infringing work actually quotes from the original work. In other cases, however, the inference of copying relies on indirect, or circumstantial, evidence. In other words, the circumstances make copying more likely than not.

That's another two-pronged test.

To show copying, the plaintiff must prove that (1) the defendant had access to the original work **and** (2) the two works are substantially similar. If the plaintiff meets this test, it becomes the defendant's burden to show that she created the infringing work independently or that her use was fair. If the defense is successful, the word label "infringing" becomes a lie and the defendant wins the case.

But these defenses are irrelevant unless the plaintiff has met its test.

You can prove access in various ways. For example, you might be able to show that you sent the original manuscript to the individual who wrote the infringing work or to the company that published it. Or maybe your book was published first or posted on the Internet where anyone could see it.

Failure to prove access is not always fatal to a copyright case, however. It just raises the stakes on the second element. If the plaintiff can show that the defendant had access to the original work, the standard for the second element is "substantial similarity." If the plaintiff can't show access, the second element becomes "striking similarity," meaning that it is highly unlikely two people could have come up with wording so alike.

While quotations are themselves evidence of copying, the courts sometimes treat them as part of the substantial similarity analysis. To avoid confusion, this book will do the same.

The flow chart on the next page shows how the litigation process works.

Substantial Similarity—A Quiz

So how do you know if two works are substantially similar?

The substantial similarity test applies to fiction, non-fiction, visual arts, and music. It is neither a one-size-fits-all nor a mathematical test, and not all courts figure it the same way. In the end, it is a subjective determination based on objective information. Not quite "I know it when I see it," but close.

How well do you know it when you see it? Take the quiz located after the chart. The earlier work is described first, followed by the one that may—or may not—have been based on it.

Copyright Litigation

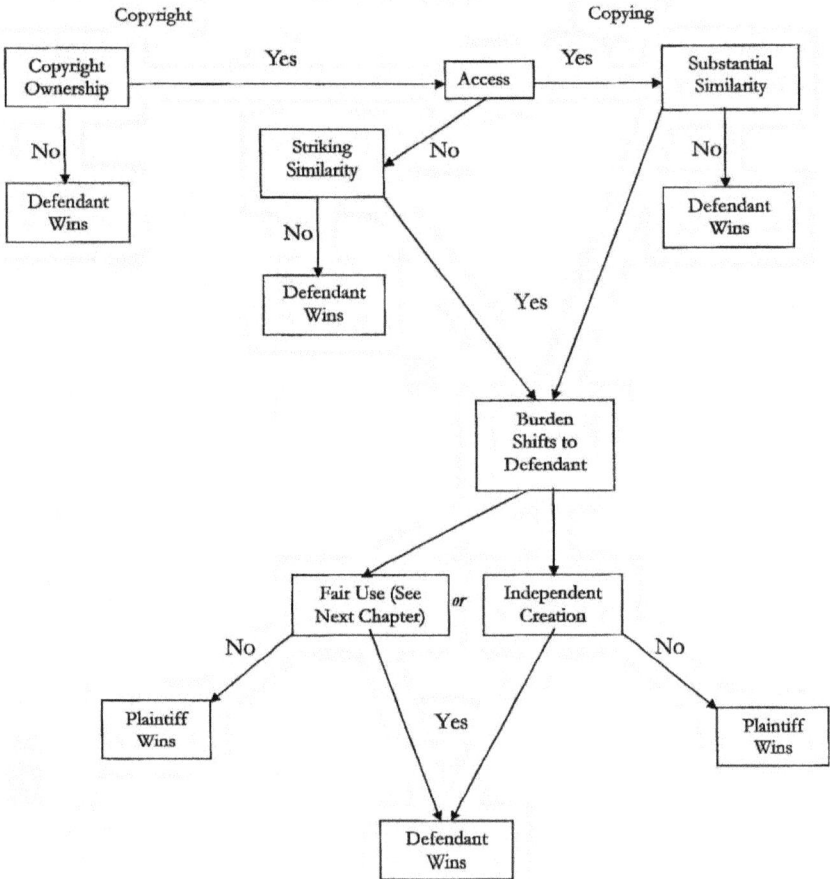

Copyright   Copying

```
Copyright                 Yes                        Yes       Substantial
Ownership  ─────────────────────► Access ──────────────►  Similarity

   │ No                    Striking      No                    │ No
   ▼                       Similarity                          ▼
Defendant                      │ No                       Defendant
Wins                           ▼                          Wins
                           Defendant
                           Wins            Yes

                              Burden
                              Shifts to
                              Defendant

                  Fair Use (See   or   Independent
                  Next Chapter)        Creation
           No                                        No
      Plaintiff              Yes                      Plaintiff
      Wins                                            Wins
                           Defendant
                           Wins
```

NOTE: A showing of **either** fair use **or** independent creation is sufficient to defeat a claim of copyright infringement.

(1) Is the illustrated children's magazine story "The Most Beautiful
    Woman in the World" substantially similar to the children's
    picture book *My Mother is the Most Beautiful Woman in the World*?

My Mother is The Most Beautiful Woman in the World

This thirty-five page book begins by describing life in the
Ukraine as lived by a Russian father, mother, and six-year-old
daughter. It shows the family harvesting wheat and the mother and
daughter preparing distinctively Russian dishes for an upcoming
feast day. About halfway through the book the girl becomes
separated from her parents. After she describes her mother as the
most beautiful woman in the world, the local leaders send for the
best candidates, but none is her mother. Then a homely woman
approaches the crowd and is reunited with her daughter. The village
leader notes that we don't love people because they are beautiful: we
see them as beautiful because we love them.

One of the illustrations shows the reunion between the girl and
her mother.

"The Most Beautiful Woman in the World"

This two-page story opens with a little boy crying in a field
because he has lost his mother. After he describes her as the most
beautiful woman in the world, the village leader gathers all of the
beautiful women from the surrounding villages. Then an old,
unattractive woman shows up and claims the boy as her son,
showing that beauty is in the eye of the beholder (although the story
does not use those words).

One of the illustrations shows the reunion between the girl and
her mother.

Although the story doesn't say where it takes place, the
illustrations show details of African village life.

(2) Is the novel *The DaVinci Code* substantially similar to the novel
    Daughter of God?

Daughter of God

As the novel opens, a former Nazi sends for art assessor Zoe
Ridgeway and her husband, Seth. The dying man asks Zoe to help
him return his vast art collection to the Jews he stole it from during
World War II.

The dying man also provides information about a second
Messiah who lived during the fourth century A.D. The second
Messiah was a woman named Sophia, who performed great miracles
until the Roman Church murdered her and her followers. Centuries
later, the Church discovered her empty shroud and hid it.

The Russians want to find the shroud and use it to blackmail
the Russian Orthodox Church. When they learn that Zoe knows
something, they kidnap her.

Learning that his wife has disappeared, Seth discovers a clue in a
painting the old Nazi had sent to Zoe. With the help of a
government agent, Seth finds and rescues his wife.

The painting hides an account number and safe deposit box key,
and the safe deposit box contains instructions for finding Sophia's
empty shroud in a booby-trapped salt mine.

After fighting gun battles at various locations and dodging booby-
traps and villains in the salt mine, Seth, Zoe, and the government
agent find the shroud. The agent shows his true colors as he steals it
and takes it to the Cardinal, who intends to use it to blackmail the
Pope into stepping down. But the Cardinal's home burns as he tries
to save the shroud from the fire, and all that is left of the shroud
and the building is a portion of the floor in the shape of a woman.

The DaVinci Code

The curator of the Louvre Museum is murdered by a member of a devout Catholic sect. Before dying, the curator leaves a message for his granddaughter, Sophie, asking her to locate Professor Robert Langdon. The curator has left clues directing them to a daVinci painting and the key to a safe deposit box. The safe deposit box contains a stone cryptex that can only be opened with a password.

The curator has been the Grand Master of a secret society charged with keeping the secret of the Holy Grail. The secret is that Jesus married Mary Magdalene, they had children, and their bloodline continues.

Robert and Sophie hook up with historian Sir Leigh Teabing. The three look for clues to the password that will unlock the cryptex, which they believe holds the secret to the location of the Holy Grail.

Sir Teabing is obsessed with finding the Holy Grail and releasing it to the public, and Robert and Sophie discover he was instrumental in the curator's murder. As Robert throws the cylinder into the air to destroy it, Sir Teabing is arrested by the police.

It turns out that Robert has already discovered the password and removed the contents of the cylinder—another riddle. Then Sophie's grandmother reveals that Sophie is a descendant of Jesus and Mary Magdalene.

Although Robert has figured out the last piece of the puzzle, the book ends without his pursuing it.

(3) Is the novel *60 Years Later: Coming Through the Rye* substantially
    similar to the novel *The Catcher in the Rye?*

The Catcher in the Rye

Sixteen-year-old Holden Caulfield has been kicked out of yet
another boarding school just a few days before he is due home for
Christmas vacation. Instead of going straight home, he checks into a
hotel and spends the next three days wandering around New York
City.

The story is told from Holden's first-person point of view. As
the judge describes it, Holden is "a sarcastic, often uncouth
protagonist who relies heavily on slang, euphemisms, and
colloquialisms, makes constant digression and asides, refers to
readers in the second person, constantly assures the reader that he is
being honest and that he is giving them the truth." Holden is also
rebellious, depressed, and has trouble connecting with people.

During his wanderings in New York, Holden almost has sex but
ultimately decides not to, finds himself drawn to Central Park,
ponders where the ducks go during the winter when the ice freezes,
stands on a hill next to a cannon while watching a sporting
competition, and thinks about the metaphor that life is a game.

Holden has a vision of himself saving little children who are
playing in a field of rye. His ambition in life is to catch them as they
run toward or over a cliff.

When the book ends (and at the beginning) the reader is given
hints that Holden is currently in a mental institution. He expects to
attend a new boarding school in the fall.

---

60 Years Later: Coming Through the Rye

"Mr. C" is seventy-six years old and living in a nursing home. During the course of the story it becomes clear that he has the same memories, acquaintances, and family as Holden Caulfield, the hero of *The Catcher in the Rye*.

The story is told from Mr. C's first-person point of view. As the judge describes it, Mr. C is "a sarcastic, often uncouth protagonist who relies heavily on slang, euphemisms, and colloquialisms, makes constant digression and asides, refers to readers in the second person, constantly assures the reader that he is being honest and that he is giving them the truth." Mr. C is also rebellious, depressed, and has trouble connecting with people.

Mr. C leaves the nursing home and spends time in New York City. While there, he almost has sex but ultimately decides not to, finds himself drawn to Central Park, ponders where the ducks go during the winter when the ice freezes, stands on a hill next to a cannon while watching a sporting competition, and thinks about the metaphor that life is a game.

Mr. C has a vision of children playing in a park. A child lands in his arms and he runs through the rye and over a cliff. When he lands, he sees that he is holding himself.

When the book ends, Mr. C is in a different institution than the one he left.

(4) Is the book *Seinfeld Aptitude Test* substantially similar to the TV show *Seinfeld*?

Seinfeld TV Show

Seinfeld is a half-hour situational comedy about a group of friends. Its main star, Jerry Seinfeld, uses his own name and profession in the show, although the situations are fictional.

By the time *The Seinfeld Aptitude Test* was published, the TV show had aired 86 episodes.

Seinfeld Aptitude Test

The Seinfeld Aptitude Test is a 132-page trivia quiz book for fans of the *Seinfeld* TV show. It contains 643 questions that each refer to a particular moment in a *Seinfeld* episode.

There is at least one question from each of 84 episodes. Forty-one questions include dialogue, and 20 come from a single episode ("The Cigar Show Indian"). Depending on who does the math, the book includes somewhere between 3.6% and 5.6% of that single episode.

---

(5) Is the cookbook *Deceptively Delicious: Simple Secrets to Get Your Kids Eating Good Food* substantially similar to the cookbook *The Sneaky Chef: Simple Strategies for Hiding Healthy Food in Kids' Favorite Meals*?

The Sneaky Chef

This cookbook includes thirteen different methods for sneaking healthy food into children. Pureeing is one of the thirteen.

The recipes are divided into five sections: breakfast, lunch, snacks, dinner, treats. Each recipe includes comments and nutritional information. One or more icons by the recipe show which of the thirteen methods it uses. The sneaky ingredients are printed in gray, and the book primarily uses muted colors.

The cookbook discusses child behavior, food philosophy, and parenting. It also includes several pages of photos of prepared dishes.

Deceptively Delicious

This cookbook provides recipes for hiding pureed fruits and vegetables in foods children like. It also contains some general cooking and nutritional information.

The recipes are divided into three sections: breakfast, mealtime, and dessert. Each recipe is accompanied by a drawing of the pureed fruit or vegetable it contains, and most are supplemented with a short comment or tip. Bright colors give the book a cheerful look.

Most of the dishes are shown in color photographs. Some photographs include a member of the Seinfeld family with that person's comments.

(6) Is the rap song "D.O.G. in Me" substantially similar to the rap
    song "Atomic Dog"?

"Atomic Dog"

   The song uses the refrain "bow wow wow, yippie yo, yippie
yea." It also repeats the word "dog" in a low tone of voice at regular
intervals and includes rhythmic panting.

"D.O.G. in Me"

   The song uses the refrain "bow wow wow, yippie yo, yippie
yea." It also repeats the word "dog" in a low tone of voice at regular
intervals and includes rhythmic panting.

   These elements are only a portion of the song, which appears to
have a different theme, mood, and tone from "Atomic Dog."

Substantial Similarity—The Answers

The courts start by eliminating all of the unprotectable elements. The basic theme or plot is an idea, and you can't copyright an idea. As mentioned in the last chapter, you also can't copyright *scènes à faire*—those elements that arise naturally from that theme or plot. That's why the law takes these elements out of the substantial similarity analysis.

In the following cases, the plaintiff's copyright ownership in the original work and the defendant's access to that work have either been established or are assumed for the limited purpose of reaching the question of "substantial similarity." And unless that question is answered "yes," the defendant has no need to prove fair use or independent creation. Although these cases may raise other issues, the following discussion is limited to the question of whether the works are substantially similar.

Here are the answers to the quiz.

(1) **The illustrated children's story "The Most Beautiful Woman in the World" IS NOT substantially similar to the children's picture book *My Mother is the Most Beautiful Woman in the World*.** (*Reyher v. Children's Television Workshop*, 533 F.2d 87 (2nd Cir. 1976))

The Second Circuit Court of Appeals held that the overall story line is an unprotectable concept or idea and the remaining similarities are *scènes à faire*. When a child is lost, it is natural for adults to help the child find his or her parents and for the family to have a loving reunion when they are reunited. It is also natural for a child to think of his or her mother as the most beautiful woman in the world.

As the court put it, "[The] book presents a picture of family life in the Russian Ukraine and develops the characters of the little girl and her mother. The [magazine] story is barren of meaningful setting or character development in an attempt to present its theme. The two stories are not similar in mood, details or characterization." (*Reyher v.*

Children's Television Workshop, 533 F.2d 87, 92 (2d Cir. 1976)) Therefore, the two stories are not substantially similar.

(2) **The novel *The DaVinci Code* IS NOT substantially similar to the novel *Daughter of God*.** (*Brown v. Perdue*, No. 04 Civ. 7417, 2005 WL 1863673, 76 U.S.P.Q.2d 1012 (S.D.N.Y., 2005))

According to the judge, the concept and feel of the two novels are very different. *Daughter of God* is an action thriller filled with gun fights and a perilous journey through a salt mine while *The DaVinci Code* is an intellectual treasure hunt based on codes and hidden messages. The judge also said the plots were different, with *Daughter of God* focusing on a husband's search for his kidnapped wife while *The DaVinci Code* focuses on uncovering the secret in the cryptex. Finally, the judge found little similarity in the characters, sequence, pace, and setting of the two books.

(3) **The novel *60 Years Later: Coming Through the Rye* IS substantially similar to the novel *The Catcher in the Rye*.** (*Salinger v. Colting*, 641 F.Supp.2d 250 (S.D.N.Y. 2009), *rev'd*, 607 F.3d 68 (2nd Cir. 2010))

J.D. Salinger believed that *60 Years Later* infringed his copyright in *The Catcher in the Rye*, so he sued the author and publisher and asked for an injunction. An injunction is a legal order prohibiting someone from doing something. In this case, Salinger wanted the order to prohibit Colting and his publishers from producing and selling *60 Years Later*.

One of the requirements for an injunction is to show that the copyright owner is likely to succeed on the merits of the case. That means Salinger had to show substantial similarity. He also had to refute Colting's fair use defense. The district court judge briefly stated that *60 Years Later: Coming Through the Rye* was substantially similar to *The Catcher in the Rye*, but she spent the bulk of the decision discussing fair use. Still, her discussion of the fair use factors makes it clear that she found *60 Years Later* to be not only substantially similar but also basically the same story with an older protagonist. Because the judge felt that Salinger was likely to prove copyright infringement, she granted him a preliminary injunction.

This happened early in the case. The Second Circuit Court of Appeals later reversed the preliminary injunction but did not disturb the judge's finding that Salinger was likely to succeed on the merits. An educated guess says that a trial would have reached the same conclusion on substantial similarity and Salinger would have won the case. No one will ever know, however. Salinger died and his executors settled the case before it went any farther.

(4) The book *Seinfeld Aptitude Test* IS substantially similar to the TV show *Seinfeld*. (*Castle Rock Entertainment v. Carol Publishing Group*, 150 F.3d 132 (2nd Cir. 1998))

The test for substantial similarity changes somewhat when comparing works in different genres, such as fiction and non-fiction. In this case, the Second Circuit looked at how much creative expression the aptitude test had copied from the TV show, holding that the copied portions must be both quantitatively and qualitatively significant when compared with the original work.

Plaintiffs met the first prong because the aptitude test borrowed a significant percentage of the expression in the TV show. They met the second prong because that expression was protectable. As the Second Circuit stated, "The SAT did not copy from *Seinfeld* unprotected facts, but, rather, creative expression." (*Castle Rock Entertainment v. Carol Publishing Group*, 150 F.3d 132, 138-139 (2nd Cir. 1998))

Another case involving a non-fiction book based on fictional works had a similar result. Steven Vander Ark was a huge fan of J.K. Rowling's *Harry Potter* stories, so he prepared an online encyclopedia—or lexicon—of the people, places, and things from the series. Neither

Rowling, her publishers, nor the company that purchased the movie rights objected to the website. They even said good things about it.

Then RDR Books approached Vander Ark and asked him to write a print version of the lexicon. Vander Ark was hesitant for two reasons. First, he had copyright concerns. Second, he was a true fan and did not want to do anything that Rowling might object to. However, the owner of RDR Books assured Vander Ark that neither of these concerns was valid and even wrote the contract so that the publisher would indemnify the author against a copyright lawsuit—the opposite of the normal clause.

Vander Ark wrote the book and RDR began advertising its upcoming release. When Rowling became aware of it, her attorneys asked the company to stop publication. RDR's president did not cooperate, and Rowling sued.

While most of the case revolved around fair use, the judge first found that the two works were substantially similar. In regard to the quantitative component of the test, the judge stated: "The Lexicon draws 450 manuscript pages worth of material primarily from the 4,100-page *Harry Potter* series. Most of the Lexicon's 2,437 entries contain direct quotations or paraphrases, plot details, or summaries of scenes from one or more of the *Harry Potter* novels." (*Warner Bros. Entertainment, Inc. v. RDR Books*, 575 F.Supp.2d 513, 535 (S.D.N.Y. 2008) (footnote omitted)) As to the qualitative component, the judge noted that the lexicon drew its content from Rowling's original, creative expression.

These cases do not mean that preparing reference materials about fictional works will always violate the copyrights on the original materials. If Vander Ark's lexicon had used more generic descriptions of Rowling's characters, places, and things, RDR might have won the case. Of course, the lexicon would also have been less useful.

The fictional nature of the original work was an important element in both the Seinfeld and the Harry Potter cases. Substantial similarity is harder to prove when the original work is nonfiction.

Mark Landsberg prepared a strategy book for winning at Scrabble and asked the company that owned the game's trademark to let him use it in his book. The company asked Landsberg to send in a copy of the book for review. When he did, the company sent it to its own Scrabble expert. Landsberg didn't receive a response from the company, so he requested his manuscript back. He received it shortly before the company produced a different strategy handbook, which contained a chapter on Scrabble written by the company's expert.

The district court held that the company acted in bad faith and intentionally held on to Landsberg's book while using it to prepare its own strategy materials. The judge found that the company had violated Landsberg's copyright in the process.

The Ninth Circuit Court of Appeals reversed the district court's legal findings. As the Ninth Circuit put it, "One consequence of the policy in favor of free use of ideas is that the degree of substantial similarity required to show infringement varies according to the type of work and the ideas expressed in it." (*Landsberg v. Scrabble Crossword Game Players, Inc.*, 736 F.2d 485, 488 (9th Cir. 1984)) The decision went on to say that authors of factual works—as this one was—have limited ways to say the same thing, so those works need to be virtually identical before copyright infringement occurs. Then it found that the two works were not substantially similar under that test. Therefore, the company was not guilty of copyright infringement.

(5) The cookbook *Deceptively Delicious: Simple Secrets to Get Your Kids Eating Good Food* **IS NOT** substantially similar to the cookbook *The Sneaky Chef: Simple Strategies for Hiding Healthy Food in Kids' Favorite Meals.* (*Lapine v. Seinfeld*, No. 08 Civ. 128, 209 WL 2902584, 92 U.S.P.Q.2d 1428 (S.D.N.Y. 2009), *aff'd* 375 Fed. Appx. 81 (2d Cir. 2010))

This case involves a lawsuit brought by a classically trained chef against a lay cook who also happened to be Jerry Seinfeld's wife. The author of *The Sneaky Chef* had submitted her cookbook proposal to HarperCollins, which rejected it. HarperCollins subsequently published Jessica Seinfeld's *Deceptively Delicious*, and the chef sued.

As noted in Chapter 3, recipes cannot be copyrighted. Neither can an idea such as camouflaging vegetables in children's favorite foods. General organization and basic information on cooking styles and measurements are common to most cookbooks. Therefore, the court ignored these elements when comparing the total concept and feel of the two books.

As the judge described it, *The Sneaky Chef* covers thirteen methods for sneaking healthy ingredients into children's food, is printed in muted colors, and is dry and text-heavy with a lecturing tone. Seinfeld's *Deceptively Delicious*, on the other hand, centers around one method for hiding fruits or vegetables in children's food, is bright and cheerful, and focuses on the recipes—providing simple, step-by-step instructions for busy parents. Therefore, the judge found that *Deceptively Delicious* is not substantially similar to *The Sneaky Chef*.

(6) The rap song "D.O.G. in Me" IS substantially similar to the rap song "Atomic Dog." (*Bridgeport Music, Inc. v. UMG Recordings, Inc.*, 585 F.3d 267 (6th Cir. 2009))

In this case, the Sixth Circuit Court of Appeals recognized that the traditional substantial similarity analysis is not a good fit when a small fragment of the work is copied into a new piece with a different overall theme or concept than the original work. The court held that, in this situation, copying even a small amount may be enough to find substantial similarity if the copied material is an integral part of the original piece. Since the bow wow refrain and the use of the other elements were integral parts of "Atomic Dog," the court found that "D.O.G. in Me" was substantially similar.

In another case, the question was whether the theme from *E.T.* was substantially similar to an earlier composition titled "Joy." On a pre-trial motion, the district court judge decided that it was not. However, substantial similarity is normally a question for the trier of fact—usually a jury—and cannot be decided as a pre-trial motion if reasonable persons could disagree on the answer. Since the Ninth Circuit Court of Appeals felt that reasonable people could disagree, it sent the case back for a jury trial. As the appeals court stated, "Even if a copied portion be relatively small in proportion to the entire work, if qualitatively important, the finder of fact may properly find substantial similarity." (*Baxter v. MCA, Inc.*, 812 F.2d 421, 425 (9th Cir. 1987))

The case went to trial, and the jury found that the copied portion was not sufficiently original to "Joy" to be copyrighted, so "Theme from E.T." did not infringe the copyright for "Joy." This time, the Ninth Circuit affirmed the finding.

Remedies for Copyright Infringement

The most common remedies for copyright infringement are actual damages and profits, statutory damages, and attorneys' fees. Some cases also result in an injunction against publishing the infringing work.

Actual damages are available even if you registered the copyright after the infringement occurred. They are just what they say: the amount of additional money you would have made but for the infringement, minus expenses you would have incurred. You can also get any profits the infringer made from the infringement if they weren't part of the actual damage calculation. On the other hand, the infringer may be entitled to retain some of its profits if it can prove that those profits are the result of its own efforts or reputation.

If you registered your copyright before the infringement occurred, you may choose to take statutory damages instead of actual damages. You cannot get both, however.

You can receive statutory damages even if the infringement did not affect your profits, so they are a good choice if your actual damages are minimal or hard to prove. The statute sets a minimum and a maximum amount for infringement of any one work, and the judge decides how much to award within that range. At the time of this writing, the range was $750-$30,000 for a non-willful violation, with the upper limit increasing to $150,000 for a willful violation.

But how do you count the number of works involved? A company published a book with extensive plot summaries taken from various episodes of the television show *Twin Peaks*. After the judge found that the book infringed the show's copyrights, the publisher argued that the entire series was one work, while the show's producer argued that each episode was a separate work. The Second Circuit Court of Appeals agreed with the producer, significantly increasing the damage amount. Subsequent printings of the same book are part of the original violation, however, so you cannot collect additional statutory damages for those additional print runs. In that situation, you may be better off asking for actual damages.

If you registered the copyright before the infringement occurred, you may also be able to recover your attorneys' fees if you win the case. Even then, courts do not normally award attorneys' fees unless the losing party's actions in filing or defending the lawsuit were frivolous, objectively unreasonable, or done in bad faith.

Injunction is another potential remedy. As mentioned above, an injunction is an order by a court prohibiting a party from doing something. In copyright cases, an injunction usually prohibits an infringer from publishing or selling the infringing work.

Traditionally, the person requesting an injunction has to show that (1) it has suffered an irreparable injury, (2) money isn't enough to compensate for the injury, (3) the hardship to the defendant from granting the injunction would be less than the hardship to the plaintiff from denying it, and (4) granting the injunction would not harm the public. To get a permanent injunction, the plaintiff must also win the case.

But what if the defendant is threatening to publish and sell the book before the case is decided? The plaintiff can ask for a preliminary injunction to keep his copyright from being infringed while the case is pending. To get a preliminary injunction, he must show that he is likely to win the case on the merits, meaning that he will probably prove copyright infringement.

The copyright law specifically authorizes courts to grant permanent and preliminary injunctions in copyright cases. Because of this, some courts have ignored most of the traditional tests and required plaintiffs to show only the probability of success on the merits (for a preliminary injunction) or actual success (for a permanent injunction).

This has begun to change. As already mentioned, D. Salinger filed a lawsuit in 2009 against an author and publishing company for violating Salinger's copyright in *The Catcher in the Rye*. The district court granted a preliminary injunction after looking at Salinger's probability of success on the merits. It did not address whether he would be irreparably harmed without the injunction, however. On appeal, the Second Circuit vacated the preliminary injunction and sent the case back to the district court to consider whether Salinger had met the other prongs of the traditional test. The case settled before the judge had a chance to decide that question.

If other courts follow the Second Circuit's lead, injunctions will be harder to obtain in copyright cases. That's because money is usually sufficient to put the author in the same place he or should would have been without the infringment.

But consider an earlier J.D. Salinger case, decided in 1987.

Although Salinger was a very private person, he had written a number of personal letters over the years. Some of their recipients donated the letters to university library collections, where Ian Hamilton located and read them. Hamilton intended to use portions of those letters in an unauthorized biography, and Salinger objected.

The letters were already available to anyone who had access to the university library collections, but that limited the number of people who saw them. The Hamilton biography would have released the material in a public forum. Since there would have been no way to erase Salinger's private matters from the public's memory, that was irreparable harm.

The law gave Salinger a copyright in his personal letters, and a copyright includes the right to decide when, or even if, to publish the material, so Salinger sued and won.

Still, money cures a number of evils. Even without injunctive relief, authors have effective remedies against copyright infringement.

CHAPTER FIVE

Who Stole the Tarts?

(Fair Use, Public Domain)

> The King and Queen of Hearts were seated on their throne when they arrived, with a great crowd assembled about them—all sorts of little birds and beasts, as well as the whole pack of cards; the Knave was standing before them, in chains, with a soldier on each side to guard him; and near the King was the White Rabbit, with a trumpet in one hand, and a scroll of parchment in the other. In the very middle of the court was a table, with a large dish of tarts upon it; they looked so good that it made Alice quite hungry to look at them—"I wish they'd get the trial done," she thought, "and hand round the refreshments!"

> Lewis Carroll, *Alice in Wonderland*

Alice didn't realize that the tarts were evidence in a court case; she thought they were just refreshments. Copying can also have two uses. It may be evidence of copyright infringement, or it may be the food that feeds someone else's creative muse.

This chapter covers the defenses mentioned in the last chapter. It starts with a brief discussion of independent creation but spends most of its time on fair use. Then it moves on to the ultimate defense—that there is no copyright to be infringed—and provides guidelines for determining whether the material is in the public domain.

Independent Creation

As noted in earlier chapters, copyright prevents copying but not independent creation. If two people write the exact same ten-stanza poem without any knowledge of the other work, there is no copyright infringement. Obviously, this is an extreme example, and it is unlikely that the person who wrote the later poem could prove he created it independently. But if he could, both poets would have untarnished copyrights.

In *Positive Black Talk v. Cash Money Records*, rap artists Juvenile and D.J. Jubilee each recorded songs that included the four-word phrase, "back that ass up." Jubilee's song, titled "Back that Ass Up" was released in the spring of 1998. Juvenile's song, titled "Back that Azz Up," was released in November 1998.

When Jubilee's record company sued for copyright infringement, Juvenile testified that he recorded his song before ever hearing Jubilee's. The jury believed Juvenile, and that was all he needed to win the lawsuit.

Fair Use

Copyrights exist to inspire new works. But too rigid an application of the copyright laws could actually suppress creativity. (See the discussion in *Stewart v. Abend*.) In those situations, the copyright law protects the newer material as a fair use.

The fair use doctrine has an additional function. The First Amendment to the U.S. Constitution prohibits government—which includes courts—from interfering with the free flow of ideas. Copyright law employs two safeguards to protect First Amendment rights. First, the law distinguishes between ideas and expression, providing that only the expression can be copyrighted. Second, it establishes the fair use doctrine, which allows even expression to be borrowed in appropriate circumstances. (See *Eldred v. Ashcroft* for a more detailed explanation.)

So what is a fair use? The courts look at all the circumstances, and there is no fail-safe test. Still, the law provides four factors that courts must consider. They are

- The purpose and character of the allegedly infringing use;
- The nature of the copyrighted work;
- The amount and substantiality of the portion used in relation to the copyrighted work as a whole; and
- The effect upon the potential market for the copyrighted work.

These factors do not all carry the same weight. They don't even always carry the same proportionate weight. In fact, the second factor becomes almost non-existent if the allegedly infringing work is a parody.

The plagiarism chart in Chapter 2 quotes material from a number of fictional works. Since they are quotes, they qualify as copying. Even so, the chart would easily pass the fair use test. The following discussion uses the plagiarism chart to show how the four factors work. The discussion also describes how the courts have applied the factors in actual cases.

1. The purpose and character of the use

The preamble to the statutory fair use section states that "**the fair use** of a copyrighted work . . . for purposes such as criticism, comment, news reporting, teaching (including multiple copies for classroom use), scholarship, or research, is not an infringement of copyright." (17 U.S.C. § 107 (emphasis added)) These uses often—although not always—meet the first factor.

Take the case of *Harper & Row v. Nation Enterprises*. Harper & Row and Reader's Digest Books had purchased the rights to former

President Gerald Ford's memoirs. They then sold *Time Magazine* the exclusive right to print prepublication excerpts. But someone leaked the Ford manuscript to the editor of *The Nation* magazine, who quickly wrote an article to scoop *Time*. *Nation*'s article focused on passages of the Ford manuscript that related to the Nixon pardon, and it included information that had not yet been made public. After the article appeared, *Time* cancelled its agreement with Ford's publishers.

The case went all the way to the U.S. Supreme Court, which agreed with the Second Circuit Court of Appeals that the *Nation* article was news reporting. Although news reporting is one of the uses listed in the preamble, that didn't end the Supreme Court's analysis.

As part of the first factor, the copyright statute requires courts to consider whether the use is of a commercial nature or is for nonprofit educational purposes. The courts are aware that even the high-minded uses listed in the preamble usually have a commercial motive. News reporting sells newspapers, and teachers are paid to teach. Still, the more commercial the use, the more likely it is to fail this factor.

The Nation's motive was highly commercial. According to the Court, "The crux of the profit/nonprofit distinction is not whether the sole motive of the use is monetary gain but whether the user stands to profit from exploitation of the copyrighted material without paying the customary price. . . . The *Nation*'s use had not merely the incidental effect but the intended purpose of supplanting the copyright holder's commercially valuable right of first publication." (*Harper & Row Publishers, Inc. v. Nation Enterprises*, 471 U.S. 539, 562 (1985) (internal citations omitted)) As a result, the article failed the first test.

The Supreme Court has also noted, however, that "the more transformative the new work, the less will be the significance of other factors, like commercialism, that may weigh against a finding of fair use." (*Campbell v. Acuff-Rose Music, Inc.*, 510 U.S. 569, 579 (1994)) But what does "transformative" mean in this context?

The Supreme Court in *Campbell* looked at whether the new work merely superseded the original creation or added something new and different that altered the expression, meaning, or message. Judge Posner of the Seventh Circuit described it more vividly:

> [W]e may say that copying that is complementary to the copyrighted work (in the sense that nails are complements of hammers) is fair use, but copying that is a substitute for the copyrighted work (in the sense that nails are substitutes for pegs or screws) . . . is not fair use.

Ty, Inc. v. Publications International, Ltd., 292 F.3d 512, 517 (7th Cir. 2002) (internal citations omitted)

This requires more than just copying the work for a different use. A novel written to entertain is not transformed merely because it is used to teach creative writing skills. Similarly, the fact that a use is mentioned in the preamble is not enough to make it transformative. As the courts made clear in *Princeton University Press v. Michigan Document Service* and *Basic Books v. Kinko's Graphics Corp.*, course packs sold to students are clearly for teaching purposes, but if they are merely copies of existing material, they fail this first factor.

Parody is an often-cited transformative use. *Campbell* revolved around Roy Orbison's song "Oh Pretty Woman" and 2 Live Crew's commercial parody of that song. Orbison had assigned his rights to Acuff-Rose, so the group sent a copy of its version to Acuff-Rose and asked for permission to record it for public distribution. When Acuff-Rose refused, 2 Live Crew released its version anyway, and Acuff-Rose sued.

The Supreme Court stated that "parody has an obvious claim to transformative value." (*Campbell v. Acuff-Rose Music, Inc.*, 510 U.S. 569, 579 (1994)) Simply because it is parody does not make it a fair use, however. According to the Court, each of the four factors must be considered, although they will not receive the same weight in every situation. In this particular case, the Supreme Court held that the appeals court had not weighed those factors appropriately, and it sent the matter back for further consideration.

Campbell is also important for its definition of parody. According to the Supreme Court, parody comments on the substance or style of the original in such a way as to make it appear ridiculous. Under the fair use doctrine, a new work that makes fun of something other than the original work may be a satire, but it is not a parody.

The findings in several lower court cases illustrate this difference. *The Wind Done Gone* was a parody of *Gone With the Wind* because the second book challenged *Gone With the Wind*'s idealized portrait of the South during and immediately following the Civil War. "The Cat NOT in the Hat! A Parody by Dr. Juice" was—despite its name—NOT a parody because its criticism centered on the O.J. Simpson murder trial rather than on any aspect of the Dr. Seuss book.

Frederick Colting had a different problem when he argued that *60 Years Later: Coming Through the Rye* was a parody of *The Catcher in the Rye*. Colting's original advertising materials and interviews claimed that *60 Years Later* was a sequel to a beloved classic and a tribute to Salinger and *Catcher*. When Salinger sued Colting, the latter changed his approach and claimed that *60 Years Later* was a parody. But the judge did not accept Colting's 180 degree turn in emphasis from tribute to parody.

The courts' distinction between parody and satire does not reject satire as a transformative use. But satire can make its point without taking significant—or even recognizable—amounts from previously existing works. So satire cannot take as much from the original under the third factor discussed below.

The most obvious cases of transformation are those where the basic genre changes, as from fiction to non-fiction. But transformation can occur even when the genre does not change.

Katrina Maxtone-Graham interviewed women who had become *Pregnant by Mistake* (the title of her book). Some had abortions and others carried their babies to term. Several years later, James Burtchaell used excerpts from some of those interviews in the title essay of his book *Rachel Weeping*, which had an anti-abortion slant. He tried to get permission, but Maxtone-Graham did not agree with his stance on the abortion issue and refused his request. Burtchaell published his book of essays, including "Rachel Weeping," anyway.

The Second Circuit Court of Appeals classified Burtchaell's essay as criticism and comment, both preamble uses. But the transformative nature came from Burtchaell's intellectual labor in organizing the interview material and offering his own insights and opinions.

Similarly, the *Opal Mehta* comparison chart in Chapter 2 is a transformative use. The chart changes the use from fiction to non-fiction and reorganizes the underlying material in order to make a particular point. Yes, this book is a commercial venture, but the importance of the commercial nature of the use recedes as the transformative nature increases. Therefore, this factor weighs in favor of fair use.

2. The nature of the copyrighted work

How creative is the original work's genre? Borrowing from fiction or poetry is less likely to be a fair use than borrowing from a textbook. Courts do not make judgments about the creativity of individual works, however. All works within a genre are treated similarly.

In *Harper & Row*, the Supreme Court characterized the Ford manuscript as a historical narrative or autobiography, which makes it factual material that would normally be entitled to less protection than fiction. But the written opinion went on to state that being unpublished is also part of the manuscript's nature, and that: "Publication of an author's expression before he has authorized its dissemination seriously infringes the author's right to decide when and whether it will be made public, a factor not present in fair use of published works." (*Harper & Row Publishers, Inc. v. Nation Enterprises*, 471 U.S. 539, 551 (1985)) In other words, unpublished material deserves greater protection than published material. Therefore, *The Nation*'s article failed on this second factor.

The Second Circuit Court of Appeals followed the same reasoning two years later when it prohibited Ian Hamilton from using J.D. Salinger's letters. The fact that they were unpublished helped defeat Hamilton's fair use claim.

The comparison chart in Chapter 2 uses only published works, but they are all fiction. Therefore, this factor weighs against a finding of fair use.

3. The amount and substantiality of the portion used in relation to the copyrighted work as a whole

Generally, the higher the percentage borrowed, the less likely it is to be a fair use. You can usually take more words from a book than from a blog post. But usually does not mean always, and this is not a mathematical test.

If what you borrow is the heart of the work, even a sentence can be too much. *The Nation* quoted approximately 400 words from President Ford's 200,000 word memoir, but those 400 words were the juiciest parts of the manuscript. Similarly, borrowing a small percentage from a song can be too much if that percentage includes the most distinctive and recognizable elements. (See *Bridgeport Music v. UMG Recordings*.)

Parody, on the other hand, can usually get away with taking significant portions of the original. This is because parody cannot succeed unless it borrows enough for the audience to recognize the parody's target.

Regardless of the genre, the second use may only borrow as much as is necessary to make its point. Since the line can be indistinct, the courts do provide some wiggle room. They would rather allow too much borrowing than stifle creativity by making the test too stringent.

The *Opal Mehta* plagiarism chart uses a very small percentage of any of the copyrighted works, and none is the heart. After reading all the quotes from *Opal Mehta*—and assuming no previous acquaintance with it—the reader still has no idea of the plot. Therefore, this factor weighs in favor of fair use.

4. The effect upon the potential market for the copyrighted work

If the new work can be a substitute for the original work or for a derivative of the original work, it is probably not a fair use. That's because people who buy the new work won't spend money on the original one.

In *Harper & Row*, there was a clear effect on the market. *Time* cancelled its exclusivity agreement, and Ford's publishers lost the income from that agreement. People who read the unauthorized article would have no reason to buy *Time* for the same information. All four factors weighed against a finding of fair use, and the Supreme Court accordingly decided that *The Nation*'s use was not fair.

The mere fact that a newer work harms the market for the original work isn't enough to fail this fourth factor, however. Book reviews and parodies may discourage people from buying their target works, yet the copyright law encourages these uses. In *Campbell* the Supreme Court described the distinction as whether the use usurps demand or merely suppresses it.

Pregnant by Mistake and *Rachel Weeping* appealed to different audiences, and the Second Circuit noted that Burtchaell could not have intended to replace Maxtone-Graham's book in the marketplace. In *Princeton University Press* and *Basic Books* cases, the sale of course packs replaced the demand for the materials included in them, diverting the profits from the pockets of the authors to the pockets of the companies printing the course packs. *Rachel Weeping* did not violate this fourth factor, but the course packs did.

Turning to the *Opal Mehta* comparison chart one last time, the fourth factor favors fair use. The publisher pulled the book from the shelves, so there is no market for the chart to affect. But even if it were still available, any negative effect would be comparable to that from a bad review. Therefore, this factor weighs in favor of fair use.

❧

Although the courts consider all four factors, they usually put the most weight on the first and the fourth. Again, though, usually is not always. It bears repeating that there is no sure test for fair use.

Still, it is reassuring to know that the first and fourth factors (as well as the third) weigh in favor of fair use of the quotes in the plagiarism chart in Chapter 2—a clear case of Lady Justice tipping the scales in favor of the chart's author.

Fair use is mostly common sense. Ask yourself how you would feel if the roles were reversed. As the author of the original work, would you be upset if someone used it the way you are proposing? If you would, don't do it. (Obviously, unfavorable criticism and parody can be exceptions.)

If you're still confused, here's another rule. When in doubt, contact the author and ask for permission. If you can't get approval and you are convinced that yours is a fair use, the fact that you asked does not hurt your defense.

Public Domain Materials

Just because something is highly creative doesn't mean it is covered by a copyright. If there is no copyright, or if the copyright has expired, the work is in the public domain. This means that any member of the public can use as much of the material as he or she wants.

But how do materials end up in the public domain? There are two main sources: (1) works authored by the federal government, and (2) older works for which the copyright has expired or never existed.

1. Works authored by the federal government

The copyright statute specifically states that there is no copyright protection for works of the United States Government. This means that works written by an officer or employee of the federal government as part of his or her official duties cannot be copyrighted. If the government accepts copyrighted works from another person, however, the copyright is still good.

Federal court decisions are works of the United States Government. Introductory notes written by third parties may be copyrighted, but the cases themselves are not.

2. Works for which the copyright has expired

If the copyright has expired, the work is in the public domain and can be used by anyone. But how do you know if the copyright has expired?

The term of copyright protection is governed by statute, and Congress amends the statute—and changes the copyright term—from time to time. When it changes the term, it usually extends it. Congress has even given copyright protection to materials that were previously in the public domain. The U.S. Supreme Court has held on several occasions that Congress has the right to make these changes. (See *Golan v. Holder*, *Eldred v. Ashcroft*, and *Steward v. Abend*.)

The simplest way to determine when a work was published or registered is to check the inside cover of the book. You can also search the registration records at the U.S. Copyright Office.

The chart on the next page gives the general rules for the length of copyrights based on when they were created, published, or registered. There are exceptions, but they are beyond the scope of this book.

As noted in Chapter 3, works created after 1978 are automatically copyrighted the moment they are put into tangible form. When the copyright expires depends on the author, however. If the author died in 1986, the copyright expires in 2056. If she died in 2006, the copyright expires in 2076. And if the author is still living, the copyright will last at least another 70 years.

These rules change somewhat for foreign works, which are covered in the next chapter.

Year	Comments	Length of Copyright
Created 1978 or later	Applies to most works from this period	Life of the author plus 70 years—for joint works, the 70 years comes after the death of the last surviving author
Created 1978 or later	Applies to works for hire and works by unknown authors	95 years from date of first publication or 120 years from date of creation, whichever is earlier
Created, but not published or registered, before 1978	Published before January 1, 2003, most works	Life of the author plus 70 years, but cannot expire before December 31, 2047
Created, but not published or registered, before 1978	Published before January 1, 2003, works for hire or by unknown authors	95 years from date of first publication or 120 years from date of creation, but cannot expire before December 31, 2047
Created, but not published or registered, before 1978	Still unpublished, most works	Life of the author plus 70 years
Created, but not published or registered, before 1978	Still unpublished, works for hire or by unknown authors	95 years from date of first publication or 120 years from date of creation, whichever is earlier
Published 1964-1977		95 years from date of first publication
Published 1923-1963	Original term was renewed	95 years from date of first publication
Published 1923-1963	Original term not renewed	Work is in the public domain
Published before 1923		Work is in the public domain

CHAPTER SIX

Curiouser and Curiouser

(Cyberspace, International Issues)

"Curiouser and curiouser!" cried Alice (she was so much surprised, that for the moment she quite forgot how to speak good English). "Now I'm opening out like the largest telescope that ever was! Good-bye, feet!" (for when she looked down at her feet, they seemed to be almost out of sight, they were getting so far off).

Lewis Carroll, *Alice in Wonderland*

Alice rapidly grew so tall that she couldn't see her feet. Similarly, the Internet and cellular technology have rapidly taken writing and copying far from their early roots.

This chapter will discuss two areas where copyright issues have expanded as the world grows smaller. The first deals with copyrights in cyberspace and the second with international copyright use and enforcement.

Copyrights in Cyberspace

The same standards apply to both traditional media and cyberspace. Material that would be copyrighted if it appeared in print is also copyrighted when it appears on the Internet. If an unauthorized use would be a copyright violation when taken from printed material, it is also a copyright violation when taken from the Internet. If it would be a fair use in print, it is a fair use on the Internet. These basic principles remain constant even as the ways of transmitting information multiply.

Beyond that, though, the law is continually changing as it scrambles to catch up with technology. By the time this book is published, many of the legal requirements and prohibitions in effect while it is being written could be obsolete. For that reason, this section paints the law in broad strokes.

If someone infringes your work on the Internet, check the host site or contact a lawyer who specializes in intellectual property to see what you need to do to get the material taken down. If you have an agent or publisher, they may be able to help as well. The cheapest—but least reliable—way to learn the current requirements is by reading the host site's instructions.

There are three basic types of copyright infringement. The first is direct infringement. Whoever takes copyrighted material without permission or a fair use is a direct infringer.

The second type is contributory infringement. In *Metro-Goldwyn-Mayer Studios v. Grokster*, the U.S. Supreme Court said that contributory infringement occurs when a third party intentionally induces or encourages someone else's direct infringement. This can include willful blindness to ongoing infringement. You can't avoid liability by putting your head in the sand.

The third type is vicarious infringement. A vicarious infringer receives a financial benefit from the direct infringement, has the power to stop or limit it, and declines to exercise that power.

Host sites are not usually liable for copyright infringement. Neither are hardware or software providers of products that are capable of non-infringing uses. When Sony came out with a video tape recorder that could copy programs directly from a television set, Universal City Studios sued to stop sales to the public. Universal argued that the machines could be used to reproduce and distribute the studio's copyrighted television shows. Sony countered that the recorders had several valid uses that did not infringe Universal's copyrights. One of these uses was time-shifting: the ability to record a show to view at a more convenient time. Since many purchasers bought the recorders for that purpose and time-shifting is a fair use, the Supreme Court found that Sony was not guilty of either contributory or vicarious infringement.

That conclusion changes with the facts, however. When the Supreme Court heard the Grokster case twenty years later, it held that the potential for non-infringing uses did not protect Grokster from copyright infringement.

Grokster and another company, StreamCast Networks, separately developed and sold file-sharing software that allowed individual users to share copyrighted materials—mostly songs—with other users. The songs never resided on the companies' servers but were passed directly between users.

The software also allowed users to share non-copyrighted materials or materials in which the source user owned the copyright, so there were non-infringing uses. However, the two manufacturers advertised their software as a means of sharing copyrighted music. Grokster and StreamCast induced and encouraged copyright violations by third-party users, so they were contributory infringers.

Yes, information in cyberspace is subject to the same copyright standards as other information. But it also causes additional concerns. Any individual can record copyrighted material from a television or download it from the Internet, depriving the author of profits from potential sales. Obviously, it would be prohibitively expensive to sue every small-time infringer, so going after the software developer (as in the Grokster case) or the company hosting an infringing site is the most effective way to stop copyright violations.

On the other hand, putting the onus on software or hardware providers would inhibit technological advances and the creative opportunities they provide. Since the Copyright Clause in the U.S.

Constitution is designed "To promote the Progress of Science and the Useful Arts," the result could be counterproductive.

Congress and the courts are continually struggling with this dilemma. Congress's biggest attempt to balance the two concerns came with the passage of the Digital Millennium Copyright Act (DMCA) in 1998.

The DMCA does not change the three main types of copyright infringement, but it does create additional defenses against claims of contributory or vicarious liability. These provisions are called "safe harbors" and are only available to qualifying service providers.

The conditions for each safe harbor depend on the type of service, which must fall within one of four categories. Those categories are: (1) transitory digital network communications (including peer-to-peer networks); (2) caching, such as where the system takes a static image of a site and stores it in archival form; (3) information residing on systems or networks at the direction of users, which covers everything from website hosting to YouTube; and (4) information location tools such as search engines and business directories with links to company websites.

While the requirements differ for the four types of service, the general principle is the same: a service provider who knows or has reason to know about the infringement must take reasonable steps to prevent its facilities from being used for that purpose. The following example provides an overview of how the safe harbors work.

The most extensive requirements apply to the third category— information residing on the service provider's servers. To qualify for this safe harbor, the service provider must tell the public how to contact it to report infringing material. This information must be included on the provider's website and filed with the U.S. Copyright Office.

Assume you discover your copyrighted material on the Internet, where it is being used without your permission. If it is a fair use, you grimace (or applaud) and go back to whatever you were doing.

If you believe it is an infringing use, however, your first step is to check the service provider's website for the person to notify and the procedures to follow. If you can't find the information there, check with the Copyright Office.

Your second step is to notify the service provider, in writing, of the copyright infringement and ask it to take down the unauthorized material. Some websites include a form that can be used for the notification. The take-down letter must include specific information, and if it does not comply with the DMCA, it is worthless. Blanket take-down notices and those that make the provider search for the material are not valid.

According to the DMCA, the notification must include

- The signature (physical or electronic) of the copyright owner or someone authorized to act on his behalf;

- Information identifying the copyrighted work;

- Information identifying the infringing material, including enough details so the service provider can locate it;

- Contact information for the complaining party (the copyright owner or the person authorized to act for it)—preferably mailing address, telephone number, and e-mail address;

- A statement that the complaining party "has a good faith belief that use of the material in the manner complained of is not authorized by the copyright owner, its agent, or the law"; and

- A statement that "the information in the notification is accurate, and under penalty of perjury, that the complaining party is authorized to act on behalf of the owner of an exclusive right that is allegedly infringed."

Once the service provider receives a valid notice, it takes down the material and gives the alleged infringer an opportunity to file a counter notification disputing the removal. Again, there are specific requirements for the information to be included in the counter notification. They are

- The signature (physical or electronic) of the user who posted the allegedly infringing material;

- Information identifying the material that was removed and the location it was removed from;

- A statement, under penalty of perjury, that the user "has a good faith belief that the material was removed or disabled as a result of mistake or misidentification of the material to be removed or disabled"; and

- The user's name, address, and telephone number, along with consent to be served and sued where the user is located (except for foreign users, which must agree to broader jurisdiction).

The counter notification does not have to explain why the material does not infringe a copyright.

If the service provider receives a valid counter notification, it puts the material back up unless the copyright owner files a lawsuit against the alleged infringer.

Under the DMCA, the service provider takes the notice and counter notice at face value if they contain the required information. While the service provider must act in good faith, it is not required to determine whether the material actually infringes the copyright.

The service provider will have a formal policy for terminating access by repeat offenders. To take advantage of the safe harbors, the service provider must notify users of the policy and must implement it under appropriate circumstances.

Consider consulting with a lawyer who specializes in intellectual property law before you send either a take-down or a counter notice. Your publisher or agent may also be able to assist you. But if you send a notice without first seeking advice on its content, you run the risk that it will not be valid.

Any person who "knowingly materially misrepresents" that his copyright has been infringed (for the take-down notice) or that the material was removed or disabled by mistake or misidentification (for the counter notice) is liable to the other party for any damages and attorneys' fees that resulted from the improper notice. "Knowingly materially misrepresents" requires more than just being wrong. But if you have reason to believe that the use might be fair, don't send a take-down notice, and if you have reason to believe that you might be infringing, don't send a counter notice.

Protecting copyrights in cyberspace is and will continue to be troublesome. Technology changes faster than Congress and the courts can react. But the basic principles remain the same regardless of the medium used.

International Copyright Issues

Copyright protection can also be troublesome in the international arena. International copyrights simply do not exist. If you have a global work, you may want to undertake the time-consuming and expensive process of registering it in other countries. But many third-world countries will never recognize your copyright, and there is little or nothing you can do about it.

Still, the news is more good than bad. The United States is party to a number of treaties that cover copyrights.

The most important treaty is the Berne Convention for the Protection of Literary and Artistic Works. Each of the countries that has signed the Berne Convention must give the "nationals" (citizens or permanent residents) of the other signatory countries the same copyright protections it gives its own nationals, and it may not condition protection on registration or any other formalities. Most, if not all, first and second-world countries have signed the Berne Convention.

If you sue for copyright infringement in Great Britain, you are entitled to the same rights as a British subject and are subject to the same defenses. Fortunately for Americans, the United Kingdom's copyright laws are similar—although not identical—to those in the United States.

Some foreign works that used to be in the public domain in the United States now have copyright protection because of the requirements of the Berne Convention. In *Golan v. Holder*, the U.S. Supreme Court made it clear that Congress has the authority to remove these foreign works from the public domain.

Another important treaty is the Universal Copyright Convention. If the two countries at issue have signed both the Berne Convention and the UCC, the Berne Convention controls. If both countries have signed the UCC but not the Berne Convention, the UCC provides some protection to copyright owners who prominently display the copyright notation (©, year of first publication, name) on the material.

Foreign works that are registered in the U.S. get the same rights as domestic works. If they are not registered, they can enter the public domain (1) when the copyright expires in the country of origin or (2) immediately if the country of origin does not have a treaty with the United States. When there is no treaty, the only obstacle to publication is an ethical one.

But as the world continues to change, copyright enforcement may get curiouser and curiouser.

Part III

Hunting the Snark
(Writing About Other People)

CHAPTER SEVEN

The Baker

(Defamation)

"For, although common Snarks do no manner of harm,
    Yet I feel it my duty to say,
Some are Boojums—" The Bellman broke off in alarm,
    For the Baker had fainted away.

Lewis Carroll, "The Hunting of the Snark"

In Carroll's poem, "The Hunting of the Snark," nine men and a beaver take a voyage to an island inhabited by a tasty but illusive creature. The Baker joins the hunt knowing that most Snarks are harmless but that a few (those that are Boojums) are lethal. Although the Baker is terrified, something compels him to take the risk.

Writing about real people is usually harmless, but writing about the wrong person can prove lethal to an author's reputation and finances. Yet something compels writers to take the risk.

This chapter isn't meant to discourage anyone from writing about real people. But the responsible writer will weigh both the benefits and the risks and take steps to minimize the latter.

So what can you do to avoid a lawsuit? Unless you are the Godfather of movie fame, there is no foolproof way to keep people from suing you. There are a number of things you can do to make it less likely, but first it helps to know what libel is.

What is Defamation?

Generally speaking, defamation is (1) a false statement (2) about an identifiable person (3) that is communicated to others and (4) harms the person's reputation.

For traditional libel, the statement must also be written or recorded in tangible form—handwritten, printed, video-taped, tweeted, or so on. If you say something at a party and lots of people hear it but no one records it, you are guilty of slander rather than libel. That's the old definition, anyway. These days, most states lump slander and libel together as "defamation."

But this is Wonderland, so it can't be as simple as the four elements listed above make it sound.

1. A false statement

The statement must be false. Truth is a defense, so if the statement is true and the person knows you can prove it, he probably won't sue you. In fact, the First Amendment requires some plaintiffs to prove that the statement is false. More about that in Chapter 9.

But truth and falsity aren't always what they seem. You can libel someone by using real facts that carry a false implication. "Uncle Charlie sleeps around a lot" may be literally true if he takes frequent overnight business trips to multiple locations—but that isn't what people will think you mean.

The following article appeared in the *Memphis Press-Scimitar* on June 5, 1971.

> ### WOMAN HURT BY GUNSHOT
>
> Mrs. Ruth Nichols, [address] was treated at St. Joseph Hospital for a bullet wound in her arm after a shooting at her home, police said.
>
> A 40-year-old woman was held by police in connection with the shooting with a .22 rifle. Police said a shot was also fired at the suspect's husband.
>
> Officers said the incident took place Thursday night after the suspect arrived at the Nichols home and found her husband there with Mrs. Nichols.

> *Witnesses said the suspect first fired a shot at her husband and then at Mrs. Nichols, striking her in the arm, police reported.*
>
> *No charges had been placed.*

Memphis Publishing Co. v. Nichols, 569 S.W.2d 412, 414 (Tenn. 1978)

The significant facts in the article were all true. Mrs. Nichols was treated for a bullet wound. The incident did take place at her home. The shooter also fired at her own husband, who was present when the shooter arrived.

What the article doesn't say is that the shooter's husband was one of several people attending a party at the home. It also doesn't mention that Mr. Nichols was there, too.

When you initially read the article, what impression did you get about the relationship between Mrs. Nichols and the shooter's husband? Did you think they were having an affair? Is that a reasonable implication from the write-up? Tennessee's Supreme Court thought it was a close enough question to send the case to a jury.

If a defamation case goes to a jury, the jury decides how an average reader would interpret the words. If it's clear that a reasonable reader wouldn't find a defamatory meaning, however, the court may throw the case out before it gets that far.

Samantha James was a well-known belly dancer who willingly gave an interview to a newspaper reporter. The article stated that James "admits to selling her time to lonely old men with money, for as much as $400 an evening in one case, 'just to sit with him and be nice to him.'" The article also reported that James claimed men found it easier to talk to her than to their wives and quoted her as saying, "'This is my business. Men is my business.'" (*James v. Gannett Co., Inc.*, 40 N.Y.2d 415, 418 (1976)

Although the quotes were accurate, James believed that the context implied that she was a prostitute and an adulterer. After noting that the quotes came in a conversation about providing a listening ear rather than in one about having sex, the highest court in New York held that a reasonable reader would not interpret the article the way James claimed. As a result, the newspaper won the case without it going to a jury.

The U.S. Supreme Court has also addressed this issue. In *Greenbelt Cooperative Publishing v. Bresler*, a newspaper reported on city council meetings, during which some opponents described a local builder's dealings with the city council as "blackmail." The Court held that a reasonable reader would understand the term to refer to Bresler's negotiating tactics rather than to the commission of a crime. Therefore, using that word did not defame the builder.

Here's another point that may make you breathe easier: the facts don't have to be perfectly accurate if getting them right would have conveyed the same impression. Nicholas Lemann wrote a non-fiction book titled *The Promised Land: The Great Black Migration and How it Changed America*. The book was a history of black migration from the rural areas in the South to the cities in the North between 1940 and 1970, and it looked at how the migration affected those involved. Part of Lemann's journalistic approach was to follow one participant through these events.

Lemann chose Ruby Daniels as his main subject and conducted extensive interviews with her. The interviews covered her life during the period in question, and that period included her marriage to Luther Haynes. Lemann used the information from these interviews to weave Daniels' story throughout the book.

Haynes objected to three passages in the book. Those passages depicted him (1) leaving his children alone at night when he was supposed to be watching them, (2) losing a job because of a drinking problem, and (3) spending money on a car when his children needed shoes. Haynes and Daniels disagreed about these events, but the court did not have to decide who was telling the truth. That's because the evidence showed facts not included in the book: (1) Haynes walked out on the four children he had with Daniels, refused to pay child support, and was jailed for contempt after he flouted the child support orders; (2) he drank heavily and was arrested for assaulting a police officer while drunk; and (3) he married his current wife two years before his divorce from Daniels became final. The court ruled that even if the three passages Haynes complained about were inaccurate, the truth showed Haynes in an even worse light. Therefore, Haynes could not recover for defamation.

Neither the belly-dancer case nor the *Promised Land* case is an invitation to sloppiness, however. Each situation depends on its own facts, and a jury—not the author—decides how a reasonable reader would interpret the words the writer used. So double-checking facts and considering the implications before putting fingers to keyboard may make the difference between getting sued or not and between winning or losing if you are sued.

2. About an identifiable person

A statement is not defamatory unless it refers to a recognizable individual, business, or other entity. As the courts describe the test, the statement must be "of and concerning" the person who claims to have been defamed.

Donna Newbury Dalbec was appalled when her maiden name showed up in a swinger's ad that implied certain sexual conduct. The advertisement also provided contact information for "Donna Newbury" at a post office box in the small town where Dalbec had lived all her life.

After discovering that the ad was purchased by an unrelated male, the magazine printed a follow-up. But instead of disclosing that someone had planted the ad, the "retraction" stated that Dalbec and another woman "are phonies operating out of the same company." After describing the fake advertisements, the item continued: "Their ads are come-ons designed to rip off our readers, so we've deleted them. . . . If you receive a letter from a 'swinger' that asks you to send money, please inform the GC office immediately, and we'll kick the scumbag out. *Classified Information* was designed to open up your sex life and help you meet new people, not allow these leeches to steal your money, so help us keep the section clean." (*Dalbec v. Gentlemen's Companion, Inc.*, 828 F.2d 921, 924 (2nd Cir. 1987) (omission in Second Circuit decision))

Would Dalbec rather be classified as a swinger or a swindler? She didn't like either choice, so she sued the magazine for libel.

The magazine argued that the items were not "of and concerning" Dalbec. It claimed that Dalbec's reputation was so impeccable that no one would believe she placed the ad. But the use of her maiden name and the small town where she lived, as well as the testimony of several residents, convinced the court that the advertisement was about an identifiable person and that person was Dalbec.

So are you safe if you change the names to protect the innocent? No. Changing a person's name isn't enough if readers can still recognize the person from the description.

If an author changes enough significant details, however, a court may hold that a statement is not "of and concerning" a particular individual. In *Springer v. Viking Press*, the highest court in New York held that the use of a common first name and the similarity of "physical height, weight and build, incidental grooming habits and recreational activities" were not sufficient to prove that references to a minor character in a novel were "of and concerning" the plaintiff.

3. That is communicated to others

The statement must be communicated to someone other than the person it is about. If you write something negative about your mother in your diary and she is the only one who sees it, it isn't libel.

4. And harms a person's reputation

Finally, the statement must harm the person's reputation. If it refers to something trivial or is clearly an opinion, it's not defamatory. "She can't even boil water" is trivial—unless she makes her living as a cook. But even if the subject is a professional chef, the reader (or hearer) probably understands the phrase as pure opinion. Either way, the statement does not harm the person's reputation.

What if the person's reputation is so bad that you can't possibly make it worse? Then you've found your perfect victim—theoretically. However, few people have a reputation that bad.

Geraldo Rivera heard rumors that an Ohio judge persuaded women to have sex with him by offering to rule in their favor or in favor of friends or family members. Rivera also suspected that the judge had enlisted William G. Brooks to frighten the women out of testifying against the judge when he was being investigated. So Rivera lay in wait for Brooks and tried to interview him on the street.

During the short exchange that occurred before Brooks fled, Rivera fired a series of questions at him that referred to his suspected role as a hit man for the judge. This footage appeared on the television show *20/20*, and Brooks sued.

Over the years Brooks had been convicted of breaking and entering, grand larceny, first degree manslaughter, and carrying a concealed weapon. After the failed interview but before the footage aired on *20/20*, a grand jury indicted Brooks on charges of obstruction of justice in connection with the events that were the subject of the broadcast.

ABC and Rivera argued that Brooks was "libel-proof" because his reputation was already so bad that any additional damage to it would be inconsequential. Although acknowledging that at least one circuit had recognized a "libel-proof" defense, the Sixth Circuit wasn't willing to go that far:

While prior to the broadcast, some Akron residents knew Brooks as an occasionally violent criminal, no popular nationwide television program or other publicity had portrayed Brooks as a "hitman" for a corrupt judge, a "pimp," a "muscleman," or a "street knowledgeable jive turkey." We leave it to a trier of fact [usually a jury] to determine whether, and to what extent, the "20/20" episode damaged Brooks' reputation.

Brooks v. American Broadcasting Companies, Inc., 932 F.2d 495, 502 (6th Cir. 1991)

Fortunately for Rivera and ABC, they won the case on First Amendment grounds after it went back to the district court. Freedom of speech is discussed in Chapter 9.

Defenses to Defamation Claims

How do you avoid a defamation claim? You can't libel the dead, so write about Abraham Lincoln or Jane Austen or Michael Jackson.

Amalgams work, too. If you use a few of your Aunt Becky's traits for a character in your novel but give her a different name and physical description and mix in several noticeable characteristics she doesn't have, she is no longer recognizable. Or at least you have changed her enough so that the reader who knows her will realize the character is mostly fictional.

But what about all those autobiographies, biographies, and other non-fiction books that say negative things about living people? These writers take a calculated risk that they can defend against a defamation charge, and they hope the defense is so obvious that the person won't bother to sue. Here are the most common defenses.

1. "Nobody in their right minds would believe it."

This isn't, "she has such a pristine reputation that nobody who knows her would believe it." If that were the argument, Donna Dalbec might have lost her case. No, this defense is closer to, "even if they don't know her they'd be fools to believe it."

Baton-twirling Kimerli Pring represented Wyoming at the 1978 Miss America pageant. She didn't win the crown, but she did win millions of dollars from Penthouse International. Then she lost that prize as well.

In 1979, *Penthouse* published a spoof about a baton-twirling Miss Wyoming who engages in oral sex in plain view of the audience and levitates her "subject" while the cameras are rolling. Pring claimed that the article defamed her, and a jury agreed.

The appeals court had a different view. It found that the actions depicted in the story were so impossible that they could not reasonably be understood as statements of fact. Based on that ruling, Pring emerged with neither the crown nor the money.

The "nobody in their right minds would believe it" defense appears to be a favorite among a certain type of men's magazines. *Hustler Magazine* printed a liqueur advertisement that portrayed Jerry Falwell's "first time" as occurring in an outhouse during a drunken rendezvous with his mother. Although the facts weren't impossible, as they were in the *Penthouse* case, the advertisement was a clear parody of a Campari Liqueur ad and wasn't meant to be believed. The jury found that the advertisement could not reasonably be understood as describing actual facts about Falwell or actual events in which he participated.

One word of caution. Kimerli Pring lost her case at the appellate level by a two-to-one vote. The dissenting justice agreed that the levitation and the public performance were clearly fiction, but he felt that readers might think otherwise about the oral sex, and he would have let the jury award stand. These cases aren't always as obvious as you might think, so if you are worried about being sued, don't write the piece.

2. "It was just my opinion."

Most opinions can't libel anyone. But if the opinion implies that it is based on facts and the implied facts are themselves untrue, the speaker (or writer) could find himself liable for defamation.

So how do you know when something is purely opinion? Context matters. The test is how a reasonable reader would interpret the statements, and a reasonable reader always considers the context. When you read a book review, don't you assume you are reading the reviewer's opinion? That's what the appeals court said when Dan Moldea sued the *New York Times* over a review of his book on organized crime influences in professional football. The review said the book contained sloppy journalism and gave a number of examples. The appeals court did, however, say that statements in a book review could be actionable if the reviewer did not support them with references to the work being reviewed. Since the *New York Times* reviewer gave examples of his opinion from the book itself, the court found that the statements were opinion and the paper was not guilty of libel.

Context also includes a manuscript's tone. When *Boston Magazine* printed an article on the best and worst in local sports, it chose James Myers as the worst sportscaster and described him as "the only newscaster in town who is enrolled in a course for remedial speaking." (*Myers v. Boston Magazine Co., Inc.*, 380 Mass. 336, 338, 403 N.E.2d 376, 377 (1980)) Since Myers wasn't taking remedial speaking classes, he sued. The state's highest court described the article as loaded with one-liners that were obvious attempts at humor. Given the tone of the article, the court held that a reasonable reader would understand the remedial speaking remark as an opinion (that Myers should be enrolled in a course for remedial speaking) rather than as a fact (that Myers was actually enrolled).

But labeling something as opinion is not enough if the statement implies that you know the facts and the implied facts turn out to be untrue. Thomas Diadiun's newspaper column suggested that former high school wrestling coach Michael Milkovich perjured himself in connection with an inquiry over an altercation at a wrestling match. The column used the words "Diadiun says" and "TD says" to describe its content, and the paper claimed that the statements in the column were clearly opinion.

The United States Supreme Court disagreed. According to the Court, if "a reasonable factfinder could conclude that the statements in the Diadiun column imply an assertion that petitioner Milkovich perjured himself in a judicial proceeding," then the newspaper could be liable for defamation. The Court went on to say that "the connotation that petitioner committed perjury is sufficiently factual to be susceptible of being proved true or false." (*Milkovich v. Lorain Journal Co.*, 497 U.S. 1, 21 (1990)) Based on these conclusions, the Supreme Court sent the case back to the lower court for trial.

3.   "I have a right to comment on public issues."

Closely related to the opinion defense is the defense of fair comment. This defense is at the heart of the First Amendment cases, which are covered in Chapter 9. One lower court case is sufficient here to show how the defenses of opinion and fair comment can intersect.

After William Buckley said that Gore Vidal's novel, *Myra Breckenridge*, was pornography, Vidal claimed that he had been defamed. Buckley's defense was that his statements were fair comment.

According to the judge:

> When an author submits his work to the public he must, of necessity, expect criticism of that work. He is said, in fact, to invite criticism, and no matter how hostile such criticism may be, the critic enjoys a privilege to make such critical comments as long as the

comment does not go beyond the published work itself
to attack the author personally, the facts are truly
stated, the comment is fair, and the comment is an
honest expression of the writer's real opinion.

Buckley v. Vidal, 327 F.Supp. 1051, 1052-1053 (S.D.N.Y. 1971)
(internal cites omitted))

The judge went on to analyze these factors as they applied to
Buckley's comments about *Myra Breckenridge*. First, the judge noted
that, although calling the book "pornography" suggests its author is a
pornographer, Buckley directed the criticism at the book rather than its
author. The judge noted that Buckley's statements were opinion, not
fact, and that there was no evidence to show they were not Buckley's
true opinion. The judge also found that Buckley's characterization—
whether accurate or not—was based on the content of the book and
was not so clearly wrong as to be unfair or dishonest.

4. "He consented."

A writer isn't liable for libel if the person gave his consent. Wait,
you say. Why would someone agree to be defamed? For the same
reason people agree to go on reality television shows where they come
across looking like jerks. Some individuals will do anything for
publicity or money. Or they don't realize how something looks until
they read it on paper, see it on tape, or hear their friends' comments.

Consent is a defense to libel. Just make sure you get it in writing
and that the consent is broad enough to cover everything you want to
say.

5. "I told the truth."

Once upon a time, the person who made a statement had to prove
that it was true. Then the United States Supreme Court decided
Philadelphia Newspapers v. Hepps and held that the First Amendment
requires the person suing a media defendant to prove the statement is
false, shifting the burden and making it harder to win a case brought

against a newspaper. The Supreme Court said that the *Hepps* decision was limited to the media and matters of public concern, so some states may still require non-media defendants—and media defendants writing about matters that are not of public concern—to prove the statement is true.

Is Fiction Exempt?

No. Calling it fiction gives you some leeway, but only a little.

You've heard the old adage: write what you know. But have you ever had someone tell you to write **who** you know? Probably not.

Even so, fiction writers do write who they know. Most characters are amalgams of several people rather than based on a single person, but that isn't always the case.

Imagine yourself living in the glow that follows your first published book. Then the sheriff knocks on the door and hands you a summons. Your brother has sued you for defamation.

Oh, you say, that won't happen to me. I'll have a disclaimer at the beginning of my book saying that any resemblance to any person living or dead is purely coincidental. Besides, I only write fiction, and everybody knows fiction isn't true.

That may have been what Andrew Fetler thought when he published *The Travelers*. If so, he soon discovered that he was wrong.

Andrew Fetler's novel involved a family of thirteen children who traveled around Europe in an old bus giving family band and choir concerts. Their father was an itinerant preacher, and the oldest son—who was 23 in 1938 when the novel took place—was responsible for his siblings.

In real life, the author was one of thirteen children who traveled around Europe in an old bus giving family band and choir concerts. Their father was an itinerant preacher, and Andrew's oldest brother—who was 23 in 1938—was responsible for his siblings. The setting and a number of other facts were also practically identical to those in the novel.

Andrew was more creative in developing his plot. The older brother in the novel would do almost anything for money, including cooperating with the Nazis and abandoning his dying father. It was these aspects of the story that Andrew's older brother, Daniel, felt were defamatory. He sued Andrew and the publisher, and the entire family took sides.

A federal appeals court said Daniel had the right to try the case. The similarities were strong enough to let a jury decide whether readers would identify the real brother as the fictional one.

A more recent incident divided long-time friends. Haywood Smith's novel, *The Red Hat Club*, included a character named "SuSu." SuSu's first husband got killed in a car accident, and she received a large insurance settlement. Later, she became engaged to a man who owned nursing homes in Florida and was already secretly engaged to another woman. This man eventually stole SuSu's insurance settlement, moved to Florida, and transferred his assets to his mistress. Although a court awarded SuSu $750,000, she was unable to collect it. Then, at the age of 50, SuSu became a flight attendant.

Unfortunately for Smith, that description also fit her real-life friend, Vickie Stewart. The details they didn't share, according to Stewart, were SuSu's foul mouth, alcoholism, and sexual promiscuity. So Steward sued for defamation.

The appeals court held that Stewart and SuSu shared enough characteristics for a jury to conclude the two were the same woman. And after a trial, the jury did just that.

The basic test is whether people who know the person claiming to be defamed could reasonably believe that the fictional character portrays the real person. If they **could** believe it, the jury gets to decide whether they **would** believe it. But the mere fact that some people make the connection isn't enough if the belief isn't reasonable.

Anatomy of a Murder was a fictionalized version of an actual crime. In real life and in the novel, one man shot and killed another after the victim raped the killer's wife. No one disputed that the fictional victim and the fictional killer portrayed the real-life victim and the real-life killer. But the libel case wasn't about them.

The real victim's wife and daughter—Hazel Wheeler and Terry Ann Chenoweth—sued over the way the book portrayed the fictionalized victim's wife and daughter. As the appeals court saw it, however, other than the characters' relationship to the victim, the fictional wife and daughter had little in common with Wheeler and Chenoweth. Therefore, the court held that a person who knew Wheeler and Chenoweth could not reasonably conclude that they were the same as the fictional characters, and that was the end of the case.

Giving a character the same name as a real person can also get you into trouble. Melanie Geisler found her name and physical traits attached to a character in a book written by a former co-worker. Since the character's actions were not very flattering, Geisler was not amused.

The same thing happened to Kimberly Bryson, who objected to the portrayal of a girl named "Bryson" in a short story. The real Bryson also identified twenty-five similarities between herself and the character in the story.

The appellate courts allowed Geisler's and Bryson's cases to proceed because the authors appropriated some of their physical characteristics as well as their names. The results tend to be different if the name is the only significant characteristic the fictional person and the flesh-and-blood person share.

The author of a short story liked the ring of his childhood friend's middle and last name, so he used them. After Larry Esco

Middlebrooks objected, the author changed the character's name to Esco Brooks. According to the Fourth Circuit Court of Appeals, the story took place at a time when Middlebrooks was absent from the area, Middlebrooks and the character were of different ages and occupations, and the story did not resemble Middlebrooks' life. Therefore, the court held that no reasonable person would believe that Larry Esco Middlebrooks and Esco Brooks were the same person,

Writers are also not liable for the coincidental use of someone's name. When Bernard Clare discovered that his name was the title of a book, he sued and lost. The author did not know Clare, the shared name was pure coincidence, and none of the other details matched. The judge wasn't willing to make authors responsible for searching records across the country when selecting a character name. Although the case happened before Internet searches, the principle should be the same today. So don't worry if you later discover that your character's name isn't unique.

It's too bad these cases weren't decided before Mark Twain published *The Gilded Age,* which he coauthored with Charles Dudley Warner. One of the characters was Colonel Sellers, and Warner suggested giving the colonel a first name of Eschol. Years earlier Warner had known an Eschol Sellers and thought the name was quaint. Twain worried that the real Eschol Sellers might show up and object, but Warner assured him that the man was a small-time farmer and probably dead. Shortly after *The Gilded Age* was published, an unknown Eschol Sellers showed up and threatened a libel suit. Rather than take the risk, the publishing company apologized and changed the name for subsequent printings. Today, it could have cited cases and saved the time and money involved in the name change.

Still, each case depends on its facts, and courts don't always agree on how many similarities are required to send a defamation case to the jury. Furthermore, defamation cases are based on state law. Although those laws are similar, they are not identical, so you can't always handicap the race in advance. That means the best advice is simply this: when in doubt, don't.

If you want to write about real people and situations in your fiction, change enough facts to disguise the characters. This requires time and creativity, but it could avoid hard feelings and a lawsuit. And your writing will be better for the effort.

A Final Word About Defamation

As discussed in Chapter 9, the First Amendment limits some actions for libel—particularly when the person suing is a public figure—but it doesn't give you free reign to say anything you want. If you intentionally lie about specific conduct that can harm someone's reputation, or if you have reason to believe it isn't true and say it anyway, neither the First Amendment nor any state law will protect you.

❧

So you've passed all the legal tests, and you're ready to proceed. But what about your personal relationships? Are you willing to put up with the cold shoulder at family gatherings after you tell the world that your cousin is an alcoholic? And is what you said about your old college roommate worth losing her friendship? If so, go ahead. If not, disguise, disguise, disguise; get permission from the person you are writing about; or turn the computer off and walk away. Because there may be more than a lawsuit at stake when you write about family and friends.

CHAPTER EIGHT

The Beaver

(Right to Privacy)

The Boots and the Broker were sharpening a spade—
    Each working the grindstone in turn:
But the Beaver went on making lace, and displayed
    No interest in the concern:

Though the Barrister tried to appeal to its pride,
    And vainly proceeded to cite
A number of cases, in which making laces
    Had been proved an infringement of right.

               Lewis Carroll, "The Hunting of the Snark"

As the hunters prepared to pursue the snark, the beaver ignored his responsibilities to the group and continued making lace. He didn't care if his actions violated someone else's rights.

Most writers aren't as callous as the beaver, but ignorance can produce the same results. Assume that you read the previous chapter and concluded that your magazine article or the use of a thinly veiled "fictional" character is not defamatory. Does that mean you can use it to reveal private information or to appropriate someone's name or likeness for commercial use?

Not if it violates an individual's right to privacy.

Like defamation, invasion of privacy and appropriation of someone's name or likeness for commercial reasons are state causes of action. Whether a writer wins or loses depends on state law, even if the case is in federal court.

The requirements for showing privacy violations vary from one state to another. This chapter provides a general overview, but you should consult a lawyer if you have specific concerns.

Right of Privacy

Depending on the state, the courts recognize four basic violations of individual privacy rights: (1) intruding into an individual's private space or affairs, (2) publicly disclosing private facts, (3) portraying an individual to the public in a false light, and (4) appropriating an individual's name or likeness for the appropriator's own advantage. This last violation is less invasion of privacy and more commercial exploitation, so it will be discussed separately.

1. Intruding into private affairs

The first, and least common, type of privacy violation is also the most invasive. It results when someone intrudes into an individual's private space or affairs. This violation isn't as much about writing or publishing information as it is about how that information is obtained in the first place.

Examples of intrusion include unauthorized wiretapping, eavesdropping by mechanical and electronic means, using a ruse to gain entry into an individual's home, and clandestine photography taken when the individual is in a place where she can reasonably expect privacy.

Not every invasion into someone's privacy is actionable, however. Interviewing an individual's family and friends is not a privacy violation, nor is taking photographs of an individual in a public place if the photographer maintains a reasonable distance.

Are Internet searches unlawful intrusions? Not under normal circumstances. In 2004, an Associated Press reporter did a Google search using the name of a Navy SEAL facility in Iraq. The search results included a www.smugmug.com folder labeled with the facility's name, and the folder contained a number of photographs. Some of the pictures showed military personnel mugging for the camera while sitting, lying, or stepping on prisoners. In other photographs, military personnel pointed guns at a prisoner's bloody head.

One of the SEALs sent the photos to his wife, and she posted them in her personal smugmug account. If she thought it was private, she was wrong. The reporter was able to download the pictures without being prompted for a password or encountering any other security measures. The judge found that the Associated Press and its reporter's Internet search had not invaded the wife's privacy. If the reporter had hacked into the account, however, the result would probably have been different.

The Second Circuit Court of Appeals described the general rule in *Galella v. Onassis* when it said, "legitimate countervailing social needs may warrant some intrusion despite an individual's reasonable expectation of privacy and freedom from harassment. However the interference allowed may be no greater than that necessary to protect the overriding public interest." (*Galella v. Onassis*, 487 F.2d 986, 995 (2nd Cir. 1973)) The decision classifies newsgathering as a legitimate social need that warrants some intrusion. In the Jackie Onassis case, however, the court found that a paparazzo's actions, which included jumping out at her children and bribing doormen, were excessive.

2. Disclosing private facts

The second type of privacy violation requires that the individual have a reasonable expectation of privacy **and** that embarrassing personal information is publicly disclosed. If the information is not of legitimate concern to the public, the individual's right to privacy will prevail. But if the matter is newsworthy, the courts will balance the individual's right to privacy, the public's right to know about newsworthy people and events, and the protections of the First Amendment (which are discussed in the next chapter).

Whether an individual has a reasonable expectation of privacy depends on the circumstances. For example, there is no reasonable expectation of privacy for information in public records, even if few people see them. The name of a rape victim is not protected when the name is included in an indictment, and the name of a sexual assault victim loses its confidentiality when listed on a police blotter available to reporters. (See *Florida Star v. B.J.F.* and *Cox Broadcasting v. Cohen*.)

Whether an expectation of privacy is reasonable also depends on who you are. A public figure cannot expect the same privacy as an unknown person. This principle extends to a public person's family and friends, so they also lose their privacy rights.

Being in the limelight for a brief period is enough to shatter the expectation of privacy. William Sidis was a child prodigy who graduated from Harvard at sixteen, after which he dropped out of public view. He reentered it against his will when *The New Yorker* featured him in a "Where Are They Now" article. The magazine described William's shabby lodgings and eccentric personal habits, and the judge characterized the piece as "merciless in its dissection of intimate details of its subject's personal life." (*Sidis v. F-R Publishing Corp.*, 113 F.2d 806, 807 (2nd Cir. 1940))

William lost anyway. According to the court, he gave up his expectation of privacy by thrusting himself into the limelight 25 years earlier. And without a reasonable expectation of privacy, it doesn't matter how embarrasing the information is.

If an individual does have a reasonable expection of privacy, however, there is another requirement. To violate privacy by disclosing public facts, the disclosure must involve information that would embarrass the average person in the community. In some states the standard is set higher: the disclosure must be highly offensive to a reasonable person.

Before she was famous, a teenage Janet Leigh eloped with her high school sweetheart, John Carlisle. Although the marriage was quickly annulled, the episode was a bittersweet story. Still, the teenage players were guilty of little more than first love and bad judgment.

Years later, Janet talked to a reporter about her first marriage and described how it affected her. When Carlisle sued for invasion of privacy, the court held that the facts were not embarrassing enough.

Flora Graham took her sons through the fun house at the country fair. As they exited, they walked across a platform with air jets. Mrs. Graham's skirt rose up and exposed her panties. A news photographer snapped a picture without Mrs. Graham's knowledge and consent, then ran it on the front page of the local paper.

The photograph of Mrs. Graham with her dress flying up embarrassed her. It wasn't that she was overly sensitive, either. The test was whether the average person in her community would have been embarrassed or offended in the same circumstances. In Alabama in 1961, Mrs. Graham's Marilyn Monroe moment met that test.

Normally, people who are in a public place do not expect privacy there, so what made this scenario different? Mrs. Graham did not expect to find herself in an embarrassing situation, nor did she create it. According to the judge, that was enough to give her a right to privacy.

After concluding that information is private and disclosure is embarrassing (or highly offensive), the court considers whether the information is of legitimate concern to the public. If it is not newsworthy, there is no right to disclose it.

Unfortunately, there is no black and white test to tell writers which events are newsworthy. Common sense is your best guideline. But it also helps to know which situations the courts have held are or are not newsworthy.

Information that relates to a candidate's qualifications for public office is always newsworthy. So is official misconduct. The public also has an interest in knowing about a convicted killer's psychological background or a teacher who was arrested on drug-related charges. Furthermore, the matter remains newsworthy even though the events are in the past or the person is no longer in the public eye.

On the other hand, the photograph of Mrs. Graham was not newsworthy. The public had no legitimate reason to know what she looked like with her skirt flying up.

3. Portraying an individual in a false light

What happens when the information is not legally defamatory but leads the public to reach an erroneous conclusion? Using private facts to portray an individual in a false light is another violation of the individual's right to privacy.

Three escaped convicts took the Hills hostage and held them prisoners in their own home for 19 hours. The convicts eventually deserted the house, releasing the family unharmed. According to the father, James Hill, the convicts were courteous and had not been violent or abusive. The police subsequently shot and killed two of the convicts and apprehended the third.

Shortly after this event, Joseph Hayes published his novel, *The Desperate Hours*. The book told the story of a family held hostage by escaped convicts but, unlike the Hill situation, the convicts were brutish and were captured and/or killed in the hostages' home. Although Hayes said the Hill situation was a triggering incident in writing *The Desperate Hours*, he characterized the book as a fictionalized amalgam of several hostage dramas and denied that it portrayed the Hill family or its particular experience.

When the novel was turned into a play, *Life* published an article that equated the events in the book to the Hill hostage drama. A *Life* photographer took pictures at the house the Hills had lived in during their ordeal, and the on-location photographs showed actors in situations that appeared in the book but not in real life. James Hill sued the magazine, claiming that the article violated his family's privacy.

The article wasn't defamatory. In fact, it was sympathetic to the Hills and made them out to be heroes. But it also brought them back into the limelight they had sought to avoid. If that was all it did, the Hills would not have had a case. As with William Sidis, the Hills' story was still newsworthy. But the article put the Hill family's experience in a false light, and *Life* lost the case.

Cantrell v. Forest City Publishing Co. is another example of invasion of privacy by portraying individuals in a false light. In 1967, the Silver Bridge across the Ohio River collapsed and killed 44 people, including Melvin Cantrell. At the time, a reporter for a Sunday magazine wrote a story that talked about how Cantrell's death affected his family.

Five months later, the reporter returned to write a follow-up story. He interviewed the Cantrell children while their mother was absent, and the magazine's photographer took pictures of their residence. The resulting article implied that Mrs. Cantrell had been present and had spoken to the reporter, and it exaggerated the family's poverty and the slovenly state of the home. This was enough to support the jury's finding that the magazine and its reporter were liable for damages under the false light claim.

Photographs can also be the basis for a false light claim. *M.G. v. Time Warner, Inc.* involved a *Sports Illustrated* article about a Little League coach who pled guilty to child molestation. The article included a team picture. Although the caption did not list the children's names, their faces were identifiable.

Four of the children were not molested, and their false light claims alleged that publishing the photograph invaded their privacy by implying that they had been victims of child molestation. The

California court agreed that this was enough to send the case to the jury.

Appropriation of an Individual's Name or Likeness

The fourth type of privacy violation doesn't involve privacy at all, as some states implicitly recognize by calling it a publicity right. This cause of action doesn't apply unless the individual is in the public spotlight and has exploited that position.

Abdul-Jabbar v. General Motors Corp. is a typical case. Lew Alcindor was an outstanding college basketball player while at UCLA. He went on to become an equally outstanding professional player under the name Kareem Abdul-Jabbar.

In 1993, General Motors Corporation aired a commercial comparing one of its automobiles with Lew Alcindor, calling them both outstanding players. General Motors did not ask Abdul-Jabbar's permission, nor did it pay him for using his name in the spot. The company withdrew the commercial after Abdul-Jabbar complained, but he sued anyway and requested damages for the times it had already aired.

One of Abdul-Jabbar's claims was that General Motors had appropriated his name to its advantage without his consent, resulting in financial injury. The financial injury is loss of the money he could have made by selling his name for commercial use. This is almost an anti-privacy right because an individual who does not already have a sellable identity cannot show financial injury. Abdul-Jabbar did have a sellable identity, so he was entitled to pursue his claim.

Not every commercial use of a public figure's name violates the right of publicity, however. For example:

- A publisher may quote from a book review that compares an upcoming author to an established one. (See *Rand v. Hearst Corp.*)

- A trading card company may use parody to lampoon professional athletes. (See *Cardtoons, L.C. v. Major League Baseball Players Association*.)

- A magazine may advertise itself by using names and pictures of celebrities that have appeared within its pages. (See *Cher v. Forum International, Ltd.* and *Namath v. Sports Illustrated*.) The magazine cannot, however, imply that the celebrity has endorsed it when that is not true.

❧

In Lewis Carroll's "The Hunting of the Snark," the beaver put his own interests ahead of the community's interests. For writers delving into someone's private life, the community's interests are paramount. If the information is not newsworthy—meaning of legitimate concern to the public—the writer could be liable for invasion of privacy.

CHAPTER NINE

The Snark

(First Amendment Freedom of Speech)

"He remarked to me then," said that mildest of men,
  "'If your Snark be a Snark, that is right:
Fetch it home by all means—you may serve it with greens,
  And it's handy for striking a light.

* * *

"'But oh, beamish nephew, beware of the day,
  If your Snark be a Boojum! For then
You will softly and suddenly vanish away,
  And never be met with again!'"

Lewis Carroll, "The Hunting of the Snark"

Like the Snark, First Amendment freedom of speech can be worth pursuing. But beware of placing too much reliance on it. If you don't understand its limits, the First Amendment could become the Boojum that makes your money vanish away in damages and attorneys' fees.

Contrary to what some people believe, the First Amendment does not allow you to say whatever you want. Its protections are designed to promote open discussion, but it does not authorize anarchy.

The U.S. Supreme Court developed the rules for media in a line of cases that began in 1964. Most of these cases deal with traditional mass media such as newspapers, magazines, and television. Still, one thing is clear: if traditional media would not be protected by the First Amendment in a particular situation, blogs and self-published books won't be protected either. And some states may give them even less protection.

This line of cases began with *New York Times Co. v. Sullivan*. A civil rights group prepared an advertisement soliciting funds and submitted it to the *New York Times*. Newspaper staff reviewed the ad and accepted it for publication.

The advertisement mentioned some of the actions taken by the Montgomery city police to suppress the civil-rights activities of local university students. It contained a few errors, such as stating that Dr. Martin Luther King, Jr. had been arrested seven times when it was only four.

Sullivan was a Montgomery, Alabama city commissioner with responsibility for overseeing the police department. He sued for defamation, and a jury awarded him $500,000.

The U.S. Supreme Court took the win—and the money—away from Sullivan. In deciding the case, it noted that America is committed to "uninhibited, robust, and wide-open" public debate on public issues. (*New York Times v. Sullivan*, 376 U.S. 254, 271 (1964)) Recognizing that no test is perfect, the Court believed it was better to err by protecting some false speech than by hindering truthful speech. According to the Court, requiring a speaker (or writer) to guarantee the truth of his statements at the pain of paying large libel judgments would inhibit criticism even when the speaker believed his statements were accurate.

For that reason, the Court held that the First Amendment "prohibits a public official from recovering damages for a defamatory falsehood relating to his official conduct unless he proves that the statement was made with 'actual malice' – that is, with knowledge that it was false or with reckless disregard of whether it was false or not." (*New York Times v. Sullivan*, 376 U.S. 254, 279-280 (1964))

The *New York Times* case was limited to comments about public officials, but the Supreme Court extended the same test to public figures in *Curtis Publishing Co. v. Butts* and *Associated Press v. Walker*. Butts was athletic director of the University of Georgia, and Walker was an activist. The Court held that both were public figures—Butts because of his high profile position, and Walker because he had thrust himself into the limelight by his activities. As a result, they had to prove actual malice.

In this context, malice is not synonymous with ill will. You can have the best intentions and even admire the person you write about. But if you know that what you write is false or have serious doubts, that is enough for a jury to find that you acted with actual malice.

When the Supreme Court decided *Time, Inc. v. Hill* (discussed in the previous chapter), it applied the *New York Times* rule. Since the jury had awarded the Hills damages based on a lower standard, the Court sent the case back to the state courts. The Supreme Court's statement of facts noted that *Life* had news clippings in its files describing the Hill family's experiences and other clippings where the author of *The Desperate Hours* denied that he based the book on those experiences. This could have been enough for a jury to find that *Life* knew that the parallels it drew between the actual events and those in the play were wrong.

But what if you aren't sure, or if you believe your facts are correct but your investigation is careless or incomplete? It takes more than that to show actual malice.

While running for public office, Phil St. Amant went on television and read a series of questions he had put to a member of the local Teamsters Union. St. Amant also read the member's answers, including one that seemed to implicate Deputy Sheriff Thompson in unlawful activities involving the local union president. Thompson sued St. Amant for defamation and won, and St. Amant appealed.

As a deputy sheriff, Thompson was a public official who had to meet the actual malice standard. The state supreme court ruled that St. Amant acted recklessly because he had no personal knowledge and relied on the union member's affidavit without verifying the information with union officials. The state supreme court also noted that the record did not contain any information on the union member's veracity.

The United States Supreme Court reached a different conclusion. For purposes of the actual malice test, it defined recklessness this way:

> [R]eckless conduct is not measured by whether a reasonably prudent man would have published, or would have investigated before publishing. There must be sufficient evidence to permit the conclusion that the defendant in fact entertained serious doubts as to the truth of his publication. Publishing with such doubts shows reckless disregard for truth or falsity and demonstrates actual malice.

St. Amant v. Thompson, 390 U.S. 727, 731 (1968)

In this case, St. Amant knew his informant, had been able to verify some of the other information the union member had given him, and apparently had no reason to doubt the man's veracity. In fact, the union member had sworn to his answers and placed himself in personal danger by giving them. St. Amant believed the information was correct, and his actions did not satisfy the actual malice standard.

How, then, does a plaintiff show that a defendant entertained serious doubts? He certainly isn't likely to admit it.

One way is by showing that the defendant purposefully avoided sources that could contradict the story. This requires more than St. Amant's failure to check with union officials, who had a strong reason to deny Thompson's charges. But failure to contact neutral sources or ones who would be expected to confirm the story is another matter.

In the *Curtis Publishing* case, the *Saturday Evening Post* article accused Butts of fixing a football game. The author based this conclusion on a conversation between the coaches of the two teams—a conversation that several people inadvertently overheard. One of those people became the source for the magazine article.

Magazine staff knew that the source had a criminal record and that another person (beside the coaches) was present during the conversation, but it did not ask that individual to confirm the source's information. *The Saturday Evening Post* assigned the story to a writer who was not a football expert and did not check with a football expert to find out whether the information disclosed during the conversation was confidential or would have made a difference in the outcome of the game. Taken with the magazine's announced policy of engaging in "sophisticated muckraking," these facts were enough to find actual malice.

Harte-Hanks Communications v. Connaughton had a similar outcome. While running for local judge, Connaughton filed a written complaint against a clerk in his opponent's office. The complaint alleged that the clerk had accepted bribes, and the allegations were based on information provided by Patsy Stephens during a taped interview at Connoughton's home.

There were eight people present at the taped interview, including Stephens' sister, Alice Thompson. After the clerk was indicted, Thompson went to the press and claimed that Connaughton had used dirty tricks to get her sister's testimony. In particular, Thompson claimed that Connaughton had offered the two sisters jobs, a vacation, and other benefits "in appreciation" for cooperating with him in the investigation.

The local paper interviewed Thompson at length. It also interviewed Connaughton, who collaborated some of the minor details but denied the allegations. The newspaper spent substantial resources interviewing most of the other participants in the conversation—whose denials could be discounted as coming from individuals loyal to Connaughton—but it did not make any serious attempts to contact Stephens. Given that she was the primary witness in the bribery case against the clerk, that omission made sense only if the paper had serious doubts about the story and was committed to running it anyway.

The newspaper also had access to tapes of the conversation between the attorney and the sisters but declined to listen to them—another omission that made sense only if the paper was purposefully avoiding sources that could contradict the story it wanted to print. These omissions were sufficient to support the jury's finding that the paper had acted with actual malice.

Unlike public officials and public figures, private individuals are not required to show actual malice. Still, the First Amendment does provide some protection. First, state law may not impose liability without fault. Negligence is enough, however. Second, the plaintiff must show actual injury—physical, emotional, or reputational—to receive compensatory damages. Third, punitive damages are available only if the actual malice standard is met.

The Supreme Court laid down these principles in *Gertz v. Robert Welch, Inc.* The case arose from an incident where a policeman killed a youth and was subsequently convicted of second degree murder. *American Opinion* published an article claiming that the policeman's prosecution was part of a communist plot to replace the regular police force with a national one.

The victim's family had hired Gertz to file a civil lawsuit against the policeman. Few people knew who he was, and the public had no interest in him. He was simply a private attorney doing his job.

Although Gertz was not responsible for and took no part in the criminal case, the *American Opinion* article portrayed him as the conspiracy's architect. The article contained other serious falsehoods that should have been easy to detect, such as claiming that Gertz had a criminal record.

The magazine's editor included an editorial introduction stating that the author had conducted extensive research, but the editor himself did not check any of the information in the article. There was no evidence that the editor knew the article was false, however. Since failure to investigate is not enough, by itself, to show recklessness, the Seventh Circuit Court of Appeals held that Gertz had not shown actual malice. It also held that Gertz's status as a private individual was irrelevant.

The Supreme Court reversed. First, it recognized that, unlike public individuals, private individuals have less access to media and fewer opportunities to correct false statements. Second, it noted that, again unlike public officials and public figures, private individuals do not place themselves in public view. The Court then held that states could adopt a negligence standard for liability to private persons. As noted above, however, punitive damages do require a showing of actual malice.

Russell and Mary Alice Firestone were not on friendly terms when their marriage ended, and the divorce proceedings were filled with acrimonious testimony from both sides. After the judge issued an order dissolving the marriage, *Time* included a short item in the "Milestones" section of the magazine. It stated in part:

> *DIVORCED: By Russell A. Firestone Jr., 41, heir to the tire fortune: Mary Alice Sullivan Firestone, 32, his third wife; . . . on grounds of extreme cruelty and adultery . . . . The 17-month intermittent trial produced enough testimony of extramarital adventures on both sides, said the judge, "to make Dr. Freud's hair curl."*

Time, Inc. v. Firestone, 424 U.S. 448, 452 (1976)

Russell Firestone filed for divorce on the basis of extreme cruelty and adultery, and the judge did say that some of the testimony described events that would have "made Dr. Freud's hair curl." But the judge did not rule that there was extreme cruelty and adultery, nor did he believe everything he heard during the trial. As he put it in the final judgment, "The court is inclined to discount much of this testimony as unreliable. Nevertheless, it is the conclusion and finding of the court that neither party is domesticated . . . ." Based on this conclusion, the judge dissolved the marriage. (424 U.S. 448, 451)

Mrs. Firestone demanded that *Time* issue a retraction. It refused, she sued, and the jury found that *Time* had libeled Mrs. Firestone. The judge had not told them to apply the actual malice test, however, so the magazine appealed. Since the divorce was widely publicized, *Time* claimed that Mrs. Firestone was a public figure.

The U.S. Supreme Court disagreed. It noted that Mary Alice Firestone did not occupy a prominent position in society and had not thrust herself into the limelight on any public controversy. Marriage to a rich man and the public's interest in their subsequent divorce did not make her a public figure, and the jury was not required to apply the actual malice test.

What about writing fiction? Does it change the test? No. In fact, the genre could work against you. If you make something up, you know it isn't true. So if the character is recognizable, you could be liable for defamation.

Regardless of whether the plaintiff is a public official, a public person, or a private individual, a media defendant cannot be found liable for defamation unless the plaintiff proves that the information is false. The U.S. Supreme Court mentioned this principle briefly in *New York Times Co. v. Sullivan*, but it addressed the issue head-on in *Philadelphia Newspapers, Inc. v. Hepps*.

The *Philadelphia Inquirer* ran a series of articles alleging that Hepps' corporation had ties to organized crime and used its connections to obtain legislative and administrative benefits. When Hepps and his company sued the newspaper for defamation, the courts were asked to decide who had the burden to show truth or falsity. If truth is a defense, it puts the burden on the newspaper to show that the information is accurate. If falsity is an element of the claim, it puts the burden on the plaintiff to show that the information is false.

The Supreme Court held that the First Amendment requires the burden to be on the person claiming to be defamed. In other words, Hepps could not collect damages unless he proved that the newspaper's information was false.

But what if the defendant isn't a newspaper? Does the plaintiff still have to prove that the information is false? That isn't clear. The Supreme Court was careful to limit its holding to media defendants discussing matters of public concern, which was enough to decide the case before it. When all the other elements of defamation exist, some states may still require non-media defendants—or anyone writing about matters that are not of public concern—to prove that the statement is true.

As a writer, the First Amendment can work for you or against you. It can work for you if you want to engage in a robust public debate without having to check and double-check every fact for accuracy. But it can—and will—work against you if you expect it to protect you even when you have doubts about the information.

So how can you guard against the First Amendment becoming a Boojum? Start by doing your homework. Then if you still have concerns about the truth of the information, turn off the computer and put down the pen. The First Amendment may or may not save you from paying damages, but it won't reimburse your attorneys' fees.

Part IV

Through the Printing Press
(Contracts and Publishing Rights)

CHAPTER TEN

The Chess Game

(Contract Basics, Grant-of-Rights Clauses)

"I declare it's marked out just like a large chessboard!" Alice said at last. "There ought to be some men moving about somewhere—and so there are!" she added in a tone of delight, and her heart began to beat quickly with excitement as she went on. "It's a great huge game of chess that's being played—all over the world—if this IS the world at all, you know. Oh, what fun it is! How I *wish* I was one of them! I wouldn't mind being a Pawn, if only I might join— though of course I should *like* to be a Queen, best."

Lewis Carroll, *Through the Looking Glass*

All serious writers—and some who aren't—have dreams of joining the great chess game of publication. While standing on the sidelines, they long to play any role, even that of a pawn. But they really yearn to be a queen.

So what happens once you are invited to join? The first step is to sign a publishing contract.

Signing is the easy part. Understanding the contract is harder.

If you are desperate to publish your book, maybe you don't care what the contract says. At least not at first. But down the road, it will matter. And if you aren't quite desperate, you should know what the contract says before you sign it. Even if you can't negotiate, you can walk away.

Contracts are governed by state law, which varies. The principles discussed in these chapters are generally applicable, but if you are unclear about a particular provision in your contract, you should check with your agent or an attorney who is familiar with publishing contacts and the laws of the relevant state. An intellectual property or entertainment attorney is usually the best choice.

What Makes It a Contract?

Contracts are legally binding documents that require each party to do what the party has agreed to do. They are valid only if the parties agree on the basic terms and exchange something of value.

1. Agreeing on Basic Terms

Both parties to the contract must have the same intent. Once a contract is signed, the courts won't let a party say he or she didn't mean what the written terms say. But a contract doesn't always have to be signed—or even written—to be valid. So what if one party says there is a contract and the other says there is not? Either the person claiming that the contract is valid has misunderstood the other person's intent, or the person disclaiming the contract is having second thoughts. How do courts decide who is correct?

One way is to look at whether there has been an offer and an acceptance.

Imagine that a publisher offers to publish your book and sends you a written contract. That is an offer. You look at the contract and say "yes," "no," or "yes if you make some changes to the contract."

"Yes" is an acceptance, and you have a contract. Or you can accept it by signing it.

If you say "no," or even "let me think about it," you have no contract. Of course, your "let me think about it" could change into a "yes" later.

"Yes if" doesn't create a contract either, but it does keep the process going. By modifying the terms offered by the publisher, you have made a counteroffer. If the publisher says "yes" to your counteroffer, that acceptance creates a contract with the revised terms. Or you may go back and forth until you and the publisher either agree to terms or reach an impasse.

Unless you are already a big name, you aren't likely to get many concessions from a publisher, and some won't negotiate at all. But you can always try. If the publisher says "no," you don't have a contract. At that point, however, you can offer to sign the original contract, and the publisher is likely to accept your offer.

2.   Exchanging Something of Value

Contracts require the parties to exchange consideration, which is a legal term to describe what the parties get and give up. The value of the consideration doesn't have to be equal, or even close, but it can't be nominal. In most cases, there must be consideration on each side or the transaction is an unenforceable gift rather than an enforceable contract.

In a typical publishing contract, the writer gives up control of his or her manuscript and receives royalties and possibly an advance. The publisher gets control of the manuscript and pays money (royalties and any advance) to the writer. Each party is getting and giving up something of value.

3.   Implied Contracts and Contracts by Estoppel

In some circumstances, the courts will find a contract even when the parties have not discussed it or the consideration is one-sided. In these situations, it isn't the parties' words that create the contract; it's their actions.

When you go to the grocery store and pick up a loaf of bread, you don't tell the clerk, "I will pay you X amount in exchange for this bread." But if you walk out with it, you had better have paid for it first. There is an implied contract that the grocer will sell and the customer will buy at the grocer's set price. As with express contracts, however, the parties understand and agree on the basic terms.

Contracts by estoppel are the exception to the rule that both sides must receive consideration. Estoppel is a fancy legal word for "stop." In these cases, one person makes a promise and a second person reasonably relies on that promise to his or her detriment. The courts then stop the person who made the promise from claiming there was no consideration.

Assume you want to study abroad for a semester but have given up that dream because you don't have the money. When your uncle finds out, he promises to pay your expenses. Relying on his promise, you buy a non-refundable airplane ticket, put a forfeitable deposit on an inexpensive apartment, and pay the extra tuition required by the foreign university. Before you can give you uncle the bills, however, he says he has changed his mind. Because you relied on his promise, the courts will stop him from claiming there is no contract. There wasn't one to begin with, but when you relied on his promise to your detriment (by paying money you can't get back), you created a contract by estoppel.

Both implied contracts and contracts by estoppel are rare in the writing business. You don't create either by sending in your manuscript when a publisher asks to see it. That is simply industry practice, and the publisher's request does not include a promise to publish it or to pay you if the publisher uses your uncopyrightable ideas.

At least, not usually.

Mark Landsberg wrote a book on how to win at Scrabble. He contacted the company that owned the Scrabble trademark and asked for permission to use it. The company requested a copy of the manuscript and entered into lengthy negotiations with Landsberg for the publishing rights. During the negotiations, the company sent the manuscript to a different Scrabble expert and asked him to write a chapter for the company's own strategy book.

You guessed it. The negotiations went nowhere and the company published its book instead of Landsberg's.

Landsberg sued for copyright infringement and breach of implied contract. The copyright claim failed because the company's expert used Landsberg's ideas rather than his expression, and—as discussed in Chapter 3—ideas are not copyrightable. But Landsberg did succeed on his implied contract claim.

The court found that Landsberg sent in the manuscript because the company had led him to believe that it would not use the manuscript without getting his consent and paying for the privilege. His belief was reasonable based on the company's conduct—primarily its expressed interest in negotiating for publishing rights rather than just reviewing it for possible publication.

Many publishers ask to see a manuscript before deciding whether to publish it, and this practice does not create an implied contract. It was the specific facts that won the case for Landsberg, including the company's apparent attempt to lead him to believe that it wanted to publish Landsberg's book when all it really wanted was to let its own expert use the manuscript as a reference.

❧

Chapters 10–12 of this book discuss clauses in contracts with traditional publishers, defined here as publishers who take all the monetary risk. Situations where you pay to publish your book are covered in Chapter 17.

The Heart of the Agreement

What is the most important part of your book contract? You might think it is royalties or subsidiary rights or who owns the copyright, but you'd be wrong. They're all important, but if you and the publisher have different ideas about what you're writing and when you'll deliver it, nothing else matters.

One of the first clauses in your book contract should describe the work. This normally includes the book's subject matter and tentative title. You also want it to include an approximate word or page count.

Some contracts, especially with smaller publishers, don't include information on the book. This can be dangerous, especially if you sold the book on a proposal. If the contract doesn't describe the book, the publisher might try to get out of the contract by claiming that you aren't giving the publisher the book it bought. Most publishers are honest, but some will try to back out of a deal when the market weakens.

If you have a specific direction you want the book to go, try to get the contract to describe it. If you haven't written the book yet, try to get the outline or synopsis attached as an exhibit. This will help ensure that the publisher is looking for the same book you are writing and is particularly important for edgy fiction or for non-fiction aimed at a limited audience.

The contract should also say when you have to deliver the completed manuscript. Sometimes it will be a single date, and sometimes the contract will ask for the manuscript in sections. Or it might set one deadline for the original manuscript and another for returning the galleys. Make sure any deadlines listed in the contract are realistic for your writing situation. Some publishers will be gracious and provide additional time, but others won't. The publishing business has certain release dates, and publishers try to fill a set number of slots for each one. If your book misses its slot, your publisher won't be happy.

Publishing contracts may also spell out how you are to deliver the manuscript. This can include both the delivery type (hard copy, disk, e-mail attachment) and the document format (e.g., Microsoft Word). Make sure you either know how to comply with these requirements or can hire someone to do it for you.

Grant-of-Rights Clauses

You've found a publisher for your masterpiece, and you want to be sure that it remains YOUR masterpiece. That's why the grant-of-rights clause is so important.

If you sell your house, you give up control. The new buyer can remodel your "perfect" kitchen or even tear the house down, and there is nothing you can do about it. If you rent it out instead, you can restrict the tenant's ability to make changes, say how long the lease will last, and even provide for early termination if the tenant trashes the house or falls behind in rent payments. While it isn't a perfect analogy, the same is true for copyrights.

Copyrights are property, and you can sell them. You can also rent out ("assign" or "license" in copyright lingo) some or all of the rights that go with them. These include the right to reproduce your book and to distribute your book to the public.

A grant-of-rights clause establishes who owns the copyright and who gets to exercise specific rights that come with it. At a minimum, traditional publishers expect authors to assign them the exclusive rights to reproduce a book and distribute it to the public. And they should expect that. These rights are the main thing a traditional publisher receives in exchange for the monetary risk of publishing a book that may or may not sell: a risk that wouldn't be worth taking if the author could compete with the publisher.

While a traditional publisher expects to have the benefit of these exclusive rights, it can protect itself by renting them from the author; it does not need to buy the copyright. If the publisher is responsible for registering the copyright, the contract should say that it will be registered in your name. Even if the contract refers to it as a sale, if the copyright stays in your name, it is really a lease. If the contract requires you to put the copyright in the publisher's name, it's a sale.

This is one place where the house analogy breaks down. A contract that sells the copyright to the publisher may contain provisions limiting what the publisher can do with it and providing for the publisher to return the copyright to the author if the publisher goes out of business or the book goes out of print. Academic publishers often buy the copyright but agree to give it back under these conditions.

So if you do decide to sell the copyright, make sure you can live with the terms of the sale.

The copyright lease may be, and often is, for an indefinite time, but the contract should contain some provisions for terminating it. Those clauses are covered in Chapter 12.

When you pay to have the book published, there is no reason to lease out your rights. You can give a the publisher permission to reproduce and sell books on your behalf and to register the copyright in your name without giving up your ability to find a different publisher or distribution method any time you want.

But if you are entering into a contract with a traditional publisher, you will have to give up some of your rights for the duration of the contract. That's just the way it is. Still, it's better to lease than to sell.

Some contracts include subsidiary rights in the grant-of-rights clause, but others deal with them separately. Subsidiary rights are covered in the next chapter.

CHAPTER ELEVEN

The White Queen

(Royalties, Subsidiary Rights, Satisfactory Manuscript Clauses)

> Alice laughed. "There's no use trying," she said. "One *ca'n't* believe impossible things."
>
> "I daresay you haven't had much practice," said the Queen. "When I was your age, I always did it for half-an-hour a day. Why, sometimes I've believed as many as six impossible things before breakfast."
>
> Lewis Carroll, *Through the Looking Glass*

Have you ever imagined six impossible things before breakfast? Writers dream that they will become rich from book sales and that their novels will be made into movies. For a few, these dreams come true, but for most writers they seem impossible. And for some people, even completing a decent manuscript turns out to be an unreachable dream.

This chapter covers contract provisions for getting paid from book sales. It also addresses subsidiary rights and unsatisfactory manuscript clauses.

Royalties and Advances

A royalty is the amount that the publisher pays you for each book it sells. Unfortunately, dealing with royalties in your publishing contract isn't as simple as asking, "How much?" You also need to ask, "How much of what?"

Royalties may be based on the suggested retail price (also called the list price) of the book. Since the list price doesn't change, you receive the same amount for every sale, which makes the math easy. While a royalty based on the retail price locks in your return, however, it can create problems for the publisher. Publishers can't sell to booksellers at retail prices, and even wholesale prices are negotiated. In order to get your book in a distributor's catalog or on a bookstore's shelves, the publisher may have to give the distributor or bookstore a deeper discount than other booksellers receive.

Some publishers handle this issue by basing royalties on "net." The term can be misleading, however, because some contracts use it to refer to the gross amount the publisher receives from the bookseller, while other contracts mean the net amount the publisher receives after subtracting its expenses. If your royalties are described as "net," make sure the contract spells out how they are calculated. Either way, the net price is quite a bit less than the retail price and makes the author's actual return vary from sale to sale.

Assume your book retails for $10.00. If you receive 8% of the list price, that is 80¢. If you receive 8% of the gross "net" and the publisher discounts the sale by 40%, you get 48¢ (.08 x $6). If you receive 8% of the true net and expenses are $3.00 per book, your royalty on that same discounted sale is 24¢ [.08 x ($6 - $3)].

While there is nothing intrinsically bad about net-based royalties, it takes a higher royalty percentage to make the same income you would receive from royalties figured on the retail price. So if your royalty is based on net, make sure the percentage is substantially higher than you would accept otherwise.

But what is the standard royalty percentage? There is none. Rates vary with the publisher and the type of book (hardcover, trade paperback, mass market paperback, e-book). Many contracts also increase the royalty rate at set sales levels. Below are some typical rates paid by established publishing companies. Small presses and children's book publishers often pay less.

Hardcover: 10% of retail for the first 5,000 copies sold, 12.5% for the next 5,000, and 15% after that.

Trade Paperback: 6-8% of retail for the first 25,000 copies sold and 8-10% after that.

Mass Market Paperback: 6-8% of retail for the first 150,000 copies sold and 8-10% after that.

E-Book: Not only is there no standard rate, but it may be a while before the industry reaches a consensus on what is fair. If you sign with an e-book publisher or a traditional publisher that also does e-books, it may offer anything from 10% of retail to 50% of net. If it is licensing the rights to a third party, you should get at least half of what the publisher receives for the license.

Other Subsidiary Rights Licensed to Third Parties: 50% of what the publisher receives. The author's percentage may increase for subsidiary rights with a higher potential return, such as movie rights.

Some publishers pay advances, and some don't. Advances are nice because you collect some money upfront and may get to keep the money even if your book bombs.

Advances are not bonuses. As the name implies, they are advances against royalties. If the publisher pays you a $5,000 advance and you make a $1 royalty on each book, the publisher won't send you any more money until it has sold 5,001 copies.

Getting Paid

Now that you know your royalty percentage, your next question is, "How often do I get paid?"

Unlike the day job where you get a paycheck at least twice a month, most publishers pay you twice a year. Others pay quarterly or annually. Even worse, publishers may send the money as much as six months after sending the royalty statement.

If your publisher issues royalty statements as of June 30 and December 31 and your book releases on March 1, you will probably receive your first statement sometime in July. But your check for the sales shown on the June 30 statement may come as late as December 31. And that's assuming you didn't get an advance or you sold enough copies in the first four months to earn the advance. If not, you'll be waiting even longer for your first royalty check.

There really isn't much you can do about this. It's just the way things work. Still, you should read the contract and make sure you know when royalty statements and checks are due. If you don't get them on time, ask for them.

If your publisher prints hundreds or thousands of copies at once, the contract will probably allow the publisher to withhold a reserve against returns. A 10% reserve means that the publisher can hold back the royalties on 10% of the books it "sells" to bookstores and other distributors during that royalty period. The reserve may be as high as 15-25% for hardcover books and trade paperbacks and 35-50% for mass market paperbacks, or the contract may merely allow the publisher to withhold a "reasonable" reserve.

Withholding a reserve is fair because distributors can return unsold books for a refund. If a book is returned, you don't have a right to receive a royalty on it. What isn't fair is when the reserve amount is higher than the expected return rate or the contract gives the publisher complete discretion by leaving out the word "reasonable." A good contract will also provide that amounts held for a certain period of time (usually two accounting periods or a year) without being offset by returns will be released from the reserve fund and sent to the author with the next royalty payment.

Returns aren't common for print-on-demand (POD) and e-books, so those contracts should not allow the publisher to keep a reserve against returns. If the contract covers more than one format, make sure the reserve applies to only those formats with multiple-copy print runs.

You **don't** want your contract to contain a joint accounting clause. This provision allows the publisher to pay the unearned advance and author's expenses on one book with the royalties from another. If your first book doesn't earn back its advance but the second one does (or vice versa), a joint accounting clause would let the publisher apply the excess royalties from the more successful book to the remaining advance on the less successful one. Until the two books together earn back both advances, you won't see another cent.

There is some justification for joint accounting among the books covered by a multi-book contract since they are all part of the same deal. But watch out for joint accounting clauses that let the publisher apply royalties earned under one contract to the shortfall on a different contract with the same publisher.

On the other hand, you **do** want your contract to include an audit clause. This clause gives you the right to audit the publisher's financial records that show sales and expenses for your book. Ideally, you also want the contract to say that the publisher will pay the auditor's fees if the audit shows a discrepancy of 5% or more in your favor, but most writers don't have the bargaining power to insist on it.

Audits are expensive, so this clause is rarely applied. Even so, if you believe the publisher is paying you less than it owes you, simply threatening an audit may convince it to review its own records and pay you any discrepancy. But the threat is worthless unless you have an audit clause.

Subsidiary Rights

The book contract gives the publisher the exclusive right to publish your book in hardback, paperback, and maybe (as is increasingly common) as an e-book. But your dreams are bigger than that. In your mind, you have already cast Julia Roberts or Reese Witherspoon or Emma Watson to play your heroine when the novel hits the big screen. And of course it will be picked for Oprah's book club and translated into every language from Spanish to Russian to Japanese.

These are called subsidiary rights because they are not the main reason you entered into the book contract. Common subsidiary rights include the following:

- First serialization, or the right to publish all or part of the book as a series in a magazine or newspaper **before** the book comes out (following in Charles Dickens's footsteps);

- Second serialization, or the right to publish all or part of the book as a series **after** the book comes out;

- Movies, plays, and broadcasts;

- Audio books;

- Book club selections;

- Translations and foreign sales;

- Abridgments and condensations (think *Readers Digest Condensed Books*); and

- Anthologies.

E-book rights may be either primary rights or subsidiary rights, depending on the publisher's expertise and intent.

Returning to the leasing analogy, who gets to find the tenants for these secondary rights? And why does it matter?

As an aside, the contract won't call them tenants, and neither will the people you deal with. The people who purchase these secondary rights are usually referred to as licensees or rights holders. The landlord/tenant analogy is easier to understand, however.

A building manager who finds tenants gets paid for the service, and so does a publisher. If the book contract includes subsidiary rights, the publisher gets to keep part of the rent. If you retain the subsidiary rights, you can find the tenants and retain the entire rent, or you can let your agent do it for a lower percentage than the publisher would take.

But what if neither you nor your agent has connections in the movie industry? A small cut of something is better than a large cut of nothing, so you may want to let the publisher find a tenant for the movie rights. The same is true for other subsidiary interests.

Your contract should list the subsidiary rights the publisher gets to find tenants for, and it should also state that any rights not on the list are yours to do with as you wish. You also want a provision that lets you look for a tenant if the publisher hasn't found one within a certain period of time. The contract may refer to it as "selling" these rights, but unless the actual copyright changes hands, it is really a lease.

Approval Rights and Satisfactory Manuscript Clauses

You've signed the contract, submitted the book, and told your Facebook friends that you are going to be a published author.

Then you get the publisher's edits and gasp because they change the look and feel of the story and eliminate your voice. Or worse, the publisher turned your family-friendly story into an X-rated one.

Researching publishers before you submit is your best defense against the publisher that doesn't understand or accept the purpose of your book. The contract is your next best defense.

Ideally, you want your contract to require your consent to any changes except copyedits that conform the manuscript to the publisher's style manual. Second-best is language requiring the publisher to consult with you before making changes. If the contract lets the publisher make the final decision and you are worried that it won't honor your message, you may be better walking away without signing.

Here's a different scenario. You get a letter from the publisher telling you the book isn't good enough and it has decided not to publish your masterpiece. Worse yet, the publisher wants the advance back.

Most contracts contain a clause requiring the author to deliver a "satisfactory manuscript." Since many books are sold on proposals, this is how publishers protect themselves from wasting money on a bad product.

Can a publisher use this clause as an excuse to terminate a contract merely because the publisher has lost interest in the subject matter? It depends on the language in the contract. If it calls for a manuscript that is satisfactory "in form and content," most courts impose a good faith obligation on the publisher: an obligation that appears, at a minimum, to require the publisher to give the author some editorial assistance and a chance to revise and resubmit the manuscript.

Here is a sampling of cases involving unsatisfactory manuscript clauses. They are listed from most recent to oldest.

- John Nance was already an established author of action novels when he entered into a three-book contract with Random House affiliates. The contract stated that the publisher could reject the manuscript if it concluded that the manuscript "cannot be revised to [the publisher's] satisfaction within a timely period or should Publisher find the revised Work or any portion thereof unacceptable for any reason." The first book was published, but the editors rejected the manuscript for the second after substantial input from the publishers and two rewrites by the author. The judge ruled that there was no evidence the publishers had acted in bad faith and ordered Nance to repay the advances for the second and third novels.

- Doubleday & Company entered into a two-book contract with actor Tony Curtis. With the help of a skillful, hands-on editor, Doubleday turned the first novel into a commercial success. The second novel ended up with a different editor, who also provided detailed critiques and comments. Unfortunately, his efforts weren't enough to save the book. In the end, Doubleday determined that the manuscript was unsalvageable. A clause in the contract said that the manuscript must be "satisfactory to the Publisher in content and form." The Second Circuit Court of Appeals interpreted this to mean that Doubleday could terminate the contract only if it was honestly dissatisfied with the manuscript. But Doubleday met that requirement. It had expended significant time and effort to help Curtis produce a satisfactory manuscript, and the trial court found that Doubleday had acted in good faith. On appeal, the Second Circuit affirmed the finding and ordered Curtis to repay his advance.

- Julia Whedon's contract with Dell Publishing Co. contained a clause requiring that her manuscript be satisfactory "in form, style, and content." Dell entered into the contract based on an outline and appeared enthusiastic when Whedon submitted the first half of the manuscript. When she submitted the completed manuscript, however, she was told that it wasn't what Dell expected. It rejected the manuscript and sued Whedon for the advance. Dell lost the case because the judge determined that it had acted in bad faith by rejecting the manuscript without providing editorial assistance that might have made the manuscript satisfactory "in form, style, and content."

- Harcourt Brace Jovanovich, Inc. entered into a contract with Barry Goldwater to publish the senator's memoirs. The contract required that the manuscript be "satisfactory to the publisher in form and content." Unfortunately, Harcourt never liked Goldwater's choice of ghost writer. When it could not get Goldwater to agree to a different one, it rejected the manuscript in spite of repeated attempts by the authors to get Harcourt's input on how to make the manuscript satisfactory. The book subsequently found another home and became a best seller using the original ghost writer. The judge found that Harcourt had acted in bad faith and could not recover the advance.

- Eric Lasher pitched J.B. Lippincott Co. on an as yet unwritten non-fiction book about the handful of Berlin Jews who had survived the Holocaust. The decision does not disclose the actual language of the satisfactory manuscript clause, but the manuscript was to be delivered to the publisher by January 31, 1969. After Lasher requested numerous extensions (which Lippincott granted) and additional advances (which Lippincott paid) to allow him to complete his research, Lasher still had not delivered a manuscript by September 1, 1972. That's when Lippincott terminated the contract and sued to recover the advances. The judge gave Lippincott what it asked for.

Publishers do have significant leeway in determining whether a manuscript is satisfactory. The courts recognize that evaluating literary works involves an element of subjective judgment. "What in good faith may be acceptable to one publisher may be, in equally good faith, not acceptable to a different publisher." (*Nance v. Random House, Inc.*, 212 F.Supp.2d 268, 273 (S.D.N.Y. 2002)) The mere fact that one publisher accepts what another rejects does not demonstrate bad faith on the part of the rejecting publisher. That's why, in searching for a more objective test, the courts have concentrated on the editorial assistance and second chances the rejecting publisher gave the author.

Even that may not apply if the contract says you get only one shot or no editing help. Still, courts are unwilling to give a publisher an "unfettered license to act or not to act in any way it wishes and to accept or reject a book for any reason whatever. If this were the case, the publisher could simply make a contract and arbitrarily change its mind and that would be an illusory contract." (*Harcourt Brace Jovanovich, Inc. v. Goldwater*, 532 F.Supp. 619, 624 (S.D.N.Y. 1982))

For an author, the best contract allows you to keep any advances the publisher has already paid unless you sell the book to a different publisher. In that event, you would have to pay back only as much as you received from the second publisher. This is all the court required Nance to do. The courts allowed Goldwater and Whedon to keep their entire advances even though they had resold their manuscripts, but that is because the publishers had acted in bad faith.

If you miss your deadlines or supply an inferior product, you may be required to repay any advances. But if the publisher terminates the contract for reasons beyond your control—such as going out of business—the contract should allow you to keep the entire amount you have already received.

If the publisher has seen your entire manuscript before entering into the contract, it might not ask for a "satisfactory manuscript" clause. Even so, if your manuscript is a diamond in the rough, a publisher may want the clause to protect it if the polished version doesn't sparkle.

&

Six-figure royalties and movie contracts may seem like impossible dreams, but impossible dreams sometimes come true. Or those dreams may turn into nightmares if you can't write a satisfactory manuscript in the first place. Better to be a White Queen who believes and prepares for them than an Alice who is caught by surprise.

CHAPTER TWELVE
The Gnat
("Lesser" Clauses)

"I know you are a friend," the little voice went on; "a dear friend, and an old friend, and you won't hurt me, though *I am* an insect."

"What kind of insect?" Alice inquired a little anxiously. What she really wanted to know was, whether it could sting or not, but she thought this wouldn't be quite a civil question to ask.

Lewis Carroll, *Through the Looking Glass*

Insects may seem harmless until they bite or sting. In the same way, many contract clauses appear inconsequential and tend to be overlooked—until they are invoked. This chapter discusses the seemingly minor clauses that publishers often include in their book contracts.

Options on Subsequent Works

Most book contracts contain an option clause, or at least a right of first refusal. While some people distinguish those terms, others use them interchangeably. For simplicity, this discussion calls them all option clauses.

An option clause basically says you can't sell your next book to a different publisher unless the current publisher doesn't want it.

The publisher is taking a chance on you and investing resources in a book that may fail, so shouldn't the publisher have the right to benefit from subsequent books if its gamble pays off? That seems logical. Still, the option clause has no benefit for the author, so you'd rather eliminate it.

If you can't negotiate it away, what provisions should you look for or try to avoid in the clause?

- **When you can submit the next book.** Ideally, the contract should allow you to submit another manuscript shortly after you have delivered a satisfactory manuscript for the contracted book. If the contract doesn't allow you to submit the next one until the publisher can see how the first is doing, you may not be able to seek a publisher for the second book for two years or more.

- **What you can submit.** If the clause requires a completed manuscript, you will have to write the entire book first. The better clause will let you submit a detailed outline and one or two chapters.

- **How soon the publisher must respond.** Sixty days is good. If the time is open-ended, the publisher can tie up the next deal indefinitely.

- **The terms of the next deal.** Some contracts state that the author grants the publisher the right to publish the author's next book—if the publisher accepts it—"on the same terms" as the current deal. That means even the option clause carries over, so the author will never get a better deal until the publisher finally rejects a book. "On the same financial terms" is marginally better: at least you may be able to negotiate the option clause and other non-financial issues. "On terms to be mutually agreed upon" is best.

- **The scope of the clause.** A clause that simply refers to your next manuscript means **any** manuscript, regardless of genre. Try to get the contract language to say the option only applies to your next novel, your next children's picture book, or your next nonfiction book on the same or a related topic.

- **How many manuscripts.** You want to limit it to one book.
- **A "no less favorable terms" provision.** The worst case scenario is when your contract allows your publisher—after it has already rejected the manuscript—to match an offer from another publisher and get the book after all. That practically kills any chance you have to sell the next book elsewhere. No publisher wants to waste time and resources preparing a book for committee and negotiating a contract only to have another publisher take it away.

In colonial days, indentured servitude provided European immigrants with opportunities they would not otherwise have had. It was a voluntary choice by people with a strong desire to come to the New World but no money to pay the fare. Yes, sometimes the conditions were atrocious, but the indenture was a means to an end, and the end was freedom to pursue their dreams in the colonies.

For writers, option clauses are another type of indentured servitude. If that's the price of getting published, you may be happy to sign the contract anyway. Just make sure that the terms of your indentured servitude are ones you can live with.

Book Promotion

Authors and publishers have the same goal: to maximize book sales. How close you come to that goal depends on a number of factors, and most have nothing to do with the contract. But some do.

Once upon a time, the publisher took the primary responsibility for marketing. Today, that is no longer the case. Still, the publisher wants to see the book succeed, so it may at least agree to send out advance reader copies and press kits and provide postcards or bookmarks (or give you a copy of the artwork so you can make your own). If the publisher says it will create a trailer or sponsor a book tour, the contract should spell that out. If the publisher won't agree to put its promises in writing, assume you will be doing all the promotion on your own.

Some contracts explicitly turn the historical relationship around and require the author to self-promote the book. For most writers, a clause that requires them to use their best efforts is not a problem. After all, they want to do what they can to make their books successful. But beware of clauses that include objective measurements or require promotional activities that are beyond your time, resources, or talents.

Ideally, the contract will say how much of the book you can reproduce for promotional purposes. Can you post three chapters on your website? Or one? Or none? Even if you still own the copyright, you are leasing most or all of the publication rights to your publisher. That means you violate the contract if you use more than the publisher allows.

Most publishers give you several free copies and let you buy additional ones at a discount, which is often 40-50% of retail. (And no, you don't get royalties on these copies.) You can give these "author's copies" away. If you want to sell them at speaking events or book fairs, however, make sure the contract doesn't prohibit it. A clause that says the books you purchase at a discount are "for the author's own use, and not for resale" means that you can't sell them. You can, however, send free copies to reviewers and to acquaintances who will encourage others to buy the book through traditional channels.

The wrong title, front-cover design, or back-cover copy could damage your sales, so try to retain as much control over them as you can. The publisher often has a better feel for what makes a title work than the author does, and the same is true for the back-cover copy. Still, even the most experienced professionals can make mistakes. Although few publishers will allow you full control over the title and back-cover copy, some will give you approval rights. If yours won't, try for a provision that says the publisher will consult with you. That doesn't guarantee the publisher will listen to your comments, but most will try to find a compromise.

The publisher usually creates and pays for the front-cover design, so the author is not likely to get approval rights. It's also hard to get consultation rights, but you can at least ask for them and see what the publisher says.

Competing Works

Before a publisher buys your book, you may have to tell the house what other books are out there that compete with yours. By the time you sign your contract, however, the publisher is more concerned about how the book competes with itself. A competing works clause prohibits you from competing through a different publisher.

The clause isn't necessary for fiction, and many fiction contracts don't have one. If the contract for your novel contains a competing works clause, try to eliminate it. If the publisher won't agree, make sure the wording isn't so broad that it could prohibit you from using the same characters in other books. If it could, you may be better walking away.

Nonfiction is different. Say you have written a college textbook for introductory psychology classes. It will compete with other introductory college textbooks in the market, and your publisher knows that. But the publisher does not expect it to compete with a similar textbook you wrote for the same audience but self-published or sold to a different publisher. This is also true for a Bible study on Lamentations or a travel guide to Spain. It isn't fair for the author to compete with a publisher that has taken a risk and invested its money.

Still, a clause that simply talks about "competing works" could apply to anything with the same subject matter, so try to narrow it if you can. See if you can limit the prohibition to psychology textbooks or, even better, to introductory psychology textbooks. And if developments in psychology move fast enough that a textbook is obsolete after five years, maybe you can get the clause to terminate then.

Revision Clauses

What if the publisher wants to update the book and release it as a new edition? Are you required to make the changes? What happens when you don't?

This is where the revision clause comes in. This provision is especially important for textbooks and other nonfiction books containing information that changes over time. It doesn't apply to fiction, so try to remove it from the contract for your novel.

A revision clause spells out who makes the updates and who pays for them. Many clauses require you, as the original author, to make the changes. Some give you the right of first refusal, meaning that the publisher must offer you the opportunity but you don't have to accept it. Ideally, you want to retain as much control as possible over who will make the revisions if you don't.

If you are unable or unwilling to revise the book, the usual clause allows the publisher to hire someone else. That person will get paid from your royalties, so you want to make sure the amount is not excessive. It might be a flat fee, or it might be a percentage of the royalties. If you were getting a 10% royalty and the reviser gets 2%, your subsequent royalty rate will be 8%.

Then there are issues such as whether the reviser is listed as a coauthor, whether you can take your name off if the reviser ruins the book, and how many revisions the book can go through before the contract simply terminates. If you care about the answers, make sure they are addressed in the contract.

Representations, Warranties, and Indemnification

You love the sentiment in a popular love song written last year, and you want your hero to sing it to your heroine. If you include the lyrics, you probably need permission to use them. And if your autobiography says terrible things about your ex-spouse, those things had better be true.

But what do defamation and other peoples' copyrights have to do with book contracts? A lot. If your words aren't legal, the injured party may sue both you and the person with the largest bank account, which is usually the publisher. So the publisher wants to protect itself as much as it can.

The publisher does this through the representations and warranties clause in your contract. The difference between representations and warranties is too technical for most writers to worry about, so this chapter refers to them both as "warranties."

A warranty is a promise that you have or haven't done something in the past or will or won't do something in the future. For practical purposes, the warranties clause makes you promise that nothing in your book is likely to get the publisher sued.

The main warranties promise that

- You own the copyright and nobody else has a legal interest in it;
- You didn't plagiarize or infringe on anyone else's copyright; and
- The book doesn't defame people or violate their privacy rights.

If you are selling a previously self-published book to a traditional publisher, you don't want to warrant that it has never been published. Even if the publisher knows the book's history, it may forget to remove the warranty from its standard contract, so make sure you point it out and get it deleted.

Be sure to read all of the warranties and make sure they are true—or at least that you honestly believe they are. But what if you made all these warranties and the publisher gets sued anyway?

The indemnification clause in your contract says you will reimburse the publisher for any legal fees and judgments it has to pay. If you were at fault, that's only fair. But here are some things to watch out for in the indemnification clause.

- A provision that covers **any** lawsuit, including one that is the publisher's fault. Indemnification should be limited to claims on matters you have warranted and should exclude any material added by the publisher.

- Wording that allows the publisher to settle the case without your approval. As an author, you want a clause that requires your approval of the settlement and says the publisher will pay half. After all, a settlement isn't a determination that you did anything wrong.

- Language that says you have to pay the publisher's legal fees even if you and the publisher win the case. Publishers may argue—with some validity—that this provision is fair since the publisher is defending you, too, and the case was about what you did, not what the publisher did. Still, the publisher has more incentive to keep legal fees reasonable if it bears some responsibility for paying them. A clause that says you don't have to reimburse the publisher for legal fees if you win the case is best, but one that splits the fees in half is better than making you pay them all.

- A provision that allows the publisher to withhold all royalties from all contracts until the lawsuit is over. Try to limit the withheld royalties to those earned under the contract for the book involved in the lawsuit and to no more than a reasonable estimate of the expected damages and legal fees.

"Can't I get insurance to cover this?" you ask. Probably, but a personal insurance policy is expensive. On the other hand, the publisher may be able to add you to its liability insurance for little extra cost. If your publisher agrees to do that, make sure your contract says it. Insurance isn't a perfect fix since you will still be responsible for the deductible—which may be quite high—and any amount over the limit. Still, it's better to be added to the publisher's insurance than to have no protection at all.

Permissions Clauses

You have probably warranted that you will not use copyrighted material without permission. "Fine," you say, "I'll use it **with** permission."

But whose responsibility is it to get permission and at whose expense? That's the function of a permissions clause. The typical clause requires the author to get the permissions and to pay any related costs. You may have to give that famous songwriter $1,000 to quote his lyrics. If your book is illustrated or contains photographs, maps, and charts that you didn't create, that can get expensive, too. Make sure you calculate the expenses—including a generous overrun for the unexpected—before you sign the contract. Then decide whether the royalty is high enough to make it worthwhile. Or maybe you can live without the lyrics to that popular love song.

Choice of Forum and Choice of Law Clauses

Did you notice that all of the cases discussed in Chapter 11 came from New York? The writers probably lived in various areas of the country, but most big publishing houses are located in New York City. They probably used the choice of forum clauses in their contracts to keep the cases in their backyard.

Choice of forum clauses can take several forms. The simplest clause says that you agree to be sued in the publisher's jurisdiction, meaning that a New York publisher can sue you in New York even if you live in California. These clauses may also require you to sue the publisher in the same jurisdiction. If you have a dispute that goes to court, you may have to travel but the publisher won't.

Another type of forum clause requires disputes to be mediated. You and the publisher work with a neutral third party to come to an agreement. In a sense, the mediator helps you settle the case. If an agreement is reached, it becomes binding. If you can't agree, you can take the case to either arbitration or court.

An arbitration clause requires the parties—writer and publisher— to submit disputes to arbitration rather than filing lawsuits in court. The clause will say which rules the parties must use to resolve the dispute. Either the publishing contract or the arbitration forum's rules will spell out how arbitrators are selected.

Arbitration has both advantages and disadvantages. There are two main disadvantages. First, you may give up some of the procedural protections you receive in a court case. Second, you cannot appeal the decision to the courts when you believe that the arbitrators reached the wrong result.

The main advantages are speed and cost. While arbitration doesn't happen overnight, it tends to be much quicker to arbitrate than to take the same case to court. The upfront costs may be higher and you will probably still need an attorney, but because you give up some of the procedural protections, arbitration tends to be less complicated. As a result, the amount you pay your lawyer can be substantially less than for a lawsuit. And while it is true that you can't appeal the merits of the case, neither can the publisher. This eliminates the time and expense involved in those appeals.

Even an industry forum has its advantages. Imagine explaining that pesky option clause to a jury that knows nothing about writing and publishing books. Industry arbitrators already understand these issues and don't have to be educated. This saves additional time and money.

Some writers worry that industry arbitrators will be prejudiced in favor of the publisher, but it isn't likely. Nobody is perfect, and even some judges are biased. Still, most arbitrators understand and honor their ethical obligation to render a fair decision. If they don't, that's the exception to the rule that you can't appeal the case to a court. The courts can and do overturn arbitration awards when the arbitrators are biased or the procedures are unfair.

Most contracts include a choice of law clause. This clause says which state's laws will apply to the contract, and it doesn't have to be the same state where the contract is signed or a dispute is heard. This provision benefits both parties by eliminating potential confusion on which law to use to interpret the contract.

Out-of-Print and Reversion Clauses

You hope your book will have a long life, but few stories are immortal. Yours might be another *Odyssey* (as in the one written by Homer), but it's more likely to be one of the tidal wave of books that go out of print every year. Chances are, your manuscript will eventually die.

Much as you'd like to pretend it will never happen, the birth of your publishing contract is the best time to plan the death of your book. Your contract contains its funeral instructions.

Not that the contract is trying to hasten the book's demise. Your publisher wants it to live a long, healthy life. But even a book should be prepared for death, and the out-of-print and reversion clauses (which may be combined) tell the publisher when to pull the plug.

It used to be a lot easier to know when a book was deceased. If the publisher decided that it couldn't sell enough copies to cover the cost of another print run, it would simply refuse to print more. That refusal was the book's death certificate.

Today, with e-books and POD, the publisher can print and sell single copies without losing money. As a result, books with sales that would formerly have put them out of print may now be kept alive by life support. But that may not be what you want. It's better to have a contract clause that uses more objective measures for determining that the book is out of print. Here are some examples:

- The book is out of print when the publisher has sold less than __ books of any type (e-book, print on demand, mass market paperback, trade paperback, hardback) over the past __ months;
- The book is out of print when the contract has generated less than $__ in royalties over the past __ months (or during the last accounting period);
- The book is in print only while copies of an English-language print edition are readily available and offered for sale in the U.S. through regular channels and listed in the publisher's catalog.

Since some authors want to pull the plug sooner than others do, this book doesn't fill in the blanks. But your contract should.

Why would you ever want to take your book off life support? As mentioned in Chapter 10, the contract gives your publisher an exclusive lease to certain rights. While the contract is in effect, you can't use those rights yourself. If sales are slow and you think you can sell the book to a different publisher or do better on your own, you want the lease to terminate so you will get your rights back.

The contract should state that the rights revert to you if the contract terminates under the out-of-print clause or for any other reason. It should also require the publisher to notify you when the book goes out of print. Even better is a provision that requires the publisher to also notify you when the book's vital statistics indicate that it is close to death.

The contract may terminate for other reasons, such as the publishing company's bankruptcy. The author should receive the same reversion rights as it would if the book were out of print. This is also true if the publisher wants to abort the manuscript before it is published. Ideally, the contract will require the publisher to publish the book within a specified period after receiving an acceptable manuscript and will provide for the rights to revert to you if the publisher misses its deadline.

Regardless of the cause of your book's demise, you want the right to purchase any remaining copies from the publisher at a deep discount. The best provision will also allow you to purchase—at cost—any existing electronic files, plates, and films, and any artwork owned by the publisher.

Authors shouldn't have to repay unearned advances if the book is out of print, the publisher misses its deadline, or the reasons for the termination are beyond their control. So make sure that's what your contract says.

There is another way to get your rights back even if the book is in print and the publisher is alive and well. You can wait thirty-five years and then follow the complicated termination procedure set out in Section 203 of the Copyright Act. That process is beyond the scope of this book, however.

ॐ

All of these provisions seem like harmless insects when you are excited about signing your first book contract. You can ignore them or try to swat them away, but don't be surprised later in the relationship when they come back to bite or sting. Understanding your contract is the best insect repellant.

Chapter 13

Tweedledum and Tweedledee

(Agent, Collaboration, Work-for-Hire Contracts; Magazine Rights)

So the two brothers went off hand-in-hand into the wood, and returned in a minute with their arms full of things—such as bolsters, blankets, hearth-rugs, table-cloths, dish-covers, and coal-scuttles. "I hope you're a good hand at pinning and tying strings?" Tweedledum remarked. "Everyone of these things has got to go on, somehow or other."

Alice said afterwards she had never seen such a fuss made about anything in all her life—the way those two bustled about—and the quantity of things they put on—and the trouble they gave her in tying strings and fastening buttons—"Really they'll be more like bundles of old clothes than anything else, by the time they're ready!" she said to herself, as she arranged a bolster round the neck of Tweedledee, "to keep his head from being cut off," as he said.

Lewis Carroll, *Through the Looking Glass*

Tweedledum and Tweedledee acted like children, so Alice wasn't inclined to take them seriously. Especially as they prepared to go to battle against each other and put on a confusing array of armor designed to keep their heads from getting cut off.

Writers often enter into seemingly minor contracts as they work toward that big publishing deal. But these contracts are important, too, and writers who don't take them seriously risk losing their heads.

This chapter will cover agent contracts, collaboration agreements, work for hire, and ghostwriting arrangements. It will also discuss the different kinds of rights magazines purchase.

Agent Contracts

If you decide to work with an agent, you will want a contract spelling out each party's rights and responsibilities. It could be anything from a letter to an imposing-looking legal document. Either way, make sure you understand what the relationship will involve.

1.   Exclusive arrangement

Most agency agreements are exclusive arrangements. This means that you may not use another agent to represent the same work. In fact, you might not even be permitted to sell it yourself.

An agent doesn't make money until a publisher buys the book. If that doesn't happen, the agent won't get paid for the time and effort he or she put in. So imagine how an agent would feel if she puts in time and effort—and might even be on the verge of completing a deal— when you or another agent sells the manuscript. That's a risk many agents aren't willing to take, and it is why the contract will likely require you to pay the first agent whatever commission she would have received if she had been the one to place the book. If a second agent actually sold the manuscript, you'll have to pay him, too. Although the publishing contract may still be valid, you pay twice as much in commissions.

Even if the contract doesn't say so, an agent with an exclusive arrangement has a legal responsibility to use his or her best efforts to place the manuscript and to get the best deal possible. Still, it's better to put this duty in the agreement. You also want the contract to say that the agent will notify you of every offer that comes in and will not accept an offer without your approval. Or, if you trust the agent and don't want to be bothered with offers you know you would reject, you can give the agent the authority to reject those offers for you.

An exclusive arrangement works fine if the agent is doing his or her job. But what if that isn't the case? That's why you want an agreement you can terminate at will.

2. Termination

Termination at will means you can end the contract at any time—with reasonable notice. For example, an at-will contract may require 30-days' notice before it actually terminates.

A contract that terminates at will is better than one that lasts for a specified time, such as one year. Or an agent may ask you to sign a contract that gives the relationship a sort of trial period. If you are comfortable with the length of the trial, you may decide to agree to this type of arrangement.

Just because you terminate the contract doesn't mean that everything stops, however. You still have to pay the agent commissions on any book the agent has placed with a publisher. But see if you can negotiate a limit on the number of years the agent can continue collecting commissions.

3. Works and rights covered

The contract should describe the manuscript the agent is agreeing to represent. Unless you already have a great relationship with your agent, you will want to limit it to one manuscript. You can always add additional manuscripts later.

The agreement should also describe the type of rights the agent will represent. Print rights? E-book rights? Film rights? Foreign language rights? Some agents have great contacts in the book publishing industry but none in the movie industry, or vice versa. If your book would sell well in Japan but your agent has no contacts there, you can reserve your foreign language rights—or your Japanese foreign language rights—and find another agent to represent those.

Another way to handle this is to let your agent find a subagent who has the contacts the primary agent doesn't have. In this situation, the contract should require the two agents to split a reasonable commission. If using a subagent is the only way to get your manuscript into the hands of the Japanese market, it may be worth paying an extra five percent, but you should not have to pay each agent the same amount as if that agent had done everything on his own.

4. Assignment

Your relationship with your agent is personal. The contract should require your permission before your agent can assign his or her responsibilities to a different agent.

5. Commissions and royalty payments

What is a reasonable commission to pay an agent? That depends on you. If you really want Suzie Superagent and she charges 5% more than the competition, you may feel that's a reasonable commission. At the time of this writing, however, most agents are charging 15%, although some of the rights that are harder to sell (such as foreign language rights) may be as high as 20% when a subagent is involved.

The normal arrangement has the publisher paying the entire advance and all royalties to your agent. The agent then deducts his or her share and sends you the rest. With your agent's consent, you may be able to convince the publisher to send separate payments, but you will never get the agent to allow you to receive the full amount and then pay him or her.

If the agent receives the entire advance and all royalties, make sure your contract requires the agent to send your share promptly after he or she receives it. The contract should also include an audit clause similar to that discussed in Chapter 11.

6. Expenses

Agents may require you to pay expenses such as photocopying and postage. The contract should require your approval if the expenses are unusual or exceed a set amount.

The agent contract may also include representations, warranties, and indemnification clauses and choice of forum and choice of law clauses. See Chapter 12 for more information on those provisions.

Collaboration Agreements

Writers have many opportunities to collaborate with others. You may be co-authoring a novel with another writer. Perhaps you are writing the text for a children's book and a business associate is illustrating it. Maybe a celebrity has asked you to write her biography. Or you could use a researcher to track down newspaper articles and conduct interviews for a non-fiction book. All of these situations benefit from collaboration agreements.

This discussion mentions two collaborators, but the same principles apply to agreements among three or more collaborators.

1. Copyright and authorship

The first question to ask is, "who owns the copyright, and how does that affect our relationship?" Each of the above situations has a different answer.

- Many co-authored books are integrated works where the whole is greater than the sum of the parts. If you try to separate the contributions, neither makes sense. In this situation, the copyright statute says that both writers are authors of the entire work and share the copyright. Both authors have to consent to a contract that gives a publisher the exclusive right to publish the book. But either author can rent out the publishing rights on a non-exclusive basis, and no consent is required as long as the other author receives his or her share of the proceeds. If you want to change any of these legal rights, do it in the contract.

- In the case of a writer and an illustrator, the two collaborators produce separate products, which makes each person the sole author of his or her individual contribution. (Graphics novels may be an exception.) If the illustrator wants to sign an exclusive contract for his illustrations, the copyright law says he doesn't need your consent. If you want to make sure those illustrations are used with your text, you had better put that in the contract.

- In the third example, assume the celebrity will tell you her life story and give you information but will not do any of the writing. Since facts and ideas can't be copyrighted, you are the only one providing copyrightable material. That means you are the sole author and own the entire copyright. The celebrity won't like that result and will ask you to sign a contract selling all or part of the copyright to the celebrity.

- Similarly, a researcher does not normally provide copyrightable expression, so you will be the sole copyright owner. Still, it is best to say this in the contract so the researcher doesn't expect more than he or she is legally entitled to. Or you could agree to give the researcher a limited interest in the copyright, such as a percentage of the royalties or the right to make copies of the work for academic uses.

Know who owns the copyright under the law and what the ramifications are. If the result is not what you and your collaborator want, you can change it in the contract. Read Chapter 3 for more information on copyrights.

2. Attribution

The contract should spell out how your names will appear on the book and in promotional material. If one name is more likely to sell the book, you may decide to give that person top billing. Or perhaps you give it to the person who had the initial story idea or did most of the writing. You can also list the authors alphabetically or simply flip a coin.

If one person's story is written by the other, you have several choices. You can simply list both names as joint authors, probably with the subject's name first. You can say "[subject's name] as told to [writer's name]." In a ghostwriting situation, the writer is not listed in the credits at all.

Then there is the matter of type size and prominence. Many "as told to" books list the subject's name in larger print because that is the name readers know.

Whatever you decide, include it in the contract to avoid arguments later.

3. Income and expenses

One of the first decisions you are likely to make is how to divide the income. Will you share royalties equally? Will one collaborator get a larger share of the advance in exchange for a smaller royalty percentage? Or will one collaborator—such as a ghostwriter or a researcher—simply receive a flat amount?

Payment may also vary based on publishing format and subsidiary rights. The contract should mention subsidiary rights even if it simply says that each collaborator receives 50% of all income regardless of the rights involved. If the amount will vary by type, make sure the agreement lists them separately. Since an illustrator contributes nothing to the audio version of a book, the contract might say that the illustrator receives no royalties for those sales.

The agreement should also describe how expenses will be divided. The collaborators can share them equally, or each collaborator could bear his or her own expenses. If they are shared, will approval be needed for expenses in excess of a particular amount? Spell that out in the contract.

If the collaborators sign a publishing contract and receive one or more advances before the work is completed, consider putting the money in a joint bank account. Then include a contract provision stating that it can only be used to pay expenses until the work is completed and accepted by the publisher, after which the remainder will be paid to the collaborators.

The contract should also say how payments will be handled once the work is completed. Is the publisher willing to pay the collaborators or their agents separately? If not, designate one person to receive the royalties and pay the other collaborator. In this case, make sure the person receiving the royalties is required to pay them promptly and to keep books and records, and include an audit clause.

4. Dividing the work and making creative decisions

Describe the nature and content of the project in the agreement. This summary should include the approximate length of the manuscript, the number of illustrations (if one of the parties is an illustrator), and other details relevant to that particular relationship.

The contract should also describe how the collaborators will divide the work. Writer and illustrator is easy. Two writers is harder. It might be a non-fiction work with the writers dividing the chapters by subject matter or a novel where each writer takes a point-of-view character. The working relationship depends on the personalities of the two individuals, and some arrangements are more fluid than others. As much as possible, however, make it clear who will do what.

Then there is the responsibility for making decisions about the creative aspects of the work. If the writer doesn't like the illustrations, can he tell the illustrator to change them? In that non-fiction work where the writers divide the chapters, do they both have to agree on the content before finalizing the manuscript? Or does each collaborator have final say on his or her own contribution? For that "as told to" book, does the celebrity or the writer make the final call? The answer to these questions may vary with the individuals and the project, but the contract should include them.

5. Project schedule

The collaborators should agree on a schedule, which can either be incorporated into the contract or attached as an exhibit. Attaching it as an exhibit makes it easier to revise if circumstances change. Either way, get it in writing when formalizing the collaboration agreement.

The schedule should include deadlines for completing particular parts of the work and may break the deadlines down into the first and subsequent drafts as well as the completed manuscript. It should also state when each collaborator will share his or her work with the other collaborator. Again, this depends on the individuals and the project. Some writers work together better if they exchange their work chapter by chapter, while others work better if they can complete a draft before sharing it.

6. Research material

A project may use research material purchased by the parties or provided by one party to the other. In these circumstances, the contract should state who owns the materials and should require the non-owner to return them in good condition (or in the same condition, absent normal wear and tear) when the project is completed.

7. Early termination

What happens when the parties can't work together or one person is unwilling to complete his portion of the project? Or what if death or disability prevents one collaborator from fulfilling his or her responsibilities? The contract should address these issues.

The agreement might provide that the collaborator who is not at fault has the right to finish the work independently or to find a replacement for the collaborator who did not finish. If the person who was unwilling or unable to complete his or her portion of the project has already done a significant amount of work, how will that person be compensated and what credit will he or she receive for that contribution? Spell it out.

Early termination does not mean that the contract is no longer good. Unless it says otherwise, those provisions of the agreement that relate to future rights, such as the copyright provisions and the provisions for resolving disputes, remain in effect until they no longer apply.

8. Continuing effect

Even if a project is completed in two years, the effects of the agreement last much longer. That's because certain provisions live on. Royalties may continue for years, and they will be distributed however the contract provides. The copyright clause usually lasts as long as the copyright, which is why some collaboration agreements state that they will remain in effect until the copyright expires.

What happens after the manuscript is finished and sold? Is it okay for the collaborators to publish works that compete with it? Who will prepare and own the rights to future editions and sequels? Are both parties allowed to prepare derivative works? All of these questions should be answered in the contract.

9. Assignment

Each party should be able to assign royalties from the contract to any person the collaborator chooses since that assignment does not affect the other collaborators. In contrast, the person chosen to complete the collaborator's share of the work affects the other collaborators, so the choice should require their approval. Copyright ownership may or may not affect other collaborators. If it does, the contract should require approval to assign those rights.

In the case of a collaborator's death, the collaborator's share of a copyright would normally pass to his or her heirs, as explained in

Chapter 15. If the collaborators own the copyright jointly, the contract might give the surviving collaborator the right to purchase the deceased collaborator's share at fair market value.

10. Other provisions

As with agent contracts, collaboration agreements may also contain some of the other provisions discussed in Chapter12. In particular, the agreement may include clauses covering one or more of the following:

- representations, warranties, and indemnification, with each collaborator agreeing to indemnify the other if the collaborator's work is found to violate someone else's rights;

- responsibility for obtaining and/or paying for copyright permissions;

- competing works; and

- choice of forum and choice of law.

Finally, the parties should consider who will sign and approve the publishing contract. Will they sign a joint contract, or will they enter into separate contracts? And must they all agree before any of them can sign? Collaborating writers often enter into one agreement with the publisher, while a writer and an illustrator may have separate agreements. If a collaborator is a researcher who provides no creative expression, that individual will probably not sign a publishing contract at all.

Work for Hire and Ghostwriting

As noted in Chapter 3, the copyright of a work for hire is owned by the employer or the person who commissioned the work. See that chapter for more details on what qualifies as a work for hire.

Even though the employer or person who commissioned the work is the legal author and the owner of the copyright, the parties are free to divide or share the legal rights the copyright gives the author. The work-for-hire agreement might, for example, state that the writer may re-publish the work as long as the writer acknowledges the legal author and states where the manuscript was originally published.

In the typical ghostwriting arrangement, the person whose name will go on the book provides the facts and the ideas, neither of which can be copyrighted, and the ghostwriter provides the copyrightable expression. Unless the resulting manuscript fits the work-for-hire definition, the ghostwriter owns the copyright under the law. The writer can, of course, sell the copyright to the person whose name is on the book, and the contract usually includes this sale. If you are the ghostwriter, make sure you can live with whatever terms the contract contains.

Magazine Rights

Not all writers aim for book contracts. Even those that do often write magazine articles to bolster their credibility or help sell their books.

When a magazine buys an article, story, or poem, it buys the rights to publish it once or many times, and it may limit your future use. Magazine rights also cover geographical territory and language. If you sell North American rights, you are free to do whatever you want with the piece in overseas markets. If you sell English language rights, you have not tied your hands as to Spanish or Chinese publications. Note, however, that other countries speak English, so if it isn't limited to North America, you may have sold the rights in Great Britain, Australia, and other English-speaking countries. If the rights don't mention a geographical area or language, assume the magazine has bought the rights in all countries and languages.

Your contract with the magazine determines what rights it is buying. If the magazine doesn't make you sign anything, you still have a contract. Without a separate agreement, the contract will combine the terms of your submission letter, the publisher's acceptance letter, and the submission guidelines. If your submission letter offers one type of rights and the publisher doesn't object, that is what you have sold. If the publisher says it will buy different rights and you don't object, then the acceptance letter governs. If both letters are silent but the submission guidelines tell you what the magazine buys, that is what you are selling, so read the submission guidelines carefully.

Some magazines pay kill fees, which means the magazine pays you part of your fee up front (the kill fee) and the rest when it publishes the piece. If the magazine changes its mind, you keep the kill fee but don't receive the rest of the money. You are most likely to receive a kill fee when a magazine gives you an assignment for a piece you haven't written yet. If the magazine doesn't buy the article, you are free to sell it elsewhere once the magazine rejects it.

The most common types of magazine rights have titles that describe the rights purchased. These rights can be modified by contract, however, and what the contract says is more important than the label you or the magazine put on those rights. Still, it is helpful to know what the titles mean.

1. All rights

If a periodical buys all rights, it has complete control over what happens to the item you submitted. You cannot sell it again, and you can't even post it on your website without the magazine's permission.

Selling all rights doesn't bar you from publishing another article about Aunt Maud's hat, but it must be a new article with a fresh approach. Modifying the existing article is not enough. Even this freedom can be changed by contract, however, so watch out for wording that prohibits you from writing another article or story about the same subject.

Section 203 of the Copyright Act does allow you to get your rights back eventually, but thirty-five plus years is a long time to wait.

If a magazine pays well and is a prestigious name to have among your credits, you may be happy to sell it all rights. That's your choice.

2. First rights

When a magazine buys first rights, it buys the right to be the first to publish the piece. The most common type of first rights is first North American rights (also called first North American serial rights or FNASR), which gives the publication the right to be the first publisher in North America. Once the magazine has published the item, control reverts to you and you are free to post it on your website, include it in a compilation, or resell it.

Can you sell first rights after you post the piece on your blog or website? That depends on two things: how big an audience it had on the web and how lenient the magazine is. Some magazines will still buy first rights if you can convince them that the original audience was small. However, you must be honest when you submit the article. Posting an item in a non-public forum is not usually considered publication, but check with the magazine to be on the safe side.

3. Reprint or second rights

The biggest advantage of first rights is second rights—also called reprint rights. Once the first rights holder has published your article, story, or poem, you can sell it over and over again. Because a reprint isn't the public's first chance to view the piece, second rights don't usually pay as well, and some magazines won't buy them at all. But considering that the second magazine is paying for work you already did, any size check is good. You can also sell the item a third time, and a fourth, and . . . These additional sales are also second or reprint rights.

Since you can only sell first rights once, you do not want to mislead a later purchaser. When submitting the piece for subsequent publication, you should explain where and when the item previously appeared.

When selling reprint rights, look for magazines that have separate audiences and do not compete with each other. Assume you wrote an article on traveling with grandparents and sold first rights to a parenting magazine. You are unlikely to sell reprint rights to another parenting magazine, but a publication for retirees might buy it. For Christian articles, consider selling first rights and reprint rights to publications from different denominations. Baptists don't usually read magazines aimed at Presbyterians, and Methodists rarely subscribe to periodicals meant for Roman Catholics.

The magazine that bought first rights might require you to wait one or more months after publication before sending your article, story, or poem elsewhere. Even if it doesn't, don't try to sell second rights while you are waiting for the first magazine to print your piece. Although the second periodical may agree to hold the piece until a reasonable time after the first publication, mistakes happen. If a magazine discovers that it didn't get the first rights it paid for, it isn't likely to give you another chance.

4. One-time and simultaneous rights

One-time rights allow the magazine to publish your article or story or poem once. If the publication wants to print it again, it must get your permission. While first rights can be one-time rights, the two terms are not synonymous. Reprint rights can also be one-time rights, and a contract for first rights might authorize additional printings or on-line publication.

If you grant simultaneous rights, you are probably selling the article or story or poem to more than one publication. As the name implies, simultaneous rights allow several magazines to publish the piece at the same time. They are not the same as reprint rights since you may not have sold the item before.

5. Electronic rights

This is the right to print your piece in an electronic medium. You can sell all rights, first rights, reprint rights, or any other rights that you can sell for print media.,

6. Nonexclusive rights

If you don't say what you are selling and the magazine doesn't say what it is buying, it gets nonexclusive rights. This doesn't restrict your ability to sell the article or story or poem again, but it gives the publication the right to reprint the piece in subsequent editions of its magazine and even in an anthology without further payment. You can also explicitly agree to sell nonexclusive rights.

7. Work for hire

A work for hire doesn't belong to you and never did. (See Chapter 3.) The result is similar to selling all rights. However, there are times when doing a work for hire is better than selling all rights. That's because some magazines allow the writer of a work for hire to publish the piece elsewhere—and get paid for it. Make sure you read your contract to see what you can do.

❧

Never ignore your contract, even if you think it is unimportant or childish. The terms you agree to may seem like old clothes, but they are really the armor that keeps you from losing your head.

Part V

The Voice of the Lobster
(Writing as a Business)

CHAPTER FOURTEEN

Talking About the Shark
(Taxes, Business Licenses)

'Tis the voice of the Lobster; I heard him declare,
"You have baked me too brown, I must sugar my hair."
As a duck with its eyelids, so he with his nose
Trims his belt and his buttons, and turns out his toes.
When the sands are all dry, he is gay as a lark,
And will talk in contemptuous tones of the Shark:
But, when the tide rises and sharks are around,
His voice has a timid and tremulous sound.

> Lewis Carroll, "The Voice of the Lobster"
> From *Alice in Wonderland*

The lobster was afraid of the shark, and many writers are—or should be—afraid of IRS agents and other government officials. Sharks can smell blood, and the writer who nicks a finger out of ignorance is as much a target as the writer who slices off a leg to flout the law. This chapter will show you how to stay away from sharp edges.

First, however, you should know what this chapter does not do.

- It does not provide tax advice. Tax laws change frequently, and you should talk to your accountant or tax lawyer about how to treat individual expenses. This chapter does, however, provide an overview of certain tax issues that have remained relatively constant over time.

- It does not deal with corporate taxes. Most writers are sole proprietors, which means that they conduct their writing business as individuals, and this chapter is aimed at them.

Corporations and other types of business entities may be subject to different rules.

So how do you recognize shark-infested waters? There are three main types: (1) income tax reefs inhabited by casual writers who try to deduct "business" expenses, (2) the bottom of the ocean, which attracts writers who fail to pay self-employment taxes or make estimated tax payments, and (3) underwater caves where writers sell their books without obtaining the necessary licenses. This chapter provides topographical information about each place.

Income Taxes

Can you deduct excess writing expenses from your income taxes? To answer a question with a question, are you writing to make a profit? If "yes," then "yes." If "no," then "no." That's the theory, anyway. If writing is a trade or business, you can deduct your excess expenses. If it's just a hobby, you can't.

Even casual writers can deduct ordinary writing expenses that don't exceed their writing income. If you spend $500 on paper and ink and sell an article for $200, you can deduct $200. If writing is your business, you can deduct the entire $500. But if it is only your hobby, you can't deduct the extra $300.

Many of the writers who inhabit income tax reefs see themselves as serious writers. If you ask the IRS, however, they are mere hobbyists.

On the other hand, some writers stay farther away from the reef than they need to. If writing really is your business, why give up valuable deductions?

According to the U.S. Supreme Court, "to be engaged in a trade or business, the taxpayer must be involved in the activity with continuity and regularity and . . . the taxpayer's primary purpose for engaging in the activity must be for income or profit." (*Commissioner of Internal Revenue v. Groetzinger,* 480 U.S. 23, 35 (1987)). The basic test is simple:

the IRS and the tax courts look to see if you write to make a profit. Unfortunately, they aren't going to take your word for it. Still, there are two ways to escape the shark's teeth.

1. Make a profit

If you make money three out of five years, the law presumes that writing is your business. The five years must be consecutive, however, so if you do not start making money until year four, you cannot use the presumption for year one, and if you don't make money again until year seven, you cannot use it for years two or three, either.

Even if you make money three out of five years, you may not be safe. The IRS can rebut the presumption by proving that writing is only your hobby. The shark may come looking for you if you have miniscule profits in the three profitable years and huge losses in the two losing years. You may also find yourself looking down the shark's throat if you try to write off unusual expenses, such as exotic vacations that you claim as research for the short story you never got around to writing.

2. Treat writing as a business

If you can't meet the presumption, the burden switches to you to prove your writing is a business. And, as mentioned above, the IRS and the courts aren't going to simply take your word for it.

So how do you prove that writing is your business and not your hobby? Or, if you meet the presumption, how can the IRS show that you write as a hobby rather than as a business?

The IRS and the courts look at nine objective factors when deciding if a taxpayer is engaging in a trade or business. Not every factor counts equally, and the inquiry is fact-intensive. (See *Higgins v. Commissioner of Internal Revenue*, 312 U.S. 212 (1941).) That means there is no cut-and-dried answer to the question "Do I write as a business or a hobby?"

What are the nine factors? The following discussion rewords them as questions that apply to writing.

(1) ***<u>Do you approach writing as you would any other business?</u>*** The IRS and the courts look to see if you keep good books and records, do what successful writers do, and change your approach when it proves unprofitable. Here are some things you can do to show that you carry on your writing activities in a businesslike manner.

- Maintain separate—and detailed—financial records for your writing activities. Ideally, this means maintaining a current spreadsheet showing your writing income and expenses as well as keeping copies of payment vouchers and receipts in a file or files dedicated to your writing business. A separate checking account is not necessary, but it can help keep your records separate and may limit what the IRS looks at in an audit.

- Create a business plan with short and long-term goals, and keep business-related logs (e.g., submissions, sales). It also helps if you have an annual budget.

- If you need a license, get it.

- Join professional writing organizations.

- Submit your work.

- If you have a published book, market it.

Eleanor Harris supported herself as a freelance writer before she married Jack Howard, the president and CEO of The E.W. Scripps Company. After their marriage, she continued to write some magazine articles but focused on plays. Harris belonged to a number of professional associations, kept a separate bank account for her writing income and expenses, and submitted her plays to agents and producers. All of these activities led the judge to conclude that she approached writing in a businesslike way.

There was another significant factor in the judge's finding that Harris intended to make a profit. She wrote in an office near home for several hours a day and spent additional time outside the office gathering information for articles, short stories, and plays. Even though her husband's money allowed her to branch out into a new area (plays) that was not profitable at that time, the judge found that she was a dedicated writer who intended to make a profit from her work.

(2) ***Do you know what you're doing?*** Have you looked into the business aspects of writing? Do you know how to write, and are you trying to improve your craft? Do you understand the topic or the period you are writing about? Or, if you don't, do you seek advice from those who do?

You don't have to be an English major or even have a college degree, but you should know grammar and have some writing skills. Previous writing experience isn't essential, but it does help. The IRS also looks at your efforts to improve your craft: attending writers' conferences, taking writing classes at your local college, and reading books about the craft, for example.

The IRS and the courts look at your subject-matter expertise as well. If you write about an unfamiliar subject or era, have you done your research? This goes for fiction as well as non-fiction.

Knowing your subject isn't enough, however. If you don't apply what you learn, the IRS will discount this factor.

(3) ***How much time and effort do you put in?*** Do you write regularly and continuously? Do you try to market your work? You don't have to write full-time, but you do need to be conscientious about it. If you write only when the spirit leads you, it isn't a business.

Although the courts consider every factor, this one is crucial. If you don't write regularly and continuously, you are sure to end up as some shark's meal. Putting in significant time and effort to write,

research, and market doesn't guarantee that the courts will decide you
are writing as a business. But writing sporadically or spending little
time on it is a sure way to prove it is only a hobby.

(4) ***Do you expect assets used in your writing business to
appreciate in value?*** To the IRS, neither manuscripts nor your
creative mind are assets. This factor rarely, if ever, applies to writers,
and the shark will ignore it.

(5) ***Have you been successful in other business ventures?*** This
factor looks at your history of taking unprofitable activities and turning
them into profitable ones. If you started as a starving novelist and
became a best seller, then maybe one of your frequently-rejected movie
scripts will become the next blockbuster. Mostly, though, this factor
does not affect writers.

(6-7) ***What is your income and loss history from writing?
Have you earned occasional profits?*** While these two factors are
technically different, they are closely related. Six asks how many
profitable years you've had, and seven asks if those profits were
significant. These factors are most helpful to established writers who
have had a mix of good and bad years. If you have never made a profit,
however, all is not lost. The courts recognize that writing is a highly
speculative profession and can take time to generate significant
income. As one tax judge said, "[L]osses should be viewed in the
context of the nature of petitioner's activity. Works of fiction are
difficult to write and to market. . . . This field appears to pay large
amounts of money to those who succeed in it and 'an opportunity to
earn a substantial ultimate profit in a highly speculative venture is
ordinarily sufficient to indicate that the activity is engaged in for profit
even though losses or only occasional small profits are actually
generated.'" (*Vitale v. Commissioner of Internal Revenue*, T.C. Memo 1999-
131 (quoting from 26 C.F.R. § 1.183-2))

Gloria Churchman trained as an artist and pursued her art regularly
and continuously for twenty years. During that time she taught art

courses, worked on her own art in a home studio built for that purpose, and kept records of her sales and expenses.

Churchman exhibited her paintings and sculptures at least once a year. She maintained a mailing list that she used when announcing gallery shows, and the galleries also advertised them.

When her art didn't sell quickly enough, Churchman tried new sales methods. She visited commercial art galleries to solicit shows, and at one point she even opened her own gallery to showcase her work. She also reproduced her art as posters and in books in order to make it more available to the public.

Although Churchman had some income from her artistic activities, she did not have a single profitable year. Yet, in spite of twenty years of losses, the judge looked at all the facts and held that Churchman's art was her business, not her hobby. So if you haven't made a profit yet, don't give up.

(8) ***What is your financial status without your writing income?*** Are you willing to give up everything and live in a garret? The shark assumes that the starving artist is hungrier for a profit than the lawyer who writes on evenings and weekends. People who make a comfortable living at something else can afford to indulge in a hobby that costs more than it brings in.

Fortunately for all the people who can't afford to write without another source of income, this is only one factor. The courts recognize that people can engage in more than one business and that speculative ventures may require another funding source. "One may engage in more than one occupation, calling, or business at the same time." (*Rider v. Commissioner of Internal Revenue,* 200 F.2d 524, 525 (8th Cir. 1952)) In a close situation, however, other sources of income may be the difference between business and hobby.

(9) ***Does writing give you personal pleasure?*** The final factor asks if the activity provides the type of personal pleasure or recreation

that normally comes from a hobby. The courts understand that writers often enjoy writing, and this enjoyment alone isn't enough to keep writing from being a business. Every business has some elements that aren't fun, however, and writing is no exception. If you ignore the parts you don't enjoy (which might be revising, submitting, or marketing) or give up every time writer's block barricades the road, it isn't a business.

Maurice Dreicer had an independent income from an inheritance. Sometime in the mid-1950s, he decided to write a book about searching for the perfect steak.

During the next twenty-plus years, Dreicer traveled all over the world gathering material for the book. He stayed in the finest hotels, dined in the finest restaurants, and returned to some cities more than once. Dreicer also kept meticulous records of both his expenses and the results of his restaurant visits.

After writing what Dreicer considered his completed draft (but which the judge characterized as having some parts still in outline form), he sent it to one publisher and one agent. When they rejected it, he stopped trying to get the book published.

Dreicer put greater effort into trying to deduct travel expenses and his full-time secretary's salary. The tax court judge rejected Dreicer's claim that writing was his business, but it took two appeals before Dreicer gave up.

Did his writing pursuits bring him personal pleasure? Dreicer claimed that he did not enjoy living from a suitcase while researching his book. The judge didn't believe Dreicer and found that world traveling was his lifestyle. After noting that Dreicer had been conducting his "research" for 20 years, the judge said, "if [Dreicer] were so averse to this style of living, then he would have completed his 'research' long ago and have moved on to other pursuits." (*Dreicer v. Commissioner of Internal Revenue*, T.C. Memo 1979-395) Dreicer's personal pleasure in his "research" far outweighed any factors in his favor, leading the judge to conclude that writing was not Dreicer's business.

To illustrate how the factors work, consider the case of Ralph Vitale, who wrote a novel about legal prostitution in Nevada. He researched the book by traveling to Nevada approximately three days each month, interviewing prostitutes, and paying the normal fees for their services. Vitale then paid a publishing company to produce and promote *Searchlight, Nevada*. The following table lists the facts that met (or failed to meet) the nine factors and summarizes the judge's findings.

Factor	Facts	Effect
1. approach	<ul><li>kept records;</li><li>made substantial efforts to promote and market *Searchlight, Nevada*;</li><li>searched for a new publisher after the original one filed for bankruptcy; and</li><li>continued writing (additional manuscripts).</li></ul>	business
2. expertise	<ul><li>marketing degree</li><li>while in college, earned more than 24 combined credit hours in English, journalism, and speech</li><li>some work-related writing (mostly technical)</li></ul>	business
3. time/effort	<ul><li>25-35 hours per week spent researching, writing, and marketing</li></ul>	business
4. asset appreciation	N/A	neutral
5. success in other activities	N/A	neutral
6. history	<ul><li>no income, only losses</li></ul>	hobby
7. profits	<ul><li>none</li></ul>	hobby
8. other income	<ul><li>continued to work full-time as a budget analyst for two years after he started writing</li></ul>	hobby
9. personal pleasure	<ul><li>enjoyed writing</li></ul>	hobby

A simple counting method shows three votes for business and four for hobby, but courts do not apply such a mechanical test. The judge gave more weight to the first three factors—particularly Vitale's business-like approach and the time and effort he put in—than to the last four and found that Vitale wrote as a business. This allowed him to deduct some of his expenses, including the money he paid to get his book published.

It wasn't a complete win, however. The judge held that certain expenditures are so inherently personal that they can never be deducted as business expenses, and he put Vitale's "interview" expenses in that category. So Vitale did not get to deduct his payments to prostitutes or the portion of his travel expenses attributable to those visits.

3. Shark bait

Sharks are carnivores, and they enjoy a wide variety of fish and crustaceans and plankton and mammals and reptiles and . . . But what kinds of writers do IRS agents find tastiest?

They love self-published authors. Fannie Hawkins paid to publish a 56-page book containing 43 poems. Before her book came out, Hawkins' work had appeared (rarely) in community magazines, but, as the judge described it, "Fannie did not generally publish poems in magazines as she wished to control the exposure of her works." (*Hawkins v. Commissioner of Internal Revenue,* T.C. Memo 1979-101) The only evidence regarding how much time she devoted to her literary activities was her own vague testimony that she "worked daily." The summary of the evidence doesn't say how much effort Hawkins put into marketing the book either, but she was unable to estimate how much income she made from book sales—indicating that she didn't care whether she made a profit. It's no surprise that the judge found her writing was not a business.

Gary Kalbfleisch also lost. He wrote a number of short stories and prepared a catalog offering copies of the stories for individual sale, but it was unclear what, if anything, he did to distribute the catalog. He also self-published a political leaflet. Kalbfleisch had no marketing program and devoted little capital to his writing activities, so the judge held that writing was his hobby. The IRS might not have bothered with the case if Kalbfleisch had limited his deductions to paper, ink, and normal writing expenses, but it could not ignore the "business" deductions for house cleaning services and vacations.

While self-publishing is a red flag, it is not a sure sign that the taxpayer will lose. After Hugenia Doggett became a follower of Joanna Southcott (a religious teacher and prophetess who died more than one-hundred years earlier), Doggett paid to publish Southcott's writings. Doggett devoted most of her time to printing the books, advertising them in newspapers and magazines, and traveling around the country to sell them. When the court looked at all the facts, it held that Doggett's activities in printing and selling the books were a business. Although Doggett was technically an editor or compiler rather than a writer, the case does show that self-publishing does not, by itself, defeat a claim that the taxpayer is engaged in a business rather than a hobby.

And do you remember Ralph Vitale? He paid to publish *Searchlight, Nevada,* but the judge still found that he wrote as a business.

What made the difference? Why did Doggett and Vitale win their cases while Hawkins and Kalbfleisch lost theirs? The distinction is obvious. Doggett and Vitale made serious efforts to market their work, while Hawkins and Kalbfleisch did not.

If you self-publish but don't market, the shark wants you.

Sharks also love to eat writers who submit their work to non-paying markets. Colvin Bert was an engineer who wrote on the side. Of his forty-plus articles and poems, five were published—all by non-paying markets. The opinion does not state whether Bert submitted unsuccessfully to paying markets, but it concludes that he wrote for personal reasons rather than for profit.

To repeat, the basic test is whether you are writing to make a profit. Although you don't have to make money, you do have to try.

That doesn't mean you can never submit to non-paying markets, but you should do it to gather writing credits or publicity or for another business-related reason. If you only submit to non-paying markets and then try to write off your excess expenses, beware of the shark.

Another way to catch the shark's eye is to deduct expenses that are not normal for writers. Charles Nemish wrote short stories and submitted them to various magazines, and some of them got published before he turned his attention to writing novels. Nemish was a pilot who had always been interested in writing, and the nine factors could have gone either way. But Nemish made the mistake of deducting vacation expenses at resorts he didn't write about. If the shark sees you trying to outwit him in one matter, it isn't going to give you the benefit of the doubt in another.

Maurice Dreicer and Gary Kalbfleisch also tried to write off travel expenses, and Kalbfleisch compounded it by deducting the cost of his maid service. Both lost. But Ralph Vitale was able to deduct some of his travel. And his attempt to write off his "interview" payments shows that unusual expenses don't necessarily turn a business into a hobby even if they don't qualify as deductions.

Still, if you want to keep the shark away, don't tempt it with expenses that stand out.

Self-Employment Taxes and Estimated Income Tax Payments

Another way to tempt the shark is to ignore self-employment taxes.

Writers who intentionally ignore their tax obligations hang out at the bottom of the ocean. Others may join them there out of ignorance. But however they get there, they have entered another of the shark's feeding grounds.

As a sole proprietor, you must pay self-employment taxes for any year in which you make a net profit at or above a certain threshold. At the time of this writing, the threshold is $400. The self-employment tax funds the Social Security and Medicare systems, and you must pay it even if you are already retired and receiving Social Security or Medicare.

The federal income and self-employment taxes are pay-as-you-go taxes, meaning that the IRS expects you to estimate your net profit and make payments throughout the tax year. If you overestimate, you get a refund when you file your annual tax return. If you underestimate, you must pay the difference. If you underestimate by more than $1,000, however, you may also have to pay interest and penalties.

If your estimate was reasonable based on what you made last year, but in November you sold your first book and received a big advance, the shark will not bare its teeth and go after you. If you signed the book contract in May, you will need to adjust your subsequent quarterly payments. Or, if you are not paying estimated taxes because you haven't made a profit yet, that book contract is your signal to start.

Do you have to pay estimated state income taxes? That depends on the state, so talk to your tax advisor.

If you have other employees, you must obtain an employer identification number from the IRS and deduct Social Security and income taxes from their paychecks. You may also have to pay federal and state unemployment taxes. Consult your tax advisor for the details.

State and Local Licenses

State and local governments may require licenses or business registrations for book sales. The terminology varies from state to state, county to county, and city to city. Some refer to a particular registration as a license, while others simply call it a registration. This section lumps them all together under the term "license."

If you sell copies of your books directly to consumers during speeches or book fairs or even out of the trunk of your car, check with your state revenue department. Sales through bookstores or by consignment at conferences don't count since the bookstore or consignee will use its own license to collect sales taxes.

Obtaining the license is only the first step. You must also collect sales taxes and pay them to the state. The amount you collect and the mechanics of making the payments vary by state and, in some cases, by county or city.

If you regularly sell your books from a particular location, you may also need a business license from the city or county. Depending on the locality, this may only apply to in-person sales or it may be required if you do a significant mail-order business.

There are several reasons for obtaining a license in every state where you make direct sales if a license if required there. First, it's the law. Second, if you don't get one and you are caught making unauthorized sales, the penalties you pay may far exceed your profits. This is why state revenue sharks love to go hunting in those underwater caves where writers sell their books. Third, getting and maintaining the necessary licenses is good evidence that writing is your business rather than your hobby.

Some writers sell only a few books each year and don't realize that even one sale may require a license. Those who make frequent sales are sure to get caught, but small players should also understand and obey the law. Sharks feed on plankton as well as on whales.

❧

The lobster wanted to avoid the shark, and so do you. The best way to do that is to (1) write off excess business expenses only if you write to make a profit, (2) pay self-employment and estimated income taxes if you make a profit, and (3) obtain the necessary licenses before selling your books directly to the public.

CHAPTER FIFTEEN
The Owl and the Panther
(Incorporating, Estate Planning)

I passed by his garden, and marked, with one eye,
How the Owl and the Panther were sharing a pie:
The Panther took pie-crust, and gravy, and meat,
While the Owl had the dish as its share of the treat.
When the pie was all finished, the Owl, as a boon,
Was kindly permitted to pocket the spoon:
While the Panther received knife and fork with a growl,
And concluded the banquet by [eating the owl].

Lewis Carroll, "The Voice of the Lobster"
From *Alice in Wonderland*

You work hard to earn your royalties, but your share of the pie seems awfully small. How can you keep the panther from gobbling up what you do get?

This isn't a psychology paper or a victim's handbook for avoiding fraud. Only you can keep the panther away. Know who you are dealing with before handing over money or account information, don't sign any contracts that make you uncomfortable, and don't believe people who promise to make you rich or turn your book into a best seller. If it sounds too good to be true, it probably is.

There are also several legal steps you can take to keep your money and your copyrights from falling into the wrong hands. This chapter will discuss two ways authors attempt to protect their assets: incorporating their writing businesses and preparing estate plans.

To Incorporate or Not to Incorporate?

Writers often wonder if they should incorporate. After all, writing is their business, and many businesses are corporations. But is it the best business form for a writer?

That depends on the person.

The three main types of business entities for individual writers are sole proprietorships, corporations, and limited liability companies. Writers that partner with others have additional choices, but those legal forms are beyond the scope of this book.

Most of the laws relating to business organizations are state statutes. The information in this chapter is general enough to be true throughout the country, but you should check the law of your own state for more details.

1. Sole proprietorships

If you write as a business but do not take steps to create a separate legal entity, you are a sole proprietor. You can use an alias or a pseudonym or a dba (a "doing business as" name) for business purposes, but the sole proprietor and the individual are the same person for legal purposes.

There are two significant advantages of a sole proprietorship: (1) it is easy to set up and operate (you don't have to do anything except keep good business records) and (2) it has the fewest legal requirements. A sole proprietor has the same rights and obligations as other businesses and can even hire employees. The owner-writer is not an employee, however.

The main disadvantage to being a sole proprietor is that you have no personal protection from liability. As discussed later, this is not as big a disadvantage for writers as it is for some other businesses.

Taxes are another consideration, but they don't fall in either the advantage or the disadvantage category. A sole proprietor files

Schedule C with his or her personal income tax return rather than filing separate business taxes. If your writing is a business under the test discussed in Chapter 14, you can deduct your business expenses from other personal income. This other income includes your spouse's salary (if you file jointly) and any money you make from an unrelated job.

As a sole proprietor, you will pay self-employment taxes if you make a profit of more than $400 from your freelance writing, but you would pay Social Security taxes on your salary if you incorporated, so this is basically a wash. Similarly, the business form does not affect how much sales tax you owe state or local governments when you sell copies of your book from the trunk of your car or, more likely, at workshops and other events.

2. Corporations

A corporation is a separate legal entity owned by its shareholders and run by its officers and directors. A corporation may have a single owner who is also the only officer/director, as is usually the case when writers incorporate.

If you incorporate your writing business, you become an employee of the corporation. The corporation owns the copyrights to your books, receives your royalties and fees, and pays you a salary—**if** you earn it. The corporation may also pay you dividends when it makes a profit.

As previously mentioned, the main advantage of incorporating any business is that it limits your personal liability for the corporation's activities. A later section of this chapter discusses how the limitation works for writers.

There are also disadvantages to incorporating. Unlike a sole proprietorship, you must invest money in the corporation. Although there is no hard and fast rule about how much this investment must be, a good guide is to have enough money in the corporation's name to cover the corporation's operating expenses (which include your salary) for the period it would normally take to start making a profit. If you fail to keep enough money in the corporation, you may be personally liable for the corporation's business expenses.

Even when you are the only owner, the money you invest in the corporation belongs to the corporation, not to you personally. You can't treat the corporation's money as if it were your own. Although you can earn a salary, it must be reasonable in light of the work you do. Writing and marketing your manuscripts count, but you can't pay yourself for a 40-hour week if you only put in five.

When you take dividends from the corporation, they are taxed twice—once as profits to the corporation and once as income to you. Furthermore, you can't take dividends that drain the corporation's funds: it must retain enough money to cover its debts for a reasonable period. Neither the restrictions on taking money out nor the double taxation apply to sole proprietorships.

The many legal formalities of creating and maintaining a corporation are also a disadvantage. These requirements include preparing and keeping documents that you wouldn't need as a sole proprietor (such as articles of incorporation, bylaws, and minutes) and filing documents with one or more states.

It isn't as easy to incorporate—or at least to incorporate properly—as some advertisements imply. Do-it-yourself software and kits are better than nothing, but they cannot understand your needs the way a lawyer can. Also, some programs are not updated every time the law changes. Since state law governs the process, you need someone who understands the law in your state. Hiring a lawyer costs more up front but may save you money in the long run.

Corporate tax forms can be more complicated than the Schedule C you file with your personal taxes as a sole proprietor. But does using them save you money?

Forming a corporation may lower your taxes—or it may raise them. You pay personal income taxes on the money you receive from the corporation, and the corporation pays taxes on the profits it makes after deducting its expenses (which include your salary). Whether or not you come out ahead depends on several factors, including how much profit or loss the corporation makes and the amount of income that is reportable on your personal tax forms. You cannot deduct your corporate business expenses when calculating your personal income taxes, so if your writing business loses money, you will pay more taxes than you would as a sole proprietor. If your writing business makes a profit, you may benefit if the corporation's tax rate is lower than your own.

Even this discussion makes it sound simpler than it is. There are several types of corporations, and they don't all have the same tax structure. That's another reason you should talk to a lawyer who specializes in corporate law.

3. Limited liability companies (LLCs)

A limited liability company (LLC) has the same protection against personal liability as a corporation but the same tax treatment as a sole proprietorship. Using an LLC can also help you avoid some, but not all, of a corporation's formalities. As with a corporation, an LLC also requires an initial investment. If you are considering incorporating, an LLC may be a better option. State law governs the legal requirements for forming and operating LLCs, so consult an attorney in your state.

❧

The Small Business Administration's website (www.sba.gov) provides information on forming small businesses. To find an attorney, call your local bar association for a referral to a lawyer who does corporate law.

The Problem with Incorporating to Limit Liability

The main reason people incorporate small businesses is because a corporation can limit its owners' liability. Someone who sues and wins a judgment can take everything the corporation owns, including its copyrights and the money the owners invested in it, but the person who sued cannot usually reach into the owners' pockets. Unfortunately, this advantage doesn't always apply to writers.

The following examples will help you understand when incorporating does—and doesn't—limit liability. The discussion is divided into the two main types of liability: (1) liability for negligent or wrongful acts and (2) liability for business debts.

1. Liability for negligent or wrongful acts

Assume a corporation owns a garage that employs several mechanics to repair cars. A customer brings his car in to get the brakes fixed, and one of the mechanics fails to notice a faulty brake pad. As the customer is driving home, he gets into an accident because he couldn't stop the car on time. The customer can sue the garage and the mechanic, but he can't win a lawsuit against an owner unless the owner did the work or should have known it wasn't getting done right.

Now think about your business. As a writer, you are not just the owner of the corporation; you are also the mechanic who writes the words that end up in a book or a magazine article. When someone claims that those words defamed him or violated his copyright, he can sue you individually as well as suing the corporation. If you are found liable for your own conduct, having a corporation won't protect your personal assets. Since you were acting as an employee of the corporation, incorporating won't protect the corporation's assets, either, leaving you in the same position you would have been in as a sole proprietor.

2. Liability for business debts

Now assume a corporation runs a health club. It took out a $200,000 loan to cover start-up costs, which include franchise fees, rent, and exercise equipment. Unfortunately, it chose a location that is already saturated with health clubs, and it can't attract enough members to make the loan payments. Even worse, the members it does attract are hard on the equipment, which quickly loses its value. The corporation has no choice but to file for bankruptcy. Since it is a corporation, however, the owners' personal assets are safe unless they co-signed the loan.

For writers, business debts include contractual obligations such as contracts with publishers and agents. But if you incorporate, that publisher or agent is likely to have you sign the contract personally as well as on behalf of the corporation. That means you are still on the hook even if the corporation goes bankrupt.

Think about the other expenses you incur as a writer: paper, ink cartridges, professional magazines and association dues, writer's conferences, a new laptop and printer every few years, and other modest costs. Although you may pay for some of them with your credit card, you probably don't carry a big tab. So you may not need to incorporate to protect yourself against liability for your business debts.

꙳

Most writers are—and probably should be—sole proprietors. But there are exceptions. If you have employees, incorporating can protect you from at least some of their mistakes. Or maybe you act as a publisher or have unusually high business expenses for marketing or research that you can separate from your individual liability. A corporation or LLC can also own copyrights, making it easier to deal with them after your death. Any of these may be a reason to form a separate business entity. It all depends on your particular circumstances.

Estate Planning

Copyrights and royalties from future sales are property and survive your death, so a writer's estate plan determines who inherits them. This could be as simple as lumping them in with the rest of your property, as intricate as naming the people who get particular copyrights and royalties, or as complicated as setting up a trust. You can even transfer them to a separate business entity such as a corporation. But regardless of which method you adopt, you should understand the consequences of your choices.

If you die without a will (called dying intestate), state law will determine who inherits your property. Those rules can be complicated, and it rarely all goes to the surviving spouse. In Indiana, for example, if there are surviving children, grandchildren, or great-grandchildren, the spouse gets one-half and the other half is divided equally among the children (living or dead), with a deceased child's share going to his or her descendants. But if it is a second (or third or fourth) marriage, the couple had no children, and there are children from a previous marriage, the surviving spouse only gets one-fourth. If a married person dies without children but with at least one parent who is still alive, the spouse gets three-fourths and the remaining one-fourth goes to the surviving parent or parents.

You also don't get to chose who will distribute your estate or how it will be distributed. The court will appoint an executor, who will divide the assets up according to value but might not divide them the way you would wish. See the following discussion for the different ways your copyrights and royalties could be split up.

The point? If you care who gets your copyrights, your royalties, and your other assets, you should have an estate plan. Don't leave it to the state to make those decisions.

A quick note on terminology. The law generally uses different terms to describe those people who inherit under a will (legatees) and those who inherit without a will (heirs). It also uses different terms to describe the person who is responsible for distributing the estate (an administrator under a will and an executor if there is no will). For simplicity, this chapter will refer to heirs and executors for both situations.

1.   Including copyrights with general property

If you didn't specifically mention copyrights and unearned royalties, they will be lumped in with your other property. This is the simplest method and may be the best solution if you are unpublished or if your published works are generating little income. As you become more successful, however, this approach becomes less desirable.

Assume that you have an unpublished autobiography (working title *My Life*), an unpublished novel (working title *Love*), and two published novels (*Puppies* and *Kittens*). *Puppies* was published two years ago without an advance and generated $5,000 in royalties the first year and $3,000 the second. *Kittens* was published a year ago with a $20,000 advance and earned $10,000 in royalties charged against the advance, leaving $10,000 of the advance still unearned.

You own your $250,000 home, which was part of a divorce settlement and is mortgage-free. The rest of your estate consists of $100,000 in bank accounts and liquid investments.

Then there are the copyrights and potential reprint earnings from all those magazine articles, stories, and poems. Since they make an already complicated situation even more complicated, this example will assume you never wrote anything shorter than a book.

Your will simply states that 50% of your property will go to your current spouse and 25% to each of your two children from an earlier marriage. So how will your copyrights and royalties be divided?

Co-ownership. The most likely result is that your heirs will receive a percentage of each copyright and royalty payment. As the royalties come due, the publisher or agent must pay 50% to the spouse and 25% to each child.

The copyrights work the same way. Your spouse now owns 50% of the copyright in *My Life*, 50% of the copyright in *Love*, 50% of the copyright in *Puppies*, and 50% of the copyright in *Kittens*. The children own 25% apiece. If the three heirs get along, this arrangement may work fine. But what if they don't?

Under the copyright laws, each joint copyright owner has the independent right to publish and grant permission for non-exclusive copyright use, although the proceeds must be paid in the same proportion as the copyright ownership. Maybe the children don't want *My Life* published because it tells embarrassing details about your first marriage to their father or mother. But since each copyright owner has the right to publish the manuscript, your current spouse doesn't need the children's permission as long as they receive their share of the royalties.

Valuation. The other option is for the executor to find an expert to value the copyrights and potential royalties as of the date of your death. The executor then distributes those rights among your heirs individually. It can be expensive to hire an appraiser, and his or her estimate depends on a number of unknown factors. So what if the estimates are wrong?

The appraiser considers the current nature of each manuscript (published or unpublished), the likelihood of publication and the potential sales for the unpublished manuscripts, and the royalty history for the published manuscripts, then makes the assumption that royalties will decrease over time. Based on these factors as well as others, the appraiser values the copyright for *My Life* at $100, the copyright for *Love* at $1,000, the copyright for *Puppies* at $20,000, and the copyright for *Kittens* at $30,000. The appraiser estimates the value of the royalties at $0 for *My Life*, $5,000 for *Love*, $18,000 for *Puppies*, and $25,000 for *Kittens* ($35,000 minus the $10,000 unearned portion of the advance).

This brings the total value of the estate to $449,100. Your spouse's share is $224,550 and she wants the house, so she purchases it by paying the estate the $25,450 difference.

With the proceeds from the house and your investments, the estate now has $125,450 in cash, four copyrights, and four royalty rights to be divided between the two children. The executor distributes the copyrights and royalties for *My Life* and *Kittens* (jointly valued at $55,100) and $57,175 in cash to the older child and the copyrights and royalties for *Love* and *Puppies* (jointly valued at $44,000) and $68,275 in cash to the younger child.

That's fine if the copyrights and royalties perform as the appraiser believed they would. But assume *Kittens* has already exhausted its audience and *Love* gets published and becomes a bestseller. Now the younger child has a much larger share than the older child does.

Or what if the older child wants ready money rather than copyrights and future royalties? If the younger child believes in your writing gift, maybe the two can agree to ask the executor to give the younger child all copyrights and royalties plus $21,275 in cash. If they both want the money or the copyright to the same book, however, the executor has two choices: either distribute the property as he planned and have at least one unhappy heir, or sell the copyrights and the future royalties to a third party at a discounted price and pay the heirs a reduced amount. Neither solution is ideal.

2. Choosing who gets the copyrights and royalties

Another estate planning option is to specify who gets the copyrights and royalties for each manuscript. You can even give the copyrights to your children as gifts before you die but continue to receive the royalties while you are alive.

Depending on your family dynamics, this option may avoid arguments later. Or it may create dissatisfaction if one heir believes he or she received the less desirable copyrights.

You also have the same problem with future uncertainty that you have if an executor makes the decision. If *Kittens* fizzles and *Love* soars, the elder child will receive less and could resent the younger.

3. Using a trust

Using a trust avoids most of these problems. On the downside, trusts can be expensive to set up and administer. Unless you are a best-selling or multi-published author, it may not be worth it.

A trust is a separate legal entity that holds and manages assets according to specific instructions. A trustee or group of trustees manages the trust's assets and distributes funds to the people listed as beneficiaries. The trustees may be individuals, corporations, or other legal entities. They are entitled to reasonable compensation, which is paid from trust assets.

Assume you leave your four copyrights and the royalties and fees they generate to a trust. The trust provisions require the trustee to pay 50% of the trust's annual income to your spouse and 25% to each of your children.

The trustee is responsible for managing the copyrights according to the terms of the trust. This usually means that the trustee must make a reasonable effort to maximize the income while preserving the assets. If *Love* looks like a good candidate for publication, the trustee must try to find a publisher. The trustee does not have to take actions that are unlikely to succeed, however. If *My Life* is boring and the world has no special interest in you, the trustee can throw the manuscript in a drawer and leave it there. The trustee is also responsible for managing the copyrights and granting or denying permission to use the copyrighted material. Publishing contracts follow the copyright, and the trustee must abide by the terms of those contracts.

As long as the conditions don't breach existing contracts, however, you can write the trust to limit what the trustee can do or to provide principles the trustee must follow. For example, you could direct the trustee not to sell movie rights to a film maker who will not remain true to the story in your book.

Trusts are also a good way to give the benefits of your copyrights to charity. Many nonprofit organizations do not have the resources to manage copyrights. Using a trust allows them to receive the income without having the management responsibilities. You can also use a trust to divide copyright royalties and fees among several charities.

4. Transferring copyrights and royalties to a corporation

Another way to divide up copyright royalties and fees is to transfer them to a corporation.

A corporation is owned by its stockholders, who may or may not be employees. Under a basic corporate structure, the corporation pays its owners by issuing dividends when it makes money.

When you die, your stock goes to your heirs. Assume your will says that your spouse gets 50% of your stock and each of your children gets 25%. (This could create deadlocks if the children vote their stock one way and the spouse votes hers another way, but let's keep the example as straightforward as possible.) When the corporation pays dividends, the spouse receives twice as much as each child. As with trusts, this allows your heirs to benefit in the percentage you desire without having to decide who gets which copyright.

ॐ

The best estate plan is one prepared by an attorney you talk to in person. A computer program may ask you targeted questions, but it cannot hear the doubt in your voice as you tell it how to divide your assets. Nor is it likely to question your choices and make sure you understand the consequences. This is especially important when your property includes unusual items such as copyrights. Additionally, standardized forms and computer programs may not have the most up-to-date information about your state's laws. Hiring a lawyer costs you more but may save your heirs time, money, and hard feelings.

❧

Incorporating is not right for everyone, and estate plans vary significantly. You may not have the same needs as another writer, so don't assume you should follow the same steps to protect your assets. But regardless of your final choice, you are more likely to keep your share of the pie safe if you understand the consequences and make an informed decision.

Part VI

The Walrus and the
Carpenter
(A Little of Everything)

CHAPTER SIXTEEN
The Sun Impersonates the Moon
(Trademarks)

The sun was shining on the sea,
Shining with all his might:
He did his very best to make
The billows smooth and bright—
And this was odd, because it was
The middle of the night.

The moon was shining sulkily,
Because she thought the sun
Had got no business to be there
After the day was done—
"It's very rude of him," she said,
"To come and spoil the fun!"

Lewis Carroll, "The Walrus and the Carpenter"
From *Through the Looking Glass*

The sun tried to encroach on the moon's territory. Not only did that make the moon sulk, but it probably confused the people sailing on the sea. Was it day or was it night?

If the moon owned the night like a company owns a trademark, the sun might have been liable for trademark infringement.

In simple terms, a trademark is any word, name, symbol, or device that makes you think of a particular product or group of products. If you hear someone say "McDonald's" or see the golden arches, you think of a specific chain of fast food restaurants and the menu items those restaurants sell. Technically, marks that identify services (e.g.,

FedEx for overnight delivery) rather than goods are called service marks, but they are often lumped in with trademarks. Since the law is the same for both, this chapter will refer to them all as trademarks.

The symbol ® after the word, name, symbol, or device shows that the trademark is registered with the U.S. Patent and Trademark Office. Some states also have facilities for registering trademarks. A trademark does not have to be registered to be valid, however. Unregistered trademarks—or at least those that aren't federally registered—are sometimes identified with ™ for a trademark or ℠ for a service mark.

Consumers rely on recognizable marks to tell them that they are getting a certain quality or a product with particular characteristics. When they see the Nike swoosh on a pair of shoes, they expect those shoes to last. When a counterfeiter prints the swoosh or something resembling it on shoddy-quality goods, people are misled. That harms both the consumer (who is not getting what he or she expected) and Nike (who loses sales to the counterfeiter and could suffer harm to its reputation when the shoes fall apart).

The two primary types of trademark violations are trademark infringement and trademark dilution. Writers don't have to be afraid of them, but there are a few occasions when trademark law can affect what a writer does. This chapter will begin with a primer on trademarks and then explain when they do—and do not—apply to an author's work.

What Qualifies as a Trademark?

As mentioned above, a mark is a word, name, symbol, or device that identifies a particular product or service. The word/name "Nike" is a trademark, and so is its swoosh symbol. When your manuscript mentions Google or uses "golden arches" to refer to McDonald's, it is using trademarks.

Marks vary in their ability to identify a particular product or service. The weakest marks are those that identify any brand within the same category of goods or services, while the strongest marks are those that identify only one brand. The stronger a mark is as an identifier, the more protection it receives.

There are five types of marks, and they are listed below from weakest to strongest.

- Generic marks can never qualify as trademarks. All hamburgers are hamburgers, regardless of who makes them. A ground-beef patty company could call itself "Hamburger," but it could not prevent anyone else from using the same name.

- Descriptive marks—which include surnames and geographic locations—do not qualify as trademarks unless they have acquired a secondary meaning that associates them with a particular product. "The Teaching Company" is an example of a descriptive mark that has achieved trademark status.

- Suggestive marks are marks that suggest the product. "V-8" is less direct than either the generic "juice" or the descriptive "eight vegetables," but it has a logical connection with the product it represents. Suggestive marks can be trademarks, but they are more vulnerable to challenge than the next two categories are.

- Arbitrary marks are very strong. These are marks that have a meaning that—before use as a trademark—people would not have associated with that particular type of product or service. Fruit has little or nothing to do with computers, so "Apple" is an arbitrary mark.

- Fanciful marks are the strongest of all. These are simply made-up words, like "Kodak."

The other quality of a trademark is that consumers recognize it as shorthand for that particular product or service. Trademarks to not exist until consumers begin to recognize them. A company or individual can file an "intent to use" application with the U.S. Patent and Trademark Office to warn others that it intends to use the trademark in the future, and being the first to file an application or actually use the trademark makes the case for ownership stronger, but it is not infallible.

If someone holds a valid trademark, however, how does that affect your writing? Can you let your characters meet at Starbucks without violating the coffee giant's trademark?

Types of Trademark Violations

The federal trademark law is commonly called the Lanham Act. There are also state versions, usually created by courts before Congress adopted the Lanham Act. Since the state and federal provisions are similar, this chapter will limit its discussion to the federal requirements.

1. Trademark infringement

The protection against trademark infringement is very narrow: it only applies where there is a likelihood of consumer confusion. To win a case for trademark infringement, the trademark owner needs to show that (1) it owns the trademark, (2) the alleged infringer used the trademark or a very similar mark in commerce or in commercial advertising, **and** (3) the use is likely to either cause consumer confusion over the origin of the goods or services or to imply sponsorship or approval by the trademark owner.

Proving trademark ownership is usually the easiest part of the process. Registration with the U.S. Patent and Trademark Office creates a presumption that you own it. After five years of registration and use, that presumption becomes firm.

Use in commerce means that you use the trademark to identify goods or services to consumers when selling or distributing those goods or services through normal commercial channels or other means available to the public. Most of the cases require that the consumer actually be able to see the trademark, but the law is still evolving for behind-the-scenes technology such as the use of metatags to cue Internet pop-up ads.

Trademark infringement does not require intent to deceive. It merely requires that consumers are likely to be confused as to either (1) the origin of the goods or services or (2) the trademark owner's sponsorship or approval of the use.

Because confusion is the heart of an infringement violation, the allegedly infringing product must either be of the same type as the trademarked product or be an area that the trademark owner reasonably expects to develop in the future. A fast food restaurant may protect its trademark against another fast food restaurant, an upscale restaurant, or even a hotel or resort, but it is unlikely to prevail against a sporting goods manufacturer. Consumers don't confuse roast beef sandwiches with golf clubs.

2. Dilution

The second type of violation is called "dilution." The main difference between dilution and infringement is that a dilution claim draws in the sporting goods manufacturer from the above example.

Only famous marks qualify for protection against dilution. To be famous, the trademark must be recognized nation-wide by the general consumer. "IBM" and "Pepsi" are famous marks. The name of your local bookstore is not.

To make a case for dilution, the trademark owner must show that the trademark is both famous and distinctive. Additionally, the alleged dilutor must have begun using the mark after it became famous; if it used the mark before then, it can continue to do so. Finally, the trademark owner must show that the alleged dilutor's use either blurs consumer recognition of the famous mark or tarnishes that mark. Given these requirements, writers are unlikely to face dilution claims.

Trademark Issues for Writers

So what claims do writers face?

1. Passing off

The most direct infringement is when a counterfeiter makes a similar product and tries to "pass it off" as the original. This is what happens when another manufacturer puts a swoosh on athletic shoes hoping that consumers will think they are buying Nikes.

Mentioning a product by name in your manuscript is not passing off. The references will not confuse consumers about the origin of that product, and readers do not assume that the trademark owner has endorsed the use of its trademark simply because it is used in a manuscript.

As discussed in Chapter 3, you cannot copyright names and titles. But can they become trademarks?

Raymond Cooper wrote a children's book called *Teeny-Big* and attempted to register the title as a trademark. The U.S. Patent and Trademark Office refused registration, and the appeals court affirmed the USPTO's decision. Although the court's reasoning was complicated, the bottom line is simple: the title of a book cannot be a trademark.

The court's decision was partly based on the interplay between the Lanham Act and the Copyright Act. Imagine what would happen if you could trademark book titles. Since *Tom Sawyer* is in the public domain under the copyright laws, anyone is free to publish the manuscript. But a trademark lives as long as the trademark owner continues to use it, so if Mark's Twain's publisher had a trademark in the title and continued to produce the book, anybody else would have to publish it under a different title. That result would create consumer confusion rather than eliminating it. It would also defeat the Copyright

Act's aim of removing any restraints once material enters the public domain.

There is another reason for the rule that single titles can't be trademarked. With the millions of books out there, the good titles are already taken.

Notice that the example has the publisher owning the trademark. Another consequence of the interplay between the trademark and copyright laws is that the publisher—not the author—is the source of a book in commerce. The U.S. Supreme Court put it this way:

> [R]eading the phrase "origin of goods" in the Lanham Act in accordance with the Act's common-law foundations (which were *not* designed to protect originality or creativity), and in light of the copyright and patent laws (which *were*), we conclude that the phrase refers to the producer of the tangible goods that are offered for sale, and not to the author of any idea, concept, or communication embodied in those goods. . . . To hold otherwise would be akin to finding that §43(a) created a species of perpetual patent and copyright, which Congress may not do.

Dastar Corp. v. Twentieth Century Fox Film Corp., 539 U.S. 23, 37 (2003) (emphasis in original).

Although the title of a single literary work cannot be a trademark, a magazine title can be. So can the title of a book series, such as "Chicken Soup for the Soul."

Bantam Doubleday Dell Publishing Group and Spy magazine collaborated on *Spy Notes*, which satirized three modern novels. More importantly, it was also a parody of *CliffsNotes*. The cover replicated the trademarked design with its yellow color, black stripes, and black lettering. The cover also contained significant differences, however, including the words "A Satire" printed five times in red, the Spy magazine logo, and a clay sculpture of New York City (to replace the clay sculpture of a mountain found on *CliffsNotes* covers).

As with copyrights, there is no trademark infringement if the use is fair. While parody is not a fair use by itself, it does make it less likely that consumers will be confused as to the origin or sponsorship of the goods. Intent is not enough, however. The imitating work doesn't have to be a good parody, but it must be successful to the extent that consumers recognize the subject of the parody while distinguishing the parody from that subject.

When Cliffs Notes, Inc. sued, the district court judge issued a preliminary injunction to stop the sale of *Spy Notes*. The judge thought the cover of the parody was likely to confuse consumers as to its source.

The Second Circuit Court of Appeals disagreed. While it found that there was a slight risk of consumer confusion, it did not believe that most consumers would be misled. The appeals court also rejected the district court's test for confusion where literary works were involved and replaced it with the following:

> [I]n deciding the reach of the Lanham Act in any case where an expressive work is alleged to infringe a trademark, it is appropriate to weigh the public interest in free expression against the public interest in avoiding consumer confusion.

Cliff Notes, Inc. v. Bantam Doubleday Dell Publishing Group, Inc., 886 F.2d 490, 494 (2nd Cir. 1989)

Although *Spy Notes* borrowed some of the *CliffsNotes* trademark, it did so in order to conjure up the subject of the parody. Finding that the parody was successful, the appeals court concluded that the potential for confusion over *Spy Notes'* source was outweighed by the public interest in free expression.

The Second Circuit made it clear that consumers still had an interest in not being misled, and parody is not an absolute defense to a trademark infringement claim. Bantam and *Spy* had gone out of their way to let readers know that this was a parody. Something less obvious could have led the appellate court to reach a different conclusion.

The facts are also important when celebrities claim trademarks in their names or images.

The first requirement, of course, is that consumers recognize the name as the source of goods or services. Anita Flynn was an electrical engineer and robotics scientist who co-wrote a book titled *Mobile Robots: From Inspiration to Implementation*. When the publishers wanted to revise the work, she did not have the time but agreed to let another scientist join her co-author in making the revisions. That is, she agreed until the work was finished and she had a chance to look at it. Feeling that the third author's work was substandard, she asked the publisher to take her name off the book.

When the publisher did not comply, Flynn sued, claiming that the publisher violated the Lanham Act by listing Flynn as an author on the second edition without her consent. The First Circuit Court of Appeals began its analysis by noting that personal names are descriptive and, therefore, are not protected trademarks unless they have achieved a secondary meaning among consumers. Although Flynn was well-known among the academics in her field, that was not enough to give her name a secondary meaning under the Lanham Act, and she lost the case.

Does the result change when the name belongs to someone famous?

Ginger Rogers objected to a Federico Fellini film called *Ginger and Fred*. The movie revolved around two fictional dancers who imitated Fred Astaire and Ginger Rogers during their performances. In weighing the requirements of the First Amendment against the possibility of public confusion as to the source or endorsement of a literary work, the Second Circuit Court of Appeals held that a title does not violate the Lanham Act unless it either (1) has no artistic relevance to the subject of the work or (2) has literary relevance but **explicitly** misleads the public as to the source or content of the work. The title *Ginger and Fred* was relevant to the movie's content and was not explicitly misleading, so it did not violate the Lanham Act.

The Sixth Circuit applied the same test with a different result when the rap group OutKast recorded a song titled "Rosa Parks." The song did contain the repeated line, "Everybody move to the back of the bus," but its use had nothing to do with civil rights or the incident that made Rosa Parks famous. She had allowed her name to be used to promote activities and products advancing civil rights, and the appeals court found that it had achieved trademark status. Because a jury could have found that the song's title was a blatant attempt to make money from the use of Rosa's name, the appeals court sent the case back for trial. The parties settled it instead.

An artist included Tiger Woods in a painting called "The Masters of Augusta." When a publishing company began offering a limited edition of the print, Woods sued to stop the sales. He claimed that his likeness deserved trademark protection.

Noting that the essence of a trademark is to identify the origin of goods, the Sixth Circuit Court of Appeals found that no reasonable person would believe Woods was the source of the painting merely because his image appeared in it. The court went on to hold that, as a general rule, a person's image or likeness could not be a trademark. But the "as a general rule" language leaves some leeway if the right case comes along.

Single titles cannot be trademarks, but magazine and series titles can be. A person's name or image will rarely receive trademark protection, but rarely doesn't mean never. Still, as discussed in subsection 3 below, a writer's use of a trademark in his or her manuscript is not likely to violate the Lanham Act.

2. Reverse passing off

Another type of trademark infringement is called "reverse passing off." The infringer takes the swoosh off of a real Nike shoe and replaces it with the infringer's own trademark so that the consumer thinks the high-quality product was made by the infringer. Writers occasionally claim that plagiarism (or what they view as plagiarism) is reverse passing off.

Lisa Litchfield sued Steven Spielberg and the producers of *E.T.*, claiming that they copied the movie from her copyrighted play, *Lokey from Maldemar*. The Ninth Circuit Court of Appeals first decided the copyright claims, holding that there was no substantial similarity between the two works and, therefore, no copyright violations. It then moved to the trademark claim and found that, without substantial similarity, there was also no trademark infringement.

In the *E.T.* case, the Ninth Circuit did not need—and specifically declined—to decide whether it was possible to have a trademark claim for reverse passing off in cases of substantial similarity. It decided that question six years later in connection with a television series called *The Equalizer*. The Ninth Circuit sent the case to a jury to decide the copyright claims but specifically declined to extend trademark law to cover situations where the Copyright Act provides an adequate remedy. Even so, it took a U.S. Supreme Court case to finally put the plagiarism issue to rest.

Dastar Corp. produced and sold a series of video tapes that borrowed heavily from a television series produced by Twentieth Century Fox. The television series had passed into the public domain, so Dastar was within its rights when it used the material. But Dastar did not credit the original series, which, as discussed in Chapter 2, makes it plagiarism. Still, plagiarism is an ethical issue rather than a legal one. Twentieth Century Fox tried to get around that hurdle by claiming that Dastar's actions were reverse passing off.

The Supreme Court rejected Twentieth Century Fox's argument, holding that the Lanham Act does not prohibit plagiarism. This is the same case where the Court stated that authors are not the source of goods for trademark purposes.

3. Classic vs. nominative use

Courts also look at which goods the trademark identifies. The classic use is one where a similar or identical trademark is placed on goods that are not connected with the trademark owner. Most trademark cases involve such classic use.

But what if the alleged infringer is using the trademark to refer to the trademark owner's own goods? This is called nominative use.

The New Kids on the Block were merchandisers as well as singers. Before the days of text messages and Twitter, the group made money from 1-900 numbers with recorded messages for fans. When two newspapers decided to use their own 1-900 numbers to conduct surveys about the singers, the group claimed that the newspapers' references to "New Kids on the Block" were trademark infringement.

The Ninth Circuit Court of Appeals found otherwise. Noting that the easiest way to identify the group was with its trademarked name, the court held that this nominative use was outside the purposes of trademark law. If the newspapers had suggested that the New Kids sponsored or endorsed the surveys, however, the results might have been different.

Most trademark references in manuscripts are nominative fair use. A character eats at Kentucky Fried Chicken or watches her children play with Legos or goes to Macy's to shop for clothes. These trademarks merely identify the trademarked products and do not suggest sponsorship or endorsement.

4. A note on fan fiction

Some characters are registered as trademarks, especially for visual media like graphic novels. If your Lone Ranger is too much like the official Lone Ranger, readers might think you have been commissioned, or at least authorized, to write the story. Fan fiction falls in a gray area, so make it clear that you have no connection to or endorsement by the people who own the rights to the Lone Ranger.

Or limit your reading audience to a few close friends. You are only liable for trademark infringement if you use the trademark in commerce.

First Amendment Concerns

Always cognizant of First Amendment concerns, courts provide more leeway for using another's trademarks in literary works. In the Rosa Parks and Ginger Rogers cases, the courts held that artists are free to use a celebrity's name in a title—even if there could be confusion as to the person's involvement—as long as the title has some artistic relevance to the underlying work and does not explicitly mislead the consumer as to the source or content of the work. The *CliffsNotes* and other parody cases weigh the public interest in free expression against the public interest in avoiding consumer confusion. And the New Kids on the Block case highlights the protections that are given to nominative use.

Writers do not have free reign, however. Ginger Rogers could not block the use of her name, but Rosa Parks could. The parody cases make it clear that consumer confusion is still part of the test. Even the nominative use cases state that a nominative use is not protected if the user suggests sponsorship or endorsement by the trademark holder.

Still, the First Amendment does favor authors in trademark cases.

The Bottom Line

Your characters can drink 7-Up without worrying about trademark infringement. No one is going to go out and buy counterfeit 7-Up based on your manuscript, nor will readers automatically assume that the makers of 7-Up are connected with your book. You don't have to call it lemon-lime soda in order to be safe.

Formica® has an advertising campaign that asks writers to "circle their R's." A brand name can lose its trademark protection if consumers use it generically to refer to other brands of the same type of product. After people started calling all facial tissues "kleenex" and photocopies made by any brand photocopier "xeroxes," the owners of those trademarks spent a lot of money educating consumers on the proper use of the terms. Formica is trying to prevent the same thing from happening to it.

Unfortunately, Formica's solution has its own problems. Although word processing programs include the ® among the available symbols, its absence from the keyboard means that inserting it slows down the writing process. More importantly, the ® interrupts the story for the reader, so most publishers don't use it. The ® is not legally required, and there are other ways to help trademark owners protect their property. One is to use generic terms. Or if you think "the real thing" will add authenticity, just capitalize Coke.

But if your characters want to meet at Starbucks, let them.

CHAPTER SEVENTEEN

When You Don't Like the Beach

(Author-Financed Publishing)

The sea was wet as wet could be,
The sands were dry as dry,
You could not see a cloud, because
No cloud was in the sky:
No birds were flying overhead—
There were no birds to fly.

The Walrus and the Carpenter
Were walking close at hand:
They wept like anything to see
Such quantities of sand:
"If this were only cleared away,"
They said, "it would be grand."

"If seven maids with seven mops
Swept it for half a year,
Do you suppose," the Walrus said,
"That they could get it clear?"
"I doubt it," said the Carpenter,
And shed a bitter tear.

Lewis Carroll, "The Walrus and the Carpenter"
From *Through the Looking Glass*

The Walrus and the Carpenter didn't like the beach but couldn't change it. If a writer can't find a traditional publisher, can the writer change the landscape and get published another way?

This chapter will begin with some definitions, after which it will briefly discuss e-publishing and print on demand. The bulk of the chapter will talk about the contract provisions of most importance to authors who are financing their own work, and the chapter will end with an overview of business and legal issues for those who decide to become their own distributor or publish under their own imprint.

Definitions

Self-publishing is one of those terms that gets defined various ways. Some writers use the term to refer to any publishing arrangement in which the writer foots part of the bill. To purists, however, self-publishing requires the author to have complete control over every part of the process. Under this latter definition, subsidy publishing and similar arrangements don't qualify.

To avoid confusion, this book refers to both subsidiary and self-publishing as author-financed publishing. It will distinguish between the two at times, however.

The following definitions are not precise, but they will help you understand how this chapter uses the terms.

- Most writers seek traditional publishing. In traditional publishing, as defined here, the publisher takes all of the financial risk for producing the book and pays the author royalties and maybe an advance.

- Author-financed publishing includes subsidy publishing and self-publishing. It refers to any publishing arrangement in which the author finances part or all of the publishing process. Under this definition, subsidy publishing and self-publishing are both sub-sets of author-financed publishing.

- Subsidy publishing is a hybrid between traditional publishing and self-publishing. In a subsidy publishing arrangement, the author pays money up front to produce the book and receives either a percentage or a set amount on each book sold. This amount is sometimes called a royalty, but the use of that term can be controversial. The subsidy publisher uses its own imprint (publishing company name) on the books and usually sets the price. People may also refer to these publishers as vanity presses or cooperative publishers.

- <u>Self-publishing</u> occurs when the author is the publishing company for a particular book.

- <u>E-publishing</u> is any form of publishing that delivers a product the reader will read on a screen or download and print. It covers e-readers such as Kindle and Nook as well as PDFs (portable document format) and word processing versions that a user can either print or read on a screen. E-publishing can be done through a traditional publisher or it can be author-financed.

- <u>Print on demand (POD) publishing</u> uses a digital process to print only as many books as are needed at a particular moment. This differs from the conventional printing process that requires large print runs to make it cost-effective. POD is used in both traditional and author-financed publishing.

E-Books and POD Publishing

E-books change how people receive and read books. Similarly, POD books make production and distribution easier for a publisher who does not want the expenses involved with large print runs and warehouse space. From a legal perspective, e-books and POD books are no different from paper books using a more conventional printing process.

For contract purposes, the type of printing or digital process used is largely irrelevant. What really matters is whether the book will be produced by a traditional publisher or will be author-financed.

When you enter into a contract with a "traditional" e-book publisher that takes all the financial risk, you are concerned with the clauses discussed in Chapters 10–12. Other than differences in the types of rights purchased and the royalty percentage, the contracts will be very similar to contracts for paper books produced by traditional publishers.

If, on the other hand, you decide to finance your e-book, you will share the same concerns as authors who finance their paper books. This chapter deals with those issues.

Similarly, if you sign a contract with a traditional publisher who uses a POD printing process, Chapters 10–12 describe the clauses that are likely to appear in your contract. If you are financing your own book, this chapter applies.

Contract Provisions

Self-publishing gives the author control over the process, but it takes significant time and effort and may not be a good option for someone who prefers to spend his or her time writing. POD and other new technologies are making it easier to self-publish, but critics claim the end product is of poorer quality. In general, subsidy publishing relieves you of many of the headaches of publishing the book yourself, but it also limits your ability to make a profit. Study and understand your options before you choose one.

Whether you enter into a contact with a subsidy publisher or sign multiple contracts covering different aspects of the publishing process, here are some things to look for.

- Who will register the copyright? If a subsidy publisher does it, make sure the agreement says the publisher will registered the copyright in your name. In fact, the contract should explicitly state that you are the copyright owner. You should never pay money to someone who expects to receive the copyright.

- Know who will be responsible for doing the cover design. If you commission it, your agreement with the designer should say it is a work made for hire and that the cover design is a supplementary work under Section 101 of the U.S. Copyright Act. Since cover designs are not explicitly mentioned in the statutory list of supplementary works, however, consider adding an additional clause stating that alternatively the designer assigns (sells) you all rights for the length of the copyright. Then if a court determines it is not a work for hire, you will still own the copyright. If a subsidy publisher prepares the design, read the agreement to see who owns the copyright in the cover design. If the publisher owns it, you will want the unlimited right to use the artwork in connection with publicity and book sales. If you commission the cover design, make sure the agreement requires the designer to provide you with the actual artwork and plates used for printing. Try to get the artwork from a subsidy publisher, too.

- If dealing with a subsidy publisher, get the right to approve the cover and interior design and to review the galleys.

- Similarly, know who is responsible for the interior design. If you commission it, you should have the right to receive the digital files or plates used for printing so that you can take them to another printer without having to recreate them. See if you can make the same deal with a subsidy publisher.

- Are you allowed to set your own sales price? Subsidy publishers and book printers are in business to make money, so they should be able to recoup their printing costs plus a small profit. If you use a book manufacturer or commercial printer, you will be required to pay an agreed amount for printing the books (the printing costs plus a small profit) but should have the right to set the sales price. Subsidy publishers often dictate a minimum price, which may be substantially higher than what you would pay a book manufacturer or commercial printer.

- Who will warehouse and ship the books? A subsidy publisher should provide these services. If you self-publish and don't have the resources to do it yourself, you can contract with a book manufacturer or distributor. You should also ask whether you or the shipper takes the financial loss if books are lost or damaged when shipped to you.

- Do not grant the publisher any rights to your work except the nonexclusive right to print, publish, and distribute copies of the book. You want to be able to find another printer at any time and to use the second printer simultaneously with or instead of the first publisher/printer.

- What services are included in the contract? If optional services are available, make sure you know the cost and pay for only those you need.

- A subsidy publisher will want a representations and warranties clause and an indemnification clause. It has some legal responsibility for the book's content, so this is fair. The contract may also contain a permissions clause. Read Chapter 12 for what these clauses should—and should not—contain.

When a traditional publisher takes the financial risk on a book, it has the right to set conditions that protect its investment. Those provisions are discussed in Chapters 10–12. When you finance the book, however, you should be the one in control. Subsidy publishers may try to set some conditions as well, but the more you pay the less control you should give up.

Business Requirements

If you decide to become your own distributor or publish under your own imprint, you need to be aware of certain legal provisions that apply to businesses in general. If you do everything through a subsidy publisher, however, these requirements may not apply.

1. Zoning laws

If you are running a business out of your home, check the local zoning ordinance. Most cities and counties allow some home-based business activities in residential areas as long as those activities are virtually invisible, and writers should not be concerned. The more visible your activities at that location become, however, the more likely they are to run afoul of residential zoning ordinances.

This becomes a particular problem for the author who distributes books from his or her home. Mail-order businesses, sales locations, and storage facilities may all violate residential zoning provisions, which are designed to limit noise and traffic in quiet residential areas. If you ship books from your home, you increase the number of commercial vehicles that drive down the street. If people regularly stop to buy books, they increase traffic and use parking spaces that may normally be used by residents and their non-business guests. This is what the zoning laws try to protect residents from.

Adding on to your home or building a separate storage unit on your property almost always requires approval from your city or county government. And if you are allowed to build, you must comply with the local building codes.

If the zoning ordinances do not allow you to use your home for distribution or sales, consider renting space elsewhere or paying for book distribution services.

2. Business licenses and registrations

If you run a mail-order business or have a sales office, your local government (county or city) may require a license to conduct business at that location. And if you sell books, you need to register with the state and charge and pay sales taxes. See Chapter 14 for more information.

The name you use to identify your publishing company is called an imprint. If you publish as a sole proprietor and the imprint is not your name, state or local law may require you to register the imprint as a "doing business as" or assumed name to help people locate you. Check with a business lawyer for the requirements in your city or state.

3. Trademark issues

Do not use an imprint until you have done a trademark search. First, search the Internet for identical names (leaving off descriptive words such as "publishing company") and those that are similar enough to be confusing. If your search turns up a literary business, choose a different name for your imprint. If it doesn't, take the second step and use the Trademark Electronic Search System (TESS) at www.uspto.gov. If you don't find the name on the web or in TESS, chances are good that nobody is using it. Still, that's no guarantee. TESS only includes federally registered trademarks, so it does not catch everything. If you are concerned, consider hiring a search company to check all fifty state databases.

You can file an intent to use trademark application with the United States Patent and Trademark Office at www.uspto.gov. This is expensive, so if you are confident that no one else will claim your imprint, you can take a chance and file the application after use. An imprint may have a related symbol that appears on the book spine as well as on one or more front pages, and you should register that symbol as well. You can also register your trademarks with your home state. Most states do not allow registration before use, however.

4. Business structure

The more aspects of the publishing process you handle yourself, the more beneficial it is to incorporate or become a limited liability company. If you decide to go this route, check with an attorney who regularly forms businesses for clients. See the first half of Chapter 15 for more information on business structures.

☙

If you don't like the publishing beach, you can change it. Just make sure you know the ramifications.

CHAPTER EIGHTEEN
The Ingredients
(Check Lists)

"A loaf of bread," the Walrus said,
"Is what we chiefly need:
Pepper and vinegar besides
Are very good indeed—
Now, if you're ready, Oysters dear,
We can begin to feed."

Lewis Carroll, "The Walrus and the Carpenter"
From *Through the Looking Glass*

Although they were salivating for their dinner, the Walrus and the Carpenter first gathered the ingredients to make a tasty meal. Writers salivate to see their book or article or poem in print, but they should check the ingredients first. This book concludes with a list of issues for writers to consider when attempting to minimize legal expenses from that juicy manuscript.

Copyright

Does any material in your manuscript violate the copyright laws by borrowing someone else's original work of authorship? As a reminder, the following are not original works of authorship and are not entitled to copyright protection. (See Chapter 3.)

- Titles, names, short phrases, and slogans;
- Ideas;
- Facts;

- Material composed entirely of information that is common property and contains no original elements; and

- Procedures, methods, systems, processes, discoveries, or devices.

If you did use someone else's material, is your use both legal and ethical? Ask yourself the following questions.

- Did you give the author credit? (See Chapter 2.)

- Is the material in the public domain? (See Chapter 4.) In other words, is it

  ➢ A work authored by the federal government;

  ➢ Published before 1923; **or**

  ➢ Published between 1923 and 1963 with the original copyright not renewed?

- If not in the public domain, is yours a fair use? (See Chapter 4.) Although the law provides a bias in favor of criticism, comment, news reporting, teaching, scholarship, and research, the mere fact that a use falls within one of these categories is not enough to make it fair, and the fact that it doesn't fall within one of these categories does not automatically make it unfair. The fair use analysis considers all the circumstances, with a particular emphasis on the following:

  ➢ The purpose and character of the allegedly infringing use,

  ➢ The nature of the copyrighted work,

  ➢ The amount and substantiality of the portion used in relation to the copyrighted work as a whole, and

  ➢ The effect upon the potential market for the copyrighted work.

Defamation

If your work talks about real people, does it defame them? (See Chapter 7.) This question applies even if you have fictionalized them or changed their names. For each person, consider whether the manuscript includes

- A false statement,

- About an identifiable person,

- That is communicated to others (which is always the case when a written work is published), and

- That harms the person's reputation.

If any of the four are missing, the work is not defamatory. But if they are all present in connection with the same person, don't use the material unless you have a defense against a defamation charge. The following are all potential defenses:

- Nobody in their right minds would believe it,

- You have made it clear that it is just your opinion,

- You are commenting on public issues, or

- The individual consented.

If the information is true, it is not defamatory. If the information turns out to be false and you either knew it or had serious doubts about its truth, even the First Amendment won't save you.

Rights of Privacy and Publicity

If you are writing about real people, do your words invade someone's privacy or right to control his or her own publicity? (See Chapter 8.) In particular, ask yourself the following:

- Did you intrude into an individual's private space or affairs in gathering the information? Then don't use it.

- Does your article or book disclose private facts? Don't use the information unless it is of legitimate concern to the public.

- Does the material portray any person in a false light? Then don't use it unless the work is clearly a parody.

- Have you appropriated an individual's name or likeness? Don't use the information for commercial purposes unless you have determined that the courts allow it (e.g., criticism or parody).

Trademarks

Did you use other people's trademarks in your manuscript? (See Chapter 16.) If so, consider the following:

- Have you taken care not to imply that the trademark owner has sponsored or endorsed the manuscript?

- Is your title similar to that of a book series? If it could be confused with that series, find a different title.

- If your title uses a trademark or celebrity name, does the trademark or celebrity name have artistic relevance to your work **and** have you taken care that it doesn't explicitly mislead the public as to the source or content of the work?

Book Contracts

Has a traditional publisher offered you a book contract? (See Chapters 10–12 for a discussion of contract clauses.) If so, review the contract and consider the following:

- Does the contract describe the book's subject matter and list its tentative title? Does it include an approximate page count?

- Is the deadline for delivering the work reasonable?

- Will the copyright be registered in your name?

- Which rights are you leasing to the publisher? Which are you retaining? Does the publisher have the resources and connections to find someone to develop each of the subsidiary rights it will receive? Do you?

- Are royalties based on the list price or the net price? If on the net price, how are they calculated?

- How often will you get paid? Can the publisher withhold a reserve against returns? If so, how much? Can you audit the publisher's records?

- Does your contract have a joint accounting clause? If so, can you negotiate it away?

- If the contract has a satisfactory manuscript clause, does it require the manuscript to be satisfactory "in form and content"? If the publisher saw the completed manuscript before accepting the book, can you get the clause removed? If the clause gives the publisher complete discretion, can you limit it to manuscripts that are not satisfactory "in form and content"?

- Will you get your rights back if the publisher does not publish the book within a certain period after you submit a satisfactory manuscript?

- Does your contract have an option clause? If so, can you negotiate it away? If the publisher insists on an option clause, review the clause for the following:
  - When you can submit the next book;
  - Whether you can submit a book proposal or must have a completed manuscript;
  - How soon the publisher must respond;

> ➤ Whether the next deal will be "on terms to be mutually agreed upon," "on the same financial terms," or "on the same terms," (listed from best to worst);
>
> ➤ The scope of the clause, and whether you can narrow it;
>
> ➤ The number of manuscripts you must submit before the obligation terminates;
>
> ➤ Whether there is a "no less favorable terms" provision. If so try to negotiate it away.

- Is the publisher required to do some promotion? How much?

- Does the contract include a competing works clause? Try to eliminate it for fiction and to make it as narrow as possible for nonfiction.

- If yours is the type of book that may be updated in the future, are you required to make the revisions? If someone else makes the revisions, do you get to choose who does it? How much will the reviser be paid from your royalties?

- Are you comfortable making the representations and warranties the contract requires?

- Does the indemnification clause limit your liability to lawsuits that involve your own conduct? Is your approval required before the publisher settles the case? Who pays the legal fees if you win the case? Can the publisher withhold all royalties while the case is pending or is it limited to a reasonable amount withheld only from the royalties for the book at issue?

- Will the publisher add you to its insurance policy?

- Whose responsibility is it to obtain the permissions for copyrighted material? How much is it likely to cost?

- Is there a choice of forum clause? A choice of law clause? What do they say?

- What conditions cause the book to go out of print? You should get your rights back if it does, so make sure the contract explicitly says so.

- Does the contract say you will get your rights back if the publisher goes bankrupt or out of business?

Agent Contracts

If you use an agent, you should know what the relationship involves. (See Chapter 13.) Whether the terms are in a letter or a formal-looking contract, make sure you can answer the following questions.

- Is it an exclusive arrangement? In other words, will you still have to pay the agent if someone else (including yourself) places the book with a publisher?

- Can you terminate the relationship at will if you give reasonable notice? How much notice is required? If the agreement is for a set term, how long is it?

- What works does the agreement cover? A particular book? A series? All books in a particular genre?

- What rights will the agent represent? Does the agent have contacts for all those rights? If not, does the agent have subagent relationships that it can use? Can you place certain subsidiary rights more easily than the agent can?

- Does the contract require your permission before the agent can assign his or her responsibilities to a different agent?

- What is the agent's commission? How will he or she collect it? If the publisher pays your royalties to the agent and the agent deducts his or her commission before paying you, do you have the right to audit the agent's records?

- Which expenses are you responsible for? Does the contract require your approval for unusual or large expenses?

Collaboration Agreements

Are you collaborating with others to create the work? If so, you should have a collaboration agreement. (See Chapter 13.) When entering into it, consider the following:

- Who owns the copyright under the law? Is there a reason to change that result? Do it in the agreement.

- Will all of the collaborators be listed on the book and in promotional materials? How will their names appear in the credits?

- How will the collaborators divide the income? The expenses?

- Does the agreement say who will receive and distribute the income?

- How will the work be divided and who will make creative decisions?

- Do you have a project schedule? Is it either included in the agreement or attached as an exhibit?

- Who owns research material?

- What happens if the parties can't work together or one person is unwilling or unable to complete his or her part of the project? Can the other collaborator finish it or find someone else to do so? How will this affect compensation and the names that appear on the book?

- Does each collaborator need the other collaborators' permission before assigning responsibilities or copyright ownership to third parties? Can a living collaborator purchase a deceased collaborator's share of the copyright?

- Is this a work for hire? Does it say that explicitly?
- What other provisions are included in the collaboration agreement? Consider adding the following:
  - ➢ Representations, warranties, and indemnification;
  - ➢ Responsibility for obtaining and paying for copyright permissions;
  - ➢ Restrictions on competing works; and
  - ➢ Choice of forum and choice of law.

Magazine Rights

When submitting articles, stories, and poems to magazines, consider what magazine rights you are willing to sell, including geographical area and language. (See Chapter 13.) Some common magazine rights are:

- All rights,
- First rights or first North American rights,
- Reprint rights,
- One-time or simultaneous rights,
- Electronic rights, or
- Non-exclusive rights.

On the other hand, it may be a work for hire.

Author-Financed Publishing

Are you paying to publish your book? (See Chapter 17.) Whether you sign one contract or many, here are some things to consider:

- Who will register the copyright? Make sure it is registered in your name.

- Who will be responsible for the cover design? If you commission it, your agreement should say it is a work made for hire. If you use a subsidy publisher, make sure you have the unlimited right to use the cover art for book sales and publicity.

- If working with a subsidy publisher, do you have the right to approve the cover and interior design and to review galleys?

- Who is responsible for interior design? If you commission it, you should have the right to receive the digital files or plates used for printing.

- Are you allowed to set your own sales price?

- Who will warehouse and ship the books? If you do it yourself, check the zoning laws and obtain all necessary licenses.

- Have you retained all rights? You should give the publisher/printer only nonexclusive rights to print, publish, and distribute the book.

- What services are included in the contract? Don't pay for services you don't need.

Taxes

You cannot deduct excess writing expenses on your personal income taxes unless you write to make a profit rather than as a hobby. (See Chapter 14.) If you want to deduct them but may not make a profit at least three out of five consecutive years, do you:

- Keep good records and approach writing in a businesslike manner;

- Understand or educate yourself on the craft of writing and the subjects you write about;

- Write regularly and continuously;

- Submit to paying markets or actively promote author-financed publications; and

- Put time and effort into the parts of the process that you don't enjoy as well as those you do enjoy?

If you did make a profit, have you paid any applicable self-employment taxes and made estimated income tax payments?

Business Issues

Depending on your activities, you may need to obtain state and local licenses or comply with other state and local laws applicable to businesses in general. (See Chapters 14, 15, and 17.) Have you:

- Registered to pay sales taxes and paid them to the state as required if you sell your own books;

- Applied for a business license if you run a mail-order business or sell your books from a particular location;

- Checked out the zoning laws if you run a mail-order business, sales office, or storage facility for your books;

- Conducted a trademark search before choosing an imprint for self-publishing your books;

- Registered your imprint as a "doing business as" or assumed name;

- Registered your imprint as a trademark, and

- Considered whether there is any advantage to incorporating or forming an LLC?

Estate Planning

Have you prepared an estate plan so you know where your copyrights and futures royalties will go after you die? (See Chapter 15.) If not, consider the following options:

- Including copyrights and royalties with general property,

- Writing your will to specifying who gets which copyrights and royalties,

- Giving copyrights and royalties as gifts while you are still living,

- Creating a trust to manage your copyrights and receive and distribute royalties, and

- Transferring your copyrights and royalties to a corporation.

❧

The Walrus and the Carpenter did not begin their feast until they had gathered all the ingredients. Don't publish your book or file your taxes until you have checked your list of legal ingredients and determined that you have them all.

❧

Lewis Carroll was a master at creating fantasy worlds where nothing was as it seemed. Many writers think the law is its own Wonderland, but they are wrong. Although the law can be initially confusing, when looked at the right way up everything is what it seems.

Appendices

APPENDIX I

Chapter Notes

Chapter 1—Crocodiles and Fishes (Avoiding Lawyers)

Comments:

1. To find a lawyer, contact your local bar association for a referral. Make sure you ask for a lawyer familiar with the particular issue you are concerned about (e.g., intellectual property, defamation, estate planning). The American Bar Association has a list of local bar associations by state. Find the list on the ABA website at http://apps.americanbar.org/legalservices/findlegalhelp/home.cfm.

Chapter 2—A Mad Tea-Party (Copyright Background)

U.S. Constitution:

Article I, Section 8

Cases:

Dastar Corp. v. Twentieth Century Fox Film Corp., 539 U.S. 23 (2003)

Twentieth Century Music Corp. v. Aiken, 422 U.S. 151 (1975)

Comments:

1. For articles discussing the *Opal Mehta* controversy, *see* David Zhou, "Student's Novel Faces Plagiarism Controversy," *Harvard Crimson*, April 23, 2006; Tom Zeller Jr., "In Internet Age, Writers Face Frontier Justice," *New York Times*, May 1, 2006; Dinitia Smith and Motoko Rich, "A Second Ripple in Plagiarism Scandal," *New York Times*, May 2, 2006; Motoko Rich, "'Opal Mehta' Won't Get a Life After All," *New York Times*, May 3, 2008.

2. As used in the chart, the source for the McCafferty comparison is David Zhou, "Examples of Similar Passages Between Viswanathan's Book and McCafferty's Two Novels," *Harvard Crimson*, April 23, 2006; for the Kinsella comparison is Dinitia

Smith and Motoko Rich, "A Second Ripple in Plagiarism Scandal," *New York Times*, May 2, 2006; for the Cabot comparison is Paras D. Bhayani and David Zhou, "'Opal' Similar to More Books," *Harvard Crimson,* May 2, 2006; and for the Rushdie comparison is Tom Zeller Jr., "In Internet Age, Writers Face Frontier Justice," *New York Times*, May 1, 2006.

Chapter 3—Painting White Roses Red (Obtaining a Copyright)

Statutes:

   17 U.S.C. § 101 (definitions)

   17 U.S.C. § 102 (copyrightable works)

   17 U.S.C. § 106 (exclusive rights)

Cases:

   Reed Elsevier, Inc. v. Muchnick, __ U.S. __, 130 S.Ct. 1237 (2010) (registration)

   New York Times Co., Inc. v. Tasini, 533 U.S. 483 (2001) (collective works)

   Feist Publications, Inc. v. Rural Telephone Service Co., 499 U.S. 340 (1991) (telephone books)

   Community for Creative Non-Violence v. Reid, 490 U.S. 730 (1989) (work for hire)

   Mazer v. Stein, 347 U.S. 201 (1954) (useful articles)

   Murray Hill Publications, Inc. v. Twentieth Century Fox Film Corp., 361 F.3d 312 (6th Cir. 2004) (*scènes à faire*)

   Chicago Board of Education v. Substance, Inc., 354 F.3d 624 (7th Cir. 2003) (registration)

   Murray Hill Publications, Inc. v. ABC Communications, Inc., 264 F.3d 622 (6th Cir. 2001) (derivative works)

   Thomson v. Larson, 147 F.3d 195 (2nd Cir. 1998) (joint authorship)

   Seshadri v. Kasraian, 130 F.3d 798 (7th Cir. 1997) (joint authorship)

National Basketball Association v. Motorola, Inc., 105 F.3d 841 (2nd Cir. 1997) (basketball scores)

Princeton University Press v. Michigan Document Services, Inc., 99 F.3d 1381 (6th Cir. 1996) (classroom materials)

Publications International, Ltd. v. Meredith Corp., 88 F.3d 473 (7th Cir. 1996) (cookbooks)

Williams v. Crichton, 84 F.3d 581 (2nd Cir. 1996) (*scènes à faire*)

Bellsouth Advertising and Publishing Corp. v. Donnelley Information Publishing, Inc., 999 F.2d 1436 (11th Cir. 1993) (telephone books)

Twin Peaks Productions, Inc. v. Publications International, Ltd., 996 F.2d 1366 (2nd Cir. 1993) (derivative works)

Rogers v. Koons, 960 F.2d 301 (2nd Cir. 1992) (derivative works)

Childress v. Taylor, 945 F.2d 500 (2nd Cir. 1991) (joint authorship)

M.G.B. Homes, Inc. v. Ameron Homes, Inc., 903 F.2d 1486 (11th Cir. 1990) (joint authorship)

Harper House, Inc. v. Thomas Nelson, Inc., 889 F.2d 197 (9th Cir. 1989) (pocket organizers)

Brandir International, Inc. v. Cascade Pacific Lumber Co., 834 F.2d 1142 (2nd Cir. 1987) (useful articles)

Salinger v. Random House, Inc., 811 F.2d 90 (2nd Cir. 1987) (personal letters)

Maxtone-Graham v. Burtchaell, 803 F.2d 1253 (2nd Cir. 1986) (third-party interviews)

Horgan v. MacMillan, Inc., 789 F.2d 157 (2nd Cir. 1986) (derivative works).

Walker v. Time Life Films, Inc., 784 F.2d 44 (2nd Cir. 1986) (*scènes à faire*)

Kieselstein-Cord v. Accessories by Pearl, Inc., 632 F.2d 989 (2nd Cir. 1980) (useful articles)

Gilliam v. American Broadcasting Companies, Inc., 538 F.2d 14 (2nd Cir. 1976) (derivative works)

Reyher v. Children's Television Workshop, 533 F.2d 87 (2nd Cir. 1976) (*scènes à faire*)

Morrissey v. Procter & Gamble Co., 379 F.2d 675 (1st Cir. 1967) (sweepstakes rules)

Warner Bros. Pictures, Inc. v. Columbia Broadcasting System, Inc., 216 F.2d 945 (9th Cir. 1954) (characters)

Nichols v. Universal Pictures Corp., 45 F.2d 119 (2nd Cir. 1930) (characters, *scènes à faire*)

Lapine v. Seinfeld, No. 08 Civ. 128, 2009 WL 2902584 (S.D.N.Y. Sept. 10, 2009), *aff'd* 375 F.App'x 81 (2nd Cir. 2010) (cookbooks)

Porto v. Guirgis, 659 F.Supp.2d 597 (S.D.N.Y. 2009) (*scènes à faire*)

Warner Bros. Entertainment, Inc. v. RDR Books, 575 F.Supp.2nd 513 (S.D.N.Y. 2008) (lexicon)

Brown v. Perdue, No. 04 Civ. 7417, 2005 WL 1863673 (S.D.N.Y. Aug. 4, 2005), *aff'd* 177 F.App'x 121 (2nd Cir. 2006) (*scènes à faire*)

Scholastic, Inc. v. Stouffer, 221 F.Supp.2d 425 (S.D.N.Y. 2002) (characters)

American Massage Therapy Association v. Maxwell Petersen Associates, Inc., 209 F.Supp.2d 941 (N.D.Ill, 2002) (membership directories)

Basic Books, Inc. v. Kinko's Graphics Corp., 758 F.Supp. 1522 (S.D.N.Y. 1991) (classroom materials)

Quinto v. Legal Times of Washington, Inc., 506 F.Supp. 554 (D.D.C. 1981) (collective works)

Clare v. Farrell, 70 F.Supp. 276 (D.Minn. 1947) (names)

Comments:

1. The Mark Twain incident was taken from *Autobiography of Mark Twain* by Mark Twain, ed. Harriet Elinor Smith, Vol. 1 (Berkley: University of California Press, 2010), 207.

Chapter 4—Fighting the Serpent (Copyright Litigation)

Statutes:

17 U.S.C. § 412 (registration as prerequisite to statutory damages and attorney's fees)

17 U.S.C. § 504 (injunctions)

17 U.S.C. § 505 (damages)

Cases:

Salinger v. Colting, 607 F.3d 68 (2nd Cir. 2010)

Bridgeport Music, Inc. v. UMG Recordings, Inc., 585 F.3d 267 (6th Cir. 2009)

Castle Rock Entertainment v. Carol Publishing Group, 150 F.3d 132 (2nd Cir. 1998)

Twin Peaks Productions, Inc. v. Publications International, Ltd., 996 F.2d 1366 (2nd Cir. 1993)

Baxter v. MCA, Inc., 812 F.2d 421 (9th Cir. 1987) (sending the case back for a jury to decide); *Baxter v. MCA, Inc.*, 907 F.2d 154 (9th Cir. 1990) (affirming the jury's decision)

Salinger v. Random House, Inc., 811 F.2d 90 (2nd Cir. 1987)

Landsberg v. Scrabble Crossword Game Players, Inc., 736 F.2d 485 (9th Cir. 1984)

Reyher v. Children's Television Workshop, 533 F.2d 87 (2nd Cir. 1976)

Salinger v. Colting, 641 F.Supp.2d 250 (S.D.N.Y. 2009), *rev'd*, 607 F.3d 68 (2nd Cir. 2010)

Lapine v. Seinfeld, No. 08 Civ. 128, 2009 WL 2902584, (S.D.N.Y. Sept. 10 2009), *aff'd* 375 F.App'x 81 (2d Cir. 2010)

Warner Bros. Entertainment, Inc. v. RDR Books, 575 F.Supp.2d 513 (S.D.N.Y. 2008)

Brown v. Perdue, No. 04 Civ. 7417, 2005 WL 1863673 (S.D.N.Y. Aug. 4, 2005), *aff'd* 177 F.App'x 121 (2nd Cir. 2006)

Comments:

1. For information on the settlement in *Salinger v. Colting, see* Albanese, Andrew, "J.D. Salinger Estate, Swedish Author Settle Copyright Suit," *Publishers Weekly*, January 11, 2011, located on the web at
http://www.publishersweekly.com/pw/by-topic/industry-news/publisher-news/article/45738-j-d-salinger-estate-swedish-author-settle-copyright-suit.html?utm_source=Publishers%20Weekly's%20PW%20Daily&utm_campaign=aaa5cbeae9-UA-15906914-1&utm_medium=email (accessed December 21, 2011).

Chapter 5—Who Stole the Tarts? (Fair Use, Public Domain)

Statutes:

17 U.S.C. § 105 (U.S. government works)

17 U.S.C. § 107 (fair use)

Cases:

Golan v. Holder, __ U.S. __, 132 S.Ct. 873 (2012)

Eldred v. Ashcroft, 537 U.S. 186 (2003)

Campbell v. Acuff-Rose Music, Inc., 510 U.S. 569 (1994)

Stewart v. Abend, 495 U.S. 207 (1990)

Harper & Row Publishers, Inc. v. Nation Enterprises, 471 U.S. 539 (1985)

Bridgeport Music, Inc. v. UMG Recordings, Inc., 585 F.3d 267 (6th Cir. 2009)

Blanch v. Koons, 467 F.3d 244 (2nd Cir. 2006)

Positive Black Talk, Inc. v. Cash Money Records, Inc., 394 F.3d 357 (5th Cir. 2004)

Ty, Inc. v. Publications International, Ltd., 292 F.3d 512 (7th Cir. 2002)

Suntrust Bank v. Houghton Mifflin Co., 268 F.2d 1257 (11th Cir. 2001)

Leibovitz v. Paramount Pictures Corp., 137 F.3d 109 (2nd Cir. 1998)

Dr. Seuss Enterprises, L.P. v. Penguin Books USA, Inc., 109 F.3d 1394 (9th Cir. 1997)

Princeton University Press v. Michigan Document Services, Inc., 99 F.3d 1381 (6th Cir. 1996)

Twin Peaks Productions, Inc. v. Publications International, Ltd., 996 F.2d 1366 (2nd Cir. 1993)

Rogers v. Koons, 960 F.2d 301 (2nd Cir. 1992)

Salinger v. Random House, Inc., 811 F.2d 90 (2nd Cir. 1987)

Maxtone-Graham v. Burtchaell, 803 F.2d 1253 (2nd Cir. 1986)

Salinger v. Colting, 641 F.Supp.2d 250 (S.D.N.Y. 2009), *rev'd on other grounds*, 607 F.3d 68 (2nd Cir. 2010)

Bourne Co. v. Twentieth Century Fox Film Corp., 602 F.Supp.2d 499 (S.D.N.Y. 2009)

Basic Books, Inc. v. Kinko's Graphics Corp., 758 F.Supp. 1522 (S.D.N.Y. 1991)

Comments:

1. Interesting cases discussing parody include *Campbell* ("Oh Pretty Woman"), *Blanch v. Koons* (photograph), *Suntrust Bank* (*Gone With the Wind*), *Leibovitz* (photograph), *Dr. Seuss Enterprises* (*The Cat in the Hat*), *Salinger v. Colting* (*The Catcher in the Rye*), *Rogers v. Koons* (photograph), and *Bourne Co.* ("When You Wish Upon a Star"). The information in parentheses refers to the original works.

2. For more information on conducting a copyright search, go to www.copyright.gov and download Circular 22. For more

information on when works enter the public domain, download Circular 15A.

Chapter 6—Curiouser and Curiouser (Cyberspace, International Issues)

Statutes:

17 U.S.C. § 512 (Digital Millennium Copyright Act of 1998)

Cases:

Golan v. Holder, ___ U.S. ___, 132 S.Ct. 873 (2012)

Metro-Goldwyn-Mayer Studios, Inc. v. Grokster, Ltd., 545 U.S. 913 (2005)

Sony Corp. of America v. Universal City Studios, Inc., 464 U.S. 417 (1984)

Comments:

1. The United States Copyright Office maintains information on signatories to the various treaties. For a recent listing, go to www.copyright.gov and download Circular 38A.

Chapter 7—The Baker (Defamation)

Cases:

Milkovich v. Lorain Journal Co., 497 U.S. 1 (1990)

Hustler Magazine, Inc. v. Falwell, 485 U.S. 46 (1988)

Philadelphia Newspapers, Inc. v. Hepps, 475 U.S. 767 (1986)

Greenbelt Cooperative Publishing Association, Inc. v. Bresler, 398 U.S. 6 (1970)

Moldea v. New York Times Co., 22 F.3d 310 (D.C. Cir. 1994)

Haynes v. Alfred A. Knopf, Inc., 8 F.3d 1222 (7th Cir. 1993)

Brooks v. American Broadcasting Companies, Inc., 999 F.2d 167 (6th Cir. 1993)

Brooks v. American Broadcasting Companies, Inc. 932 F.2d 495 (6th Cir. 1991)

Dalbec v. Gentleman's Companion, Inc., 828 F.2d 921 (2nd Cir. 1987)

Pring v. Penthouse International, Ltd., 695 F.2d 438 (10th Cir. 1982)

Geisler v. Petrocelli, 616 F.2d 636 (2nd Cir. 1980)

Middlebrooks v. Curtis Publishing Co., 413 F.2d 141 (4th Cir. 1969)

Fetler v. Houghton Mifflin Co., 364 F.2d 650 (2d Cir. 1966)

Wheeler v. Dell Publishing Co., 300 F.2d 372 (7th Cir. 1962)

Buckley v. Vidal, 327 F.Supp. 1051 (S.D.N.Y. 1971)

Smith v. Stewart, 660 S.E.2d 822 (Ga.Ct.App. 2008). *See also* the follow-up article by Stephen Gurr, "Jury rules for plaintiff in Red Hat Club trial," *Gainesville Times*, November 19, 2009, http://www.gainesvilletimes.com/news/archive/26196/ (accessed March 23, 2010).

Bryson v. News America Publications, Inc., 174 Ill.2d 77, 672 N.E.2d 1207 (1996)

Springer v. Viking Press, 458 N.E.2d 1256 (N.Y. 1983)

Myers v. Boston Magazine Co., Inc., 380 Mass. 336, 403 N.E.2d 376 (1980)

Memphis Publishing Co. v. Nichols, 569 S.W.2d 412 (Tenn. 1978)

James v. Gannett Co.,40 N.Y2d 415, 353 N.E.2d 834 (1976)

Clare v. Farrell, 70 F.Supp. 276 (D.Minn. 1947)

Comments:

1. The story about Mark Twain and Eschol Sellers comes from *Autobiography of Mark Twain* by Mark Twain, ed. Harriet Elinor Smith, Vol. 1 (Berkley: University of California Press, 2010), 207.

Chapter 8—The Beaver (Right to Privacy)

Cases:

Florida Star v. B.J.F., 491 U.S. 524 (1989)

Cox Broadcasting Corp. v. Cohn, 420 U.S. 469 (1975)

Cantrell v. Forest City Publishing Co., 419 U.S. 245 (1974)

Time, Inc. v. Hill, 385 U.S. 374 (1967)

Cardtoons, L.C. v. Major League Baseball Players Association, 95 F.3d 959 (10th Cir. 1996)

Abdul-Jabbar v. General Motors Corp., 85 F.3d 407 (1996)

Cher v. Forum International, Ltd., 692 F.2d 634 (9th Cir. 1982)

Galella v. Onassis, 487 F.2d 986 (2nd Cir. 1973)

Pearson v. Dodd, 410 F.2d 701 (D.C.Cir. 1969)

Sidis v. F-R Publishing Corp., 113 F.2d 806 (2nd Cir. 1940)

Four Navy SEALs v. Associated Press, 413 F.Supp.2d 1136 (S.D.Cal. 2005)

Daily Times Democrat v. Graham, 276 Ala. 380, 162 So.2d 474 (1964)

Kapellas v. Kofman, 1 Cal.3d 20, 459 P.2d 912 (1969)

M.G. v. Time Warner, Inc., 87 Cal.App.4th 623 (2001)

Carlisle v. Fawcett Publications, Inc., 201 Cal.App.2d 733 (1962)

Leopold v. Levin, 45 Ill.2d 434, 259 N.E.2d 250 (1970)

Rawlins v. Hutchinson Publishing Co., 218 Kan. 295, 543 P.2d 988 (1975)

Weiner v. Doubleday & Co., Inc., 74 N.Y.2d 586, 549 N.E.2d 453 (1989)

Chapadeau v. Utica Observer-Dispatch, Inc., 38 N.Y.2d 196, 341 N.E.2d 569 (1975)

Namath v. Sports Illustrated, 371 N.Y.S.2d 10, 48 A.D.2d 487 (App.Div. 1975)

Rand v. Hearst Corp., 31 A.D.2d 406, 298 N.Y.S.2d 405 (App.Div. 1969), aff'd 26 N.Y.2d 806, 257 N.E.2d 895 (1970)

Comments:

1. According to the courts, U.S. Senators (*Pearson*), child protégées (*Sidis*), convicted murderers (*Leopold*), and candidates for city council (*Kapellas*) have no reasonable expectation of privacy. This also extends to family members such as sons (*Kapellas*), and former husbands (*Carlisle*).

2. Matters found to be newsworthy include qualifications for public office (*Pearson* and *Kapellas*), official misconduct (*Four Navy SEALs* and *Rawlins*), and crimes (*Leopold*, *Weiner*, and *Chapadeau*).

Chapter 9—The Snark (First Amendment Freedom of Speech)

Cases:

New York Times Co. v. Sullivan, 376 U.S. 254 (1964)

Time, Inc. v. Hill, 385 U.S. 374 (1967)

Curtis Publishing Co. v. Butts, 388 U.S. 130 (1967), decided together with *Associated Press v. Walker*

St. Amant v. Thompson, 390 U.S. 727 (1968)

Gertz v. Robert Welch, Inc., 418 U.S. 323 (1974)

Time, Inc. v. Firestone, 424 U.S. 448 (1976)

Philadelphia Newspapers, Inc. v. Hepps, 475 U.S. 767 (1986)

Harte-Hanks Communications v. Connaughton, 491 U.S. 657 (1989)

Chapter 10—The Chess Game (Contract Basics, Grant-of-Rights Clauses)

Cases:

Landsberg v. Scrabble Crossword Game Players, Inc., 802 F.2d 1193 (9th Cir. 1986)

Comments:

1. To find an intellectual property or entertainment lawyer, contact your local bar association for a referral. You can locate your local

bar association through the American Bar Association website at
http://apps.americanbar.org/legalservices/findlegalhelp/home.cfm.

Chapter 11—The White Queen (Royalties, Subsidiary Rights, Satisfactory Manuscript Clauses)

Cases:

Doubleday & Co., Inc. v. Curtis, 763 F.2d 495 (2nd Cir. 1985)

Nance v. Random House, Inc., 212 F.Supp.2d 268 (S.D.N.Y. 2002)

Dell Publishing Co., Inc. v. Whedon, 577 F.Supp. 1459 (S.D.N.Y. 1984)

Harcourt Brace Jovanovich, Inc. v. Goldwater, 532 F.Supp. 619 (S.D.N.Y. 1982)

J.B. Lippincott Co. v. Lasher, 430 F.Supp. 993 (S.D.N.Y. 1977)

Chapter 12—The Gnat ("Lesser" Clauses)

Statutes:

17 U.S.C. § 203 (terminating previously assigned rights)

Chapter 13—Tweedledum and Tweedledee (Agent, Collaboration, and Work-for-Hire Contracts, Magazine Rights)

Statutes:

17 U.S.C. § 203 (terminating previously assigned rights)

Chapter 14—Talking About the Shark (Taxes, Business Licenses)

Statutes and Regulations:

26 U.S.C. § 183 (activities not engaged in for profit)

26 U.S.C. § 1401 (self-employment tax rate)

26 U.S.C. § 6654 (failure to pay estimated income tax)

26 C.F.R. § 1.183-1 (activities not engaged in for profit)

26 C.F.R. § 1.183-2 (factors that distinguish between business and hobby)

26 C.F.R. § 1.6017-1 (self-employment tax returns)

26 C.F.R. § 1.6153-1 (paying estimated taxes)

Cases:

Commissioner of Internal Revenue v. Groetzinger, 480 U.S. 23 (1987)

Higgins v. Commissioner of Internal Revenue, 312 U.S. 212 (1941)

Rider v. Commissioner of Internal Revenue, 200 F.2d 524 (8th Cir. 1952)

Doggett v. Burnet, 65 F.2d 191 (D.C. Cir. 1933)

Young v. U.S., Civ. No. 21410, 1971 WL 417 (D.Md. June 11, 1971)

Wesley v. Commissioner of Internal Revenue, T.C. Memo 2007-78 (Apr. 2, 2007)

Vitale v. Commissioner of Internal Revenue, T.C. Memo 1999-131 (Apr. 21, 1999)

Callahan v. Commissioner of Internal Revenue, T.C. Memo 1996-65 (Feb. 20, 1996)

Kalbfleisch v. Commissioner of Internal Revenue, T.C. Memo 1991-61 (Feb. 20, 1991)

Crouch v. Commissioner of Internal Revenue, T.C. Memo 1990-309 (June 20, 1990)

Bert v. Commissioner of Internal Revenue, T.C. Memo 1989-503 (Sept. 13, 1989)

Dreicer v. Commissioner of Internal Revenue, 78 T.C. 642 (1982), *aff'd,* 702 F.2d 1205 (Table) (D.C. Cir. 1983)

Howard v. Commissioner of Internal Revenue, T.C. Memo 1981-250 (May 21, 1981)

Stahnke v. Commissioner of Internal Revenue, T.C. Memo 1980-369 (Sept. 10, 1980)

Gestrich v. Commissioner of Internal Revenue, 74 T.C. 525 (1980)

Dreicer v. Commissioner of Internal Revenue, T.C. Memo 1979-395 (Sept. 24, 1979), *rev'd*, 665 F.2d 1292 (D.C. Cir. 1981)

Hawkins v. Commissioner of Internal Revenue, T.C. Memo 1979-101 (Mar. 21, 1979)

Churchman v. Commissioner of Internal Revenue, 68 T.C. 696 (1977)

Nemish v. Commissioner of Internal Revenue, T.C. Memo 1970-276 (Sept. 29, 1970)

Sheban v. Commissioner of Internal Revenue, T.C. Memo 1970-163 (June 22, 1970)

Comments:

1. For cases finding that the taxpayer acted in a business-like manner, see *Vitale, Howard, Stahnke*, and *Churchman*. For cases finding that this factor was not met, see *Wesley, Callahan*, and *Bert*.

2. For cases finding that the taxpayer had adequate expertise, see *Rider* (knowledge of subject matter), *Vitale* (a marketing degree and some writing experience), *Crouch* (knowledge of subject matter), *Howard* (substantial writing experience), and *Stahnke* (knowledge of subject matter). For cases finding that this factor was not met, see *Callahan* and *Kalbfleisch*.

3. For cases finding that the taxpayer worked at the activity on a regular and continuous basis, see *Rider* (writer), *Doggett* (editor and compiler), *Young* (photographer), *Vitale* (writer), *Crouch* (tax return preparer and writer), *Howard* (writer), *Stahnke* (scientist and writer), *Gestrich* (writer), *Churchman* (artist), and *Sheban* (writer). In each of these cases, the court held that the taxpayer was engaged in a business.

   For cases where the facts showed insufficient time and effort to meet this factor, see *Dreicer, Wesley, Callahan, Kalbfleisch*, and *Hawkins*. In each of these cases, the court determined that the taxpayer wrote as a hobby.

4. Dreicer's attempts to write off his expenses kept the courts busy. In the first decision, the tax court judge found that Dreicer's writing was a hobby, not a business. On appeal, the D.C. Circuit Court of Appeals held that the judge had used the wrong standard and sent the case back for further consideration. Applying the standard articulated by the appeals court, the judge again found that Dreicer was engaged in a hobby, and the D.C. Circuit affirmed that finding without opinion.

Chapter 15—The Owl and the Panther (Incorporating, Estate Planning)

Comments:

1. The Indiana intestate law is located at Indiana Code Title 29, Article 1, Chapter 2, Section 1 (IC-29-1-2-1 (2012)).

2. For legal purposes, joint authorship and joint copyright ownership are the same. See *Seshadri v. Kasraian,* 130 F.3d 798 (7th Cir. 1997) for an example of how the choices made by one joint author affect other joint authors.

3. Examples of trusts that own copyrights are the Stephens Mitchell Trusts, which own the copyright to *Gone with the Wind* (see *Suntrust Bank v. Houghton Mifflin Co.*, 268 F.2d 1257 (11th Cir. 2001)) and the J.D. Salinger Literary Trust (see *Salinger v. Colting*, 607 F.3d 68 (2nd Cir. 2010)).

4. To find a local attorney familiar with corporate or estate law, contact your local bar association for a referral. Locate your local bar association on the American Bar Association website at http://apps.americanbar.org/legalservices/findlegalhelp/home.cfm.

Chapter 16—The Sun Impersonates the Moon (Trademarks)

Statutes:

15 U.S.C. § 1125 (trademark violations)

Cases:

Dastar Corp. v. Twentieth Century Fox Film Corp., 539 U.S. 23 (2003)

Flynn v. AK Peters, Ltd., 377 F.3d 13 (1ˢᵗ Cir. 2004)

ETW Corp. v. Jireh Publishing, Inc., 332 F.3d 915 (6ᵗʰ Cir. 2003)

Parks v. LaFace Records, 329 F.3d 437 (6ᵗʰ Cir. 2003)

New Kids on the Block v. News America Publishing, Inc., 971 F.2d 302 (9ᵗʰ Cir. 1992)

Shaw v. Lindheim, 919 F.2d 1353 (9ᵗʰ Cir. 1990)

Cliff Notes, Inc. v. Bantam Doubleday Dell Publishing Group, Inc., 886 F.2d 490 (2ⁿᵈ Cir. 1989)

Rogers v. Grimaldi, 875 F.2d 994 (2ⁿᵈ Cir. 1989)

Litchfield v. Spielberg, 736 F.2d 1352 (9ᵗʰ Cir. 1984)

In re Cooper, 254 F.2d 611 (C.C.P.A. 1958)

Comments:

1. For other parody cases, see:

Louis Vuitton Malletier S.A. v. Haute Diggity Dog, LLC, 507 F.3d 252 (4ᵗʰ Cir. 2007) (dog chew toys resembling famous handbags)

Mattel, Inc. v. Walking Mountain Productions, 353 F.3d 792 (9ᵗʰ Cir. 2003) (photographs of Barbie dolls in compromising positions with small kitchen appliances)

Mattel, Inc. v. MCA Records, Inc., 296 F.3d 894 (9ᵗʰ Cir. 2002) (the song "Barbie Girl" by Aqua)

Nike, Inc. v. "Just Did It" Enterprises, 6 F.3d 1225 (7ᵗʰ Cir. 1993) ("Mike" T-shirts proclaiming "Just Did It"). The district court judge ruled that the T-shirts were not a parody, but the 7ᵗʰ Circuit sent the question back for a jury trial. Procedural maneuvering subsequently eliminated "Just Did It" Enterprises' right to have a jury, leaving factual questions to be decided by the judge. See *Nike, Inc. v. "Just Did It" Enterprises*, No. 91 C 4001, 1994 WL 258879, 32 U.S.P.Q.2d 1059 (N.D.Ill. June 9, 1994).

Chapter 17—When You Don't Like the Beach (Author-Financed Publishing)

Statutes:

17 U.S.C. § 101 (copyright definitions)

Comments:

1. For more information on home-based business zoning laws, check the United States Small Business Association website at www.sba.gov/content/zoning-laws-home-based-businesses.

2. For more information on registering a trademark, review the circular titled Trademark Basics, which is located at http://www.uspto.gov/trademarks/basics/index.jsp.

APPENDIX II
Resources

U.S. Government Resources

business issues The Small Business Association website at www.sba.gov provides information for small businesses, including information on forming a small business.

copyright The U.S. Copyright Office website at www.copyright.gov provides information on copyrights and provides a database of registered copyrights.

trademarks The U.S Patent and Trademark Office website at www.uspto.gov provides information on trademarks and provides a database of registered trademarks.

Finding an Attorney

Bar Associations To find an attorney, contact your local bar association for a referral and be sure to ask for someone who specializes in the area you are interested in (e.g., copyrights, defamation, taxes, estate planning). The American Bar Association website has a list of local bar associations by state at http://apps.americanbar.org/legalservices/findlegalhelp/home.cfm.

Volunteer Lawyers Organizations for the Arts Various volunteer organizations specialize in providing legal services to people working in the creative arts. Some of these services are pro bono, which means they are free to people who can't afford a lawyer. If you don't qualify, these organizations may still provide you with an attorney for a reduced fee or refer you to an attorney who will charge his or her standard fee. The Chicago-based Lawyers for the Creative Arts' website includes a listing of volunteer organizations around the U.S. and in Canada. Go to www.law-arts.org/links.html

and click on "National Volunteer Lawyers for the Arts" under
"Contents."

APPENDIX III

"The Hunting of the Snark: An Agony in Eight Fits"

by Lewis Carroll

Fit the First: The Landing

"Just the place for a Snark!" the Bellman cried,
    As he landed his crew with care;
Supporting each man on the top of the tide
    By a finger entwined in his hair.

"Just the place for a Snark! I have said it twice:
    That alone should encourage the crew.
Just the place for a Snark! I have said it thrice:
    What I tell you three times is true."

The crew was complete: it included a Boots—
    A maker of Bonnets and Hoods—
A Barrister, brought to arrange their disputes—
    And a Broker, to value their goods.

A Billiard-maker, whose skill was immense,
    Might perhaps have won more than his share—
But a Banker, engaged at enormous expense,
    Had the whole of their cash in his care.

There was also a Beaver, that paced on the deck,
    Or would sit making lace in the bow:
And had often (the Bellman said) saved them from wreck,
    Though none of the sailors knew how.

There was one who was famed for the number of things
    He forgot when he entered the ship:
His umbrella, his watch, all his jewels and rings,
    And the clothes he had bought for the trip.

He had forty-two boxes, all carefully packed,
    With his name painted clearly on each:
But, since he omitted to mention the fact,
    They were all left behind on the beach.

The loss of his clothes hardly mattered, because
    He had seven coats on when he came,
With three pairs of boots—but the worst of it was,
    He had wholly forgotten his name.

He would answer to "Hi!" or to any loud cry,
    Such as "Fry me!" or "Fritter my wig!"
To "What-you-may-call-um!" or "What-was-his-name!"
    But especially "Thing-um-a-jig!"

While, for those who preferred a more forcible word,
    He had different names from these:
His intimate friends called him "Candle-ends,"
    And his enemies "Toasted-cheese."

"His form in ungainly—his intellect small—"
    (So the Bellman would often remark)
"But his courage is perfect! And that, after all,
    Is the thing that one needs with a Snark."

He would joke with hyenas, returning their stare
    With an impudent wag of the head:
And he once went a walk, paw-in-paw, with a bear,
    "Just to keep up its spirits," he said.

He came as a Baker: but owned, when too late—
    And it drove the poor Bellman half-mad—
He could only bake Bridecake—for which, I may state,
    No materials were to be had.

The last of the crew needs especial remark,
    Though he looked an incredible dunce:
He had just one idea—but, that one being "Snark,"
    The good Bellman engaged him at once.

He came as a Butcher: but gravely declared,
    When the ship had been sailing a week,
He could only kill Beavers. The Bellman looked scared,
    And was almost too frightened to speak:

But at length he explained, in a tremulous tone,
    There was only one Beaver on board;
And that was a tame one he had of his own,
    Whose death would be deeply deplored.

The Beaver, who happened to hear the remark,
    Protested, with tears in its eyes,
That not even the rapture of hunting the Snark
    Could atone for that dismal surprise!

It strongly advised that the Butcher should be
    Conveyed in a separate ship:
But the Bellman declared that would never agree
    With the plans he had made for the trip:

Navigation was always a difficult art,
    Though with only one ship and one bell:
And he feared he must really decline, for his part,
    Undertaking another as well.

The Beaver's best course was, no doubt, to procure
    A second-hand dagger-proof coat—
So the Baker advised it—and next, to insure
    Its life in some Office of note:

This the Banker suggested, and offered for hire
    (On moderate terms), or for sale,
Two excellent Policies, one Against Fire,
    And one Against Damage From Hail.

Yet still, ever after that sorrowful day,
    Whenever the Butcher was by,
The Beaver kept looking the opposite way,
    And appeared unaccountably shy.

Fit the Second: The Bellman's Speech

The Bellman himself they all praised to the skies—
    Such a carriage, such ease and such grace!
Such solemnity, too! One could see he was wise,
    The moment one looked in his face!

He had bought a large map representing the sea,
    Without the least vestige of land:
And the crew were much pleased when they found it to be
    A map they could all understand.

"What's the good of Mercator's North Poles and Equators,
    Tropics, Zones, and Meridian Lines?"
So the Bellman would cry: and the crew would reply
    "They are merely conventional signs!

"Other maps are such shapes, with their islands and capes!
    But we've got our brave Captain to thank:
(So the crew would protest) "that he's bought us the best—
    A perfect and absolute blank!"

This was charming, no doubt; but they shortly found out
    That the Captain they trusted so well
Had only one notion for crossing the ocean,
    And that was to tingle his bell.

He was thoughtful and grave—but the orders he gave
    Were enough to bewilder a crew.
When he cried "Steer to starboard, but keep her head larboard!"
    What on earth was the helmsman to do?

Then the bowsprit got mixed with the rudder sometimes:
    A thing, as the Bellman remarked,
That frequently happens in tropical climes,
    When a vessel is, so to speak, "snarked."

But the principal failing occurred in the sailing,
    And the Bellman, perplexed and distressed,
Said he had hoped, at least, when the wind blew due East,
    That the ship would not travel due West!

But the danger was past—they had landed at last,
    With their boxes, portmanteaus, and bags:
Yet at first sight the crew were not pleased with the view,
    Which consisted to chasms and crags.

The Bellman perceived that their spirits were low,
    And repeated in musical tone
Some jokes he had kept for a season of woe—
    But the crew would do nothing but groan.

He served out some grog with a liberal hand,
    And bade them sit down on the beach:
And they could not but own that their Captain looked grand,
    As he stood and delivered his speech.

"Friends, Romans, and countrymen, lend me your ears!"
    (They were all of them fond of quotations:
So they drank to his health, and they gave him three cheers,
    While he served out additional rations).

"We have sailed many months, we have sailed many weeks,
    (Four weeks to the month you may mark),
But never as yet ('tis your Captain who speaks)
    Have we caught the least glimpse of a Snark!

"We have sailed many weeks, we have sailed many days,
    (Seven days to the week I allow),
But a Snark, on the which we might lovingly gaze,
    We have never beheld till now!

"Come, listen, my men, while I tell you again
    The five unmistakable marks
By which you may know, wheresoever you go,
    The warranted genuine Snarks.

"Let us take them in order. The first is the taste,
    Which is meager and hollow, but crisp:
Like a coat that is rather too tight in the waist,
    With a flavor of Will-o'-the-wisp.

"Its habit of getting up late you'll agree
    That it carries too far, when I say
That it frequently breakfasts at five-o'clock tea,
    And dines on the following day.

"The third is its slowness in taking a jest.
    Should you happen to venture on one,
It will sigh like a thing that is deeply distressed:
    And it always looks grave at a pun.

"The fourth is its fondness for bathing-machines,
    Which is constantly carries about,
And believes that they add to the beauty of scenes—
    A sentiment open to doubt.

"The fifth is ambition. It next will be right
　　To describe each particular batch:
Distinguishing those that have feathers, and bite,
　　And those that have whiskers, and scratch.

"For, although common Snarks do no manner of harm,
　　Yet, I feel it my duty to say,
Some are Boojums—" The Bellman broke off in alarm,
　　For the Baker had fainted away.

Fit the Third: The Baker's Tale

They roused him with muffins—they roused him with ice—
　　They roused him with mustard and cress—
They roused him with jam and judicious advice—
　　They set him conundrums to guess.

When at length he sat up and was able to speak,
　　His sad story he offered to tell;
And the Bellman cried "Silence! Not even a shriek!"
　　And excitedly tingled his bell.

There was silence supreme! Not a shriek, not a scream,
　　Scarcely even a howl or a groan,
As the man they called "Ho!" told his story of woe
　　In an antediluvian tone.

"My father and mother were honest, though poor—"
　　"Skip all that!" cried the Bellman in haste.
"If it once becomes dark, there's no chance of a Snark—a
　　We have hardly a minute to waste!"

"I skip forty years," said the Baker, in tears,
    "And proceed without further remark
To the day when you took me aboard of your ship
    To help you in hunting the Snark.

"A dear uncle of mine (after whom I was named)
    Remarked, when I bade him farewell—"
"Oh, skip your dear uncle!" the Bellman exclaimed,
    As he angrily tingled his bell.

"He remarked to me then," said that mildest of men,
    " 'If your Snark be a Snark, that is right:
Fetch it home by all means—you may serve it with greens,
    And it's handy for striking a light.

" 'You may seek it with thimbles—and seek it with care;
    You may hunt it with forks and hope;
You may threaten its life with a railway-share;
    You may charm it with smiles and soap—' "

("That's exactly the method," the Bellman bold
    In a hasty parenthesis cried,
"That's exactly the way I have always been told
    That the capture of Snarks should be tried!")

" 'But oh, beamish nephew, beware of the day,
    If your Snark be a Boojum! For then
You will softly and suddenly vanish away,
    And never be met with again!'

"It is this, it is this that oppresses my soul,
    When I think of my uncle's last words:
And my heart is like nothing so much as a bowl
    Brimming over with quivering curds!

"It is this, it is this—" "We have had that before!"
    The Bellman indignantly said.
And the Baker replied "Let me say it once more.
    It is this, it is this that I dread!

"I engage with the Snark—every night after dark—
    In a dreamy delirious fight:
I serve it with greens in those shadowy scenes,
    And I use it for striking a light:

"But if ever I meet with a Boojum, that day,
    In a moment (of this I am sure),
I shall softly and suddenly vanish away—
    And the notion I cannot endure!"

Fit the Fourth: The Hunting

The Bellman looked uffish, and wrinkled his brow.
    "If only you'd spoken before!
It's excessively awkward to mention it now,
    With the Snark, so to speak, at the door!

"We should all of us grieve, as you well may believe,
    If you never were met with again—
But surely, my man, when the voyage began,
    You might have suggested it then?

"It's excessively awkward to mention it now—
    As I think I've already remarked."
And the man they called "Hi!" replied, with a sigh,
    "I informed you the day we embarked.

"You may charge me with murder—or want of sense—
    (We are all of us weak at times):
But the slightest approach to a false pretense
    Was never among my crimes!

"I said it in Hebrew—I said it in Dutch—
    I said it in German and Greek:
But I wholly forgot (and it vexes me much)
    That English is what you speak!"

"'Tis a pitiful tale," said the Bellman, whose face
    Had grown longer at every word:
"But, now that you've stated the whole of your case,
    More debate would be simply absurd.

"The rest of my speech" (he explained to his men)
    "You shall hear when I've leisure to speak it.
But the Snark is at hand, let me tell you again!
    'Tis your glorious duty to seek it!

"To seek it with thimbles, to seek it with care;
    To pursue it with forks and hope;
To threaten its life with a railway-share;
    To charm it with smiles and soap!

"For the Snark's a peculiar creature, that won't
 Be caught in a commonplace way.
Do all that you know, and try all that you don't:
 Not a chance must be wasted to-day!

"For England expects—I forbear to proceed:
 'Tis a maxim tremendous, but trite:
And you'd best be unpacking the things that you need
 To rig yourselves out for the fight."

Then the Banker endorsed a blank check (which he crossed),
 And changed his loose silver for notes.
The Baker with care combed his whiskers and hair,
 And shook the dust out of his coats.

The Boots and the Broker were sharpening a spade—
 Each working the grindstone in turn:
But the Beaver went on making lace, and displayed
 No interest in the concern:

Though the Barrister tried to appeal to its pride,
 And vainly proceeded to cite
A number of cases, in which making laces
 Had been proved an infringement of right.

The maker of Bonnets ferociously planned
 A novel arrangement of bows:
While the Billiard-marker with quivering hand
 Was chalking the tip of his nose.

But the Butcher turned nervous, and dressed himself fine,
    With yellow kid gloves and a ruff—
Said he felt it exactly like going to dine,
    Which the Bellman declared was all "stuff."

"Introduce me, now there's a good fellow," he said,
    "If we happen to meet it together!"
And the Bellman, sagaciously nodding his head,
    Said "That must depend on the weather."

The Beaver went simply galumphing about,
    At seeing the Butcher so shy:
And even the Baker, though stupid and stout,
    Made an effort to wink with one eye.

"Be a man!" said the Bellman in wrath, as he heard
    The Butcher beginning to sob.
"Should we meet with a Jubjub, that desperate bird,
    We shall need all our strength for the job!"

Fit the Fifth: The Beaver's Lesson

They sought it with thimbles, they sought it with care;
    They pursued it with forks and hope;
They threatened its life with a railway-share;
    They charmed it with smiles and soap.

Then the Butcher contrived an ingenious plan
    For making a separate sally;
And fixed on a spot unfrequented by man,
    A dismal and desolate valley.

But the very same plan to the Beaver occurred:
    It had chosen the very same place:
Yet neither betrayed, by a sign or a word,
    The disgust that appeared in his face.

Each thought he was thinking of nothing but "Snark"
    And the glorious work of the day;
And each tried to pretend that he did not remark
    That the other was going that way.

But the valley grew narrow and narrower still,
    And the evening got darker and colder,
Till (merely from nervousness, not from goodwill)
    They marched along shoulder to shoulder.

Then a scream, shrill and high, rent the shuddering sky,
    And they knew that some danger was near:
The Beaver turned pale to the tip of its tail,
    And even the Butcher felt queer.

He thought of his childhood, left far far behind—
    That blissful and innocent state—
The sound so exactly recalled to his mind
    A pencil that squeaks on a slate!

"'Tis the voice of the Jubjub!" he suddenly cried.
    (This man, that they used to call "Dunce.")
"As the Bellman would tell you," he added with pride,
    "I have uttered that sentiment once.

"'Tis the note of the Jubjub! Keep count, I entreat;
    You will find I have told it you twice.
'Tis the song of the Jubjub! The proof is complete,
    If only I've stated it thrice."

The Beaver had counted with scrupulous care,
    Attending to every word:
But it fairly lost heart, and outgrabe in despair,
    When the third repetition occurred.

It felt that, in spite of all possible pains,
    It had somehow contrived to lose count,
And the only thing now was to rack its poor brains
    By reckoning up the amount.

"Two added to one—if that could but be done,"
    It said, "with one's fingers and thumbs!"
Recollecting with tears how, in earlier years,
    It had taken no pains with its sums.

"The thing can be done," said the Butcher, "I think.
    The thing must be done, I am sure.
The thing shall be done! Bring me paper and ink,
    The best there is time to procure."

The Beaver brought paper, portfolio, pens,
    And ink in unfailing supplies:
While strange creepy creatures came out of their dens,
    And watched them with wondering eyes.

So engrossed was the Butcher, he heeded them not,
    As he wrote with a pen in each hand,
And explained all the while in a popular style
    Which the Beaver could well understand.

"Taking Three as the subject to reason about—
    A convenient number to state—a
We add Seven, and Ten, and then multiply out
    By One Thousand diminished by Eight.

"The result we proceed to divide, as you see,
    By Nine Hundred and Ninety Two:
Then subtract Seventeen, and the answer must be
    Exactly and perfectly true.

"The method employed I would gladly explain,
    While I have it so clear in my head,
If I had but the time and you had but the brain--
    But much yet remains to be said.

"In one moment I've seen what has hitherto been
    Enveloped in absolute mystery,
And without extra charge I will give you at large
    A Lesson in Natural History."

In his genial way he proceeded to say
    (Forgetting all laws of propriety,
And that giving instruction, without introduction,
    Would have caused quite a thrill in Society),

"As to temper the Jubjub's a desperate bird,
    Since it lives in perpetual passion:
Its taste in costume is entirely absurd--
    It is ages ahead of the fashion:

"But it knows any friend it has met once before:
    It never will look at a bride:
And in charity-meetings it stands at the door,
    And collects—though it does not subscribe.

"Its flavor when cooked is more exquisite far
    Than mutton, or oysters, or eggs:
(Some think it keeps best in an ivory jar,
    And some, in mahogany kegs:)

"You boil it in sawdust: you salt it in glue:
    You condense it with locusts and tape:
Still keeping one principal object in view—
    To preserve its symmetrical shape."

The Butcher would gladly have talked till next day,
    But he felt that the lesson must end,
And he wept with delight in attempting to say
    He considered the Beaver his friend.

While the Beaver confessed, with affectionate looks
    More eloquent even than tears,
It had learned in ten minutes far more than all books
    Would have taught it in seventy years.

They returned hand-in-hand, and the Bellman, unmanned
    (For a moment) with noble emotion,
Said "This amply repays all the wearisome days
    We have spent on the billowy ocean!"

Such friends, as the Beaver and Butcher became,
    Have seldom if ever been known;
In winter or summer, 'twas always the same—
    You could never meet either alone.

And when quarrels arose—as one frequently finds
    Quarrels will, spite of every endeavor—
The song of the Jubjub recurred to their minds,
    And cemented their friendship for ever!

Fit the Sixth: The Barrister's Dream

They sought it with thimbles, they sought it with care;
    They pursued it with forks and hope;
They threatened its life with a railway-share;
    They charmed it with smiles and soap.

But the Barrister, weary of proving in vain
    That the Beaver's lace-making was wrong,
Fell asleep, and in dreams saw the creature quite plain
    That his fancy had dwelt on so long.

He dreamed that he stood in a shadowy Court,
    Where the Snark, with a glass in its eye,
Dressed in gown, bands, and wig, was defending a pig
    On the charge of deserting its sty.

The Witnesses proved, without error or flaw,
    That the sty was deserted when found:
And the Judge kept explaining the state of the law
    In a soft under-current of sound.

The indictment had never been clearly expressed,
    And it seemed that the Snark had begun,
And had spoken three hours, before any one guessed
    What the pig was supposed to have done.

The Jury had each formed a different view
    (Long before the indictment was read),
And they all spoke at once, so that none of them knew
    One word that the others had said.

"You must know———" said the Judge: but the Snark exclaimed
        "Fudge!"
    That statute is obsolete quite!
Let me tell you, my friends, the whole question depends
    On an ancient manorial right.

"In the matter of Treason the pig would appear
    To have aided, but scarcely abetted:
While the charge of Insolvency fails, it is clear,
    If you grant the plea 'never indebted.'

"The fact of Desertion I will not dispute;
    But its guilt, as I trust, is removed
(So far as related to the costs of this suit)
    By the Alibi which has been proved.

"My poor client's fate now depends on your votes."
    Here the speaker sat down in his place,
And directed the Judge to refer to his notes
    And briefly to sum up the case.

But the Judge said he never had summed up before;
    So the Snark undertook it instead,
And summed it so well that it came to far more
    Than the Witnesses ever had said!

When the verdict was called for, the Jury declined,
    As the word was so puzzling to spell;
But they ventured to hope that the Snark wouldn't mind
    Undertaking that duty as well.

So the Snark found the verdict, although, as it owned,
    It was spent with the toils of the day:
When it said the word "GUILTY!" the Jury all groaned,
    And some of them fainted away.

Then the Snark pronounced sentence, the Judge being quite
    Too nervous to utter a word:
When it rose to its feet, there was silence like night,
    And the fall of a pin might be heard.

"Transportation for life" was the sentence it gave,
    "And *then* to be fined forty pound."
The Jury all cheered, though the Judge said he feared
    That the phrase was not legally sound.

But their wild exultation was suddenly checked
    When the jailer informed them, with tears,
Such a sentence would have not the slightest effect,
    As the pig had been dead for some years.

The Judge left the Court, looking deeply disgusted:
    But the Snark, though a little aghast,
As the lawyer to whom the defense was entrusted,
    Went bellowing on to the last.

Thus the Barrister dreamed, while the bellowing seemed
    To grow every moment more clear:
Till he woke to the knell of a furious bell,
    Which the Bellman rang close at his ear.

Fit the Seventh: The Banker's Fate

They sought it with thimbles, they sought it with care;
    They pursued it with forks and hope;
They threatened its life with a railway-share;
    They charmed it with smiles and soap.

And the Banker, inspired with a courage so new
    It was matter for general remark,
Rushed madly ahead and was lost to their view
    In his zeal to discover the Snark.

But while he was seeking with thimbles and care,
    A Bandersnatch swiftly drew nigh
And grabbed at the Banker, who shrieked in despair,
    For he knew it was useless to fly.

He offered large discount—he offered a check
    (Drawn "to bearer") for seven-pounds-ten:
But the Bandersnatch merely extended its neck
    And grabbed at the Banker again.

Without rest or pause—while those frumious jaws
    Went savagely snapping around-
He skipped and he hopped, and he floundered and flopped,
    Till fainting he fell to the ground.

The Bandersnatch fled as the others appeared
    Led on by that fear-stricken yell:
And the Bellman remarked "It is just as I feared!"
    And solemnly tolled on his bell.

He was black in the face, and they scarcely could trace
    The least likeness to what he had been:
While so great was his fright that his waistcoat turned white-
    A wonderful thing to be seen!

To the horror of all who were present that day.
    He uprose in full evening dress,
And with senseless grimaces endeavored to say
    What his tongue could no longer express.

Down he sank in a chair—ran his hands through his hair—
    And chanted in mimsiest tones
Words whose utter inanity proved his insanity,
    While he rattled a couple of bones.

"Leave him here to his fate—it is getting so late!"
  The Bellman exclaimed in a fright.
"We have lost half the day. Any further delay,
  And we sha'nt catch a Snark before night!"

Fit the Eighth: The Vanishing

They sought it with thimbles, they sought it with care;
  They pursued it with forks and hope;
They threatened its life with a railway-share;
  They charmed it with smiles and soap.

They shuddered to think that the chase might fail,
  And the Beaver, excited at last,
Went bounding along on the tip of its tail,
  For the daylight was nearly past.

"There is Thingumbob shouting!" the Bellman said,
  "He is shouting like mad, only hark!
He is waving his hands, he is wagging his head,
  He has certainly found a Snark!"

They gazed in delight, while the Butcher exclaimed
  "He was always a desperate wag!"
They beheld him—their Baker—their hero unnamed—
  On the top of a neighboring crag.

Erect and sublime, for one moment of time.
  In the next, that wild figure they saw
(As if stung by a spasm) plunge into a chasm,
  While they waited and listened in awe.

"It's a Snark!" was the sound that first came to their ears,
    And seemed almost too good to be true.
Then followed a torrent of laughter and cheers:
    Then the ominous words "It's a Boo-"

Then, silence. Some fancied they heard in the air
    A weary and wandering sigh
Then sounded like "-jum!" but the others declare
    It was only a breeze that went by.

They hunted till darkness came on, but they found
    Not a button, or feather, or mark,
By which they could tell that they stood on the ground
    Where the Baker had met with the Snark.

In the midst of the word he was trying to say,
    In the midst of his laughter and glee,
He had softly and suddenly vanished away—
    For the Snark *was* a Boojum, you see.

Appendix IV

"The Voice of the Lobster"

from *Alice in Wonderland*

by Lewis Carroll

'Tis the voice of the Lobster; I heard him declare,
"You have baked me too brown, I must sugar my hair."
As a duck with its eyelids, so he with his nose
Trims his belt and his buttons, and turns out his toes.
When the sands are all dry, he is gay as a lark,
And will talk in contemptuous tones of the Shark:
But, when the tide rises and sharks are around,
His voice has a timid and tremulous sound.

I passed by his garden, and marked with one eye,
How the Owl and the Panther were sharing a pie:
The Panther took pie-crust, and gravy, and meat,
While the Owl had the dish as its share of the treat.
When the pie was all finished, the Owl, as a boon,
Was kindly permitted to pocket the spoon:
While the Panter received knife and fork with a growl,
And concluded the banquet by—[eating the owl].

"The Walrus and the Carpenter"

from *Through the Looking Glass*

by Lewis Carroll

The sun was shining on the sea,
    Shining with all his might:
He did his very best to make
    The billows smooth and bright—
And this was odd, because it was
    The middle of the night.

The moon was shining sulkily,
    Because she thought the sun
Had got no business to be there
    After the day was done—
"It's very rude of him," she said,
    "To come and spoil the fun!"

The sea was wet as wet could be,
    The sands were dry as dry.
You could not see a cloud because
    No cloud was in the sky:
No birds were flying overhead—
    There were no birds to fly.

The Walrus and the Carpenter
 Were walking close at hand:
They wept like anything to see
 Such quantities of sand:
"If this were only cleared away,"
 They said, "it would be grand!"

"If seven maids with seven mops
 Swept it for half a year,
Do you supose," the Walrus said,
 "That they could get it clear?"
"I doubt it," said the Carpenter,
 And shed a bitter tear.

"O Oysters, come and walk with us!"
 The Walrus did beseech,
"A pleasant walk, a pleasant talk,
 Along the briny beach:
We cannot do with more than four,
 To give a hand to each."

The eldest Oyster look at him,
 But never a word he said:
The eldest Oyster winked his eye,
 And shook his heavy head—
Meaning to say he did not choose
 To leave the oyster-bed.

But four young Oysters hurried up,
    All eager for the treat:
Their coats were brushed, their faces washed,
    Their shoes were clean and neat—
And this was odd, because, you know,
    They hadn't any feet.

Four other Oysters followed them,
    And yet another four;
And thick and fast they came at last,
    And more, and more, and more—
All hopping through the frothy waves
    And scrambling to the shore.

The Walrus and the Carpenter
    Walked on a mile or so,
And then they rested on a rock
    Conveniently low:
And all the little Oysters stood
    And waited in a row.

"The time has come," the Walrus said,
    "To talk of many things:
Of shoes—and ships—and sealing wax—
    Of cabbages—and kings—
And why the sea is boiling hot—
    And whether pigs have wings."

"But wait a bit," the Oysters cried,
    "Before we have our chat;
For some of us are out of breath,
    And all of us are fat!"
"No hurry!" said the Carpenter.
    They thanked him much for that.

"A loaf of bread," the Walrus said,
    "Is what we chiefly need:
Pepper and vinegar besides
    Are very good indeed—
Now, if you're ready, Oysters dear,
    We can begin to feed."

"But not on us!" the Oysters cried,
    Turning a little blue.
"After such kindness, that would be
    A dismal thing to do!"
"The night is fine," the Walrus said.
    "Do you admire the view?"

"It was so kind of you to come!
    And you are very nice!"
The Carpenter said nothing but
    "Cut us another slice:
I wish you were not quite so deaf—
    I've had to ask you twice!"

"It seems a shame," the Walrus said,
    "To play them such a trick.
After we've brought them out so far,
    And made them trot so quick!"
The Carpenter said nothing but
    "The butter's spread too thick!"

"I weep for you," the Walrus said:
    "I deeply sympathise."
With sobs and tears he sorted out
    Those of the largest size,
Holding his pocket-handerchief
    Before his streaming eyes.

"O Oysters," said the Carpenter,
    "You've had a pleasant run!
Shall we be trotting home again?"
    But answer came there none—
And this was scarcely odd, because
    They'd eaten every one.

APPENDIX VI

"You are old, Father William"

from *Alice in Wonderland*

by Lewis Carroll

"You are old, Father William," the young man said,
 "And your hair has become very white;
And yet you incessantly stand on your head—
 Do you think, at your age, it is right?"

"In my youth," Father William replied to his son,
 "I feared it might injure the brain;
But now that I'm perfectly sure I have none,
 Why, I do it again and again."

"You are old," said the youth, "as I mentioned before,
 And have grown most uncommonly fat;
Yet you turned a back-somersault in at the door—
 Pray what is the reason of that?"

"In my youth," said the sage, as he shook his grey locks,
 "I kept all my limbs very supple
By the use of this ointment—one shilling the box—
 Allow me to sell you a couple."

"You are old," said the youth, "and your jaws are too weak
 For anything tougher than suet;
Yet you finished the goose, with the bones and the beak—
 Pray how did you manage to do it?"

"In my youth," said his father, "I took to the law,
    And argued each case with my wife;
And the muscular strength, which it gave to my jaw,
    Has lasted the rest of my life."

"You are old," said the youth; "one would hardly suppose
    That your eye was as steady as ever;
Yet you balanced an eel on the end of your nose—
    What made you so awfully clever?"

"I have answered three questions, and that is enough,"
    Said his father; "don't give yourself airs!
Do you think I can listen all day to such stuff?
    Be off, or I'll kick you down-stairs!"

Appendix VII
Biographies

Lewis Carroll

The man known as Lewis Carroll was born Charles Lutwidge Dodgson on January 27, 1832, at Daresbury, England. His parents were Charles Dodgson, a country parson, and Frances Jane Lutwidge. Dodgson was the third of eleven children and the eldest son.

After beginning his education at home, a twelve-year-old Dodgson entered Richmond Grammar School. He also attended Rugby School before entering Christ Church College at Oxford University in May 1850.

Dodgson was a mathematician, and he spent his career as a lecturer in mathematics at Christ Church College. He also studied to become a minister in the Anglican Church, but he was never ordained.

An inveterate storyteller, Dodgson loved children and soon befriended the son and daughters of his college dean, Henry Liddell. One of the girls was named Alice and is credited with being the inspiration for the title character in *Alice in Wonderland*. Although Alice Liddell was involved with the story from the beginning, Dodgson denied that he had based the character on a real child.

So how did the now-famous tale grow into a book? The seed was planted when Dodgson took the three Liddell girls on a boat ride and picnic and told them the story in broad outlines. Alice begged him to write it down, and he eventually gave her a handwritten manuscript that he had illustrated himself.

By the time *Alice's Adventures in Wonderland* was published in 1863, Dodgson's illustrations had been replaced with illustrations by John Tenniel. Tenniel also illustrated the sequel, *Through the Looking Glass and What Alice Found There*, which was published in 1871.

Dodgson published mathematical books and articles under his real name, but he chose a pen name for his fantasy/nonsense works. He translated his first two names into Latin, inverted them, and Anglicized the result to come up with "Lewis Carroll."

In 1876 Dodgson published the poem "The Hunting of the Snark," illustrated by Henry Holiday. It was Dodgson's last literary masterpiece under his pen name. Dodgson did, however, continue publishing works on mathematics under his real name.

Mathematics and literature were not Dodgson's only interests. He was an excellent photographer, taking portraits of Alfred Tennyson and the actress Ellen Terry, among others. He was also an inventor, and many of his inventions show his love for reading and writing. They included a postage stamp case, a writing tablet that helped people take notes in the dark, and a number of word games.

Dodgson caught influenza shortly before his 66th birthday. The influenza turned into pneumonia, and he died on January 14, 1898.

Sir John Tenniel

Born in London on January 28, 1820, John Tenniel attended the Royal Academy but was mostly a self-taught artist. He exhibited his first painting when he was sixteen.

At the age of twenty, Tenniel was practicing fencing with his father when the protective covering came off his father's foil. As a result, Tenniel spent most of his life blind in the right eye. Tenniel concealed the extent of his vision loss from his father to keep him from feeling worse than he already did.

After beginning his career doing what he called "high art," Tenniel became a staff cartoonist for *Punch* magazine in 1850. He eventually became the main political cartoonist for the magazine, and he retained that position until he retired in 1901.

As an illustrator, Tenniel's works include Charles Dickens' *The Haunted Man*. His most famous illustrations, however, are the ones that appeared in the original editions of *Alice's Adventures in Wonderland* (1863) and *Through the Looking Glass* (1871). These illustrations have been reproduced many times since.

Married in 1852, Tenniel became a widower two years later. He was knighted by Queen Victoria in 1893 and died on February 25, 1914, at the age of 94.

Henry Holiday

Henry Holiday was born in London on June 17, 1839. He studied painting at Leigh's Art School and the Royal Academy.

Holiday spent most of his career as a stained-glass artist, eventually establishing his own workshop. Westminster Abbey contains his tribute to the engineer Isambard Kingdom Brunel. Many of Holiday's later commissions came from American churches, including Holy Trinity in Manhattan.

As a painter, Holiday's best-known work is "Dante and Beatrice." His most famous illustrations are from Lewis Carroll's poem "The Hunting of the Snark," which was originally published in 1876.

In 1864 Holiday married Catherine Raven, with whom he had one daughter. Holiday survived his wife by two years and died on April 15, 1927.

Glossary

© The internationally recognized copyright symbol.

® Symbol indicating that a trademark is registered with the United States Patent and Trademark Office.

ˢᴹ The symbol for a service mark that is not registered with the U.S. Patent and Trademark Office.

™ The symbol for a trademark that is not registered with the U.S. Patent and Trademark Office.

abridgment A shortened version of the original, a condensation.

acceptance When a party agrees to the offered contract terms.

actual damages Compensation for losses that are caused directly by wrongful conduct. For copyright infringement, actual damages are the amount of additional money you would have made but for the infringement, minus expenses you would have incurred.

actual malice In First Amendment cases (e.g., defamation or violations of privacy or publicity rights), actual malice is the publication of information knowing that the information is false or with reckless disregard for whether it is true or false.

administrator A person appointed by a court to wrap up the affairs and distribute the property left by a person who died without a will.

advance A payment to an author before a book is published; this is an advance on royalties not yet earned.

agent (literary) A professional who represents a writer to find a publisher for the writer's work and negotiates the deal with the publisher on the writer's behalf.

anthology A collection of literary pieces.

appropriation of name or likeness The unauthorized use of someone else's name or likeness for commercial purposes.

arbitrary mark A trademark consisting of a word, symbol, or device that would normally have no relationship to the type of goods or services it identifies.

arbitration A process for resolving disagreements by authorizing a third party to decide the dispute instead of going to court. In a traditional arbitration, the parties are bound by the arbitrator's decision.

assignment The transfer of rights and/or responsibilities imposed by contract.

assumed name (business) A fictitious or "doing business as" name that is different from the name of the individual or legal entity using it for business purposes. Assumed business names may have to be registered with a state or local government.

"as told to" The credit line for a book resulting from a collaboration between a writer and the book's subject, for which the writer is given credit as a co-author. The credits usually read "By [the subject] as told to [the writer]."

attribution Identifying the creator of a particular work.

author Usually the person who created the work. In a work made for hire, the author is the employer or the person who commissioned the work rather than the person who created it.

author-financed publishing Any publishing arrangement where the author finances part or all of the publishing process.

Berne Convention The Convention for the Protection of Literary and Artistic Works originally adopted in Berne, Switzerland in 1886. An intellectual property treaty.

business (writing as) Writing to make a profit rather than as a hobby.

choice of forum A contractual provision that says where a dispute will be heard. This can be a location (e.g., a particular state) and/or a type of forum (e.g., arbitration).

choice of law A contractual provision that says which state's law will apply.

classic use For purposes of trademark infringement, this refers to placing a trademark on goods that are not connected with the trademark owner.

collaboration When two or more people work together to create a manuscript or other copyrighted work.

collaborator A person who works with one or more other people to create a manuscript or other copyrighted work.

collective work A periodical, anthology, encyclopedia, or other work that combines several independent contributions in a single collection.

commission (literary agents) The amount a literary agent receives for finding a publisher. Usually a percentage of the author's advance and royalties.

condensation A shortened version of the original, an abridgment.

consideration Something of value given in exchange for something else of value. The value can come from performing an act, such as publishing a book, as well as from giving a tangible item.

contract A legally enforceable agreement between two or more parties.

contract by estoppel A contract formed when one party's actions cause another party to rely on a promise made without consideration. The promising party is prohibited (stopped) from claiming the contract is void because there was no consideration.

contributory infringement Intentionally encouraging or inducing someone to infringe a copyright.

copyright The right to publish, reproduce, distribute, prepare derivative works, perform, or display a work and to prohibit others from doing so.

Copyright Act The federal law that governs copyrights. 17 U.S.C. § 101 and following sections.

Copyright Clause Article I, Section 8 of the U.S. Constitution. It also covers patents and is sometimes referred to as the Patent Clause.

copyright infringement Use of copyrighted material without either permission or a fair use.

copyright notice Notice to the public that material is copyrighted. For legal purposes, it must be in the following form: © (or the word "copyright") followed by the date and the author.

corporation An entity owned by its shareholders and legally distinct from its owners.

cyberspace The computer network over which online communication takes place. The Internet.

defamation A false statement about an identifiable person that is communicated to others and harms the person's reputation.

defendant The person a claim is filed against. One who defends against a claim filed in court.

derivative work A work based on one or more preexisting works. Translations, musical arrangements, dramatizations, fictionalizations, motion pictures, sound recordings, art reproductions, abridgments, condensations, and annotated versions are all derivative works.

descriptive mark A name, symbol, or device that describes the particular goods or services it identifies. Descriptive marks cannot be trademarks unless they have developed a secondary meaning that associates them with a particular product (brand or manufacturer) or service.

Digital Millennium Copyright Act Law governing service provider liability for copyright infringement by users of the service. Also known as the DMCA. 17 U.S.C. § 512.

dilution When someone other than the trademark owner (1) uses a famous trademark without permission and (2) the use waters down the effectiveness or harms the reputation of the trademark.

direct infringement Using copyrighted material without permission or a fair use.

distinctive mark A trademark that is readily identified with a particular product or service (e.g., a brand or manufacturer rather than a product type).

DMCA See Digital Millennium Copyright Act.

doing business as A fictitious or assumed name that is different from the name of the individual or legal entity using it for business purposes. "Doing business as" names may have to be registered with a state or local government.

dramatization A work adapted as a movie, play, or similar presentation.

e-book A book the reader will read on a screen or download and print.

e-publishing Any form of publishing that delivers a product the reader will read on a screen or download and print.

estate planning Making legal preparations for the distribution of assets after death.

estimated taxes Quarterly payments to the IRS to cover the federal income and self-employment taxes a sole proprietor expects to owe for the tax year.

exclusive arrangement (agents) When an author and a literary agent agree that the author will not use another agent for the same work. May also prohibit the author from acting as his or her own agent while the agreement is in effect.

exclusive rights (copyright) The right to reproduce, distribute, perform, or display a copyrighted work or to prepare derivative works from the copyrighted work.

executor A person appointed by a will to wrap up the affairs and distribute the property left by the deceased person who made the will.

fair use An exception to copyright protection that allows certain uses without infringing the copyright.

famous mark A trademark that is recognized by general consumers across the nation.

fanciful mark A trademark consisting of a made-up word or words.

First Amendment The first amendment to the United States Constitution. It includes clauses protecting free speech.

Freedom of Speech The First Amendment right to express ideas and opinions without government interference.

galley Proofs showing the pages as they will be printed in the final copy.

generic mark A name, symbol, or device that refers to an entire group or class of goods or services. Generic marks do not qualify as trademarks.

ghostwriter A writer who is paid to write a book attributed to someone else.

grant-of-rights clause A clause in a publishing contract that establishes who owns the copyright and who gets to exercise specific rights that belong to the copyright owner.

heir A person who inherits property from someone who dies without a will.

hobby (writing as) Writing for recreation without caring whether it makes a profit.

implied contract An unwritten contract implied from facts and circumstances that show the parties understood and agreed on the basic terms.

imprint The name that identifies a particular publishing company.

indemnification A promise to pay another person's losses, particularly when the second person's losses resulted from the first person's actions.

infringement Using someone else's intellectual property right, such as a copyright or trademark, without permission or a fair use.

injunction A court order prohibiting a party from engaging in specified conduct or ordering a party to take a specified action.

intestate Dying without a will.

intrusion Intruding into someone's private space or affairs.

joint accounting When the royalties from one book can be used to pay off the advance for another book.

joint authorship The joint ownership of a copyright in a joint work.

joint work A work prepared by two or more authors who intend that their contributions become inseparable parts of a unified whole.

kill fee Money received by a writer in payment for work on am assigned magazine article that the publisher subsequently decides not to publish.

Lanham Act The federal law that governs trademarks. 15 U.S.C. § 1051 and following.

legatee A person who inherits property under a will.

libel Written defamation.

license (business) Formal permission from a federal, state, or local government to engage in particular business activities.

license (copyright, trademark) Permission to use someone else's copyright or trademark for certain purposes or under certain conditions. Usually refers to situations where the person receiving the license pays for the permission.

limited liability company An entity that combines the limited liability given to owners of a corporation with the tax advantages of a sole proprietorship.

list price The price printed on the cover of a book. Also referred to as the retail price or the cover price.

LLC See limited liability company.

magazine rights The publication rights a magazine receives when it buys an article, short story, poem, or other item. There are many types of magazine rights.

mass market paperback A smaller paperback, usually 4 inches by 7 inches, designed for large print runs.

mediation Using a neutral third party to help the parties settle a dispute. Traditional mediation is nonbinding.

negligence Failing to exercise the care a reasonable person would exercise under the same circumstances.

net price The price the publisher actually receives for a book (as distinguished from the list price). The price may or may not be net of the publisher's costs.

nominative use When someone other than the trademark owner uses a trademark to refer to the trademark owner's goods.

offer A proposal to enter into a contract with specific terms. The contract does not become binding until the offer is accepted.

option clause A clause in a publishing contract that gives the publisher the right, but not the obligation, to publish the author's next book.

parody For legal purposes, a work that comments on the substance or style of the original work in such a way as to make the original appear ridiculous. A successful parody is one where people recognize the subject of the parody while distinguishing the parody from that subject.

passing off When a counterfeiter tries to pass a similar product off as the original.

patent The temporary right to prohibit others from manufacturing, using, or selling an invention.

PDF Portable Document Format. A format for creating and distributing digital documents.

permission Authorization from a copyright holder or trademark owner to use any of the rights conveyed by the copyright or trademark.

plagiarism Using someone else's work without crediting the author. The work does not have to be under copyright.

plaintiff A person who files a complaint in court. This is the person who starts the lawsuit.

POD See print on demand.

presumption An assumption that a particular fact is correct. A rebuttable presumption can be proved incorrect.

primary rights The main rights a publisher intends to use. Generally, this refers to the right to publish a book in paper form and may include the right to publish an e-book.

print on demand A digital process used to print only as many books as are needed at a particular moment. Also referred to as POD.

private individual For First Amendment purposes, this term refers to a person who is neither a public official nor a public person.

public domain A work that has no copyright protection is in the public domain.

public figure For First Amendment purposes, this term refers to a person who is in the public eye, such as a celebrity, a business leader, or an activist.

public official For First Amendment purposes, this term refers to someone who is in public office (whether elected or appointed) or is a candidate for public office.

registration (business) Registering with a state or local government or obtaining a license to engage in a particular business activity.

registration (copyright) Registering a copyright with the U.S. Copyright Office.

registration (trademark) Registering a trademark with the U.S. Patent and Trademark Office or with a state.

representation (agent) When an agent agrees to work for an author to try to place the author's work with a publisher.

representation (warranty) A representation in a contract is a statement that a particular fact is true when the contract is entered into and will continue to be true for the duration of the contract.

reserve against returns Royalties that are withheld against the possibility that books will be returned to the publisher.

reverse passing off When a person misrepresents someone else's goods or services as his own.

reversion clause A clause in a publishing contract that says when all rights to the work will return to the copyright owner.

right of first refusal The right to the first chance to accept (or refuse) something, such as publishing a second book or revising an outdated work.

right of publicity An individual's legal right to control the commercial use of his/her name or image.

right to privacy An individual's legal right to be left alone and to keep one's private life private unless the information is newsworthy.

rights (copyright) The rights conveyed by copyright ownership.

royalty Payment to an author for each book sold. Usually a percentage of the list or sales price.

sales taxes Taxes owed to a state or local government on an author's book sales.

satire A literary work in which human vice or folly is attacked using irony, derision, or wit. For legal purposes, a satire is different than a parody, which must comment on the substance or style of the original work in such a way as to make the original appear ridiculous.

scènes à faire Story elements that arise naturally from an unprotectable idea.

self-employment taxes The equivalent of a self-employment social security tax.

self-publishing When the author is the publishing company for a particular book.

service mark Any word, name, symbol, or device that makes people think of a particular service vendor. Often lumped in with trademarks.

sole proprietorship When an individual conducts a business without creating a separate legal entity. The sole proprietorship and the individual are the same person.

statutory damages Damages specifically authorized by statute.

statute A law adopted by Congress or a state legislature.

subagent An agent hired by a literary agent to handle subsidiary rights that are outside the original agent's expertise.

subsidiary rights The secondary rights that may be transferred to a publisher. These are rights that the publisher may not use itself but may seek to lease to someone else.

subsidy publishing A hybrid between traditional publishing and self-publishing. In a subsidy publishing arrangement, the author pays money up-front to the publisher and receives either a percentage or a set amount on each book sold. Sometimes called vanity publishing.

substantial similarity A legal test for determining whether one work has been copied from another.

suggestive mark A trademark consisting of a word, symbol, or device that suggests, but does not describe, the particular goods or services it identifies.

termination at will The ability to terminate a contract at any time with reasonable notice.

TESS The Trademark Electronic Search System for federally registered trademarks and service marks. TESS is run by the U.S. Patent and Trademark Office.

trademark Any word, name, symbol, or device that makes people think of a particular product or group of products. Sometimes includes service marks.

trademark dilution When someone other than the trademark owner (1) uses a famous trademark without permission and (2) the use waters down the effectiveness or harms the reputation of the trademark.

trademark infringement Use of a trademark without either permission or a fair use.

trade paperback A larger paperback, usually from 5 inches by 8 inches to 7 inches by 10 inches.

traditional publishing When a publisher that is independent of the author takes all of the financial risk for producing a book and pays the author royalties and maybe an advance.

trust A legal entity created to hold, manage, and distribute property for the benefit of others.

trustee A person who manages and distributes property owned by a trust.

Universal Copyright Convention A copyright treaty that dictates the use of the copyright notice.

useful articles Useful objects that include ornamental designs.

useful arts The term used in the Copyright Clause to describe creative works.

USPTO United States Patent and Trademark Office.

vicarious infringement Receiving a financial benefit from someone else's copyright infringement if the person had the power to stop it and did not.

warranty A warranty in a contract is a promise that a particular fact is true when the contract is entered into and will continue to be true for the duration of the contract.

will A written document stating how the person's assets will be distributed upon his or her death.

work for hire/work made for hire A work 1) prepared by an employee within the
    scope of his or her employment or 2) specially commissioned and agreed to be a
    work for hire that meets the requirements set out in 17 U.S.C. § 101. The
    employer or person who commissioned the work is the author of the work for
    legal purposes.

zoning laws Laws or ordinances that say how people can use property in a particular
    location.

Case Index

General Index

Pregnant by Mistake—63, 65-66

Pring, Kimerli—89

print on demand—133, 152, 221–222, 307

procedures (copyrightability)—20, 26, 230

Promised Land, The—84–85

public domain—67–69, 78, 210–211, 215, 230, 250, 307

public figures—97, 102, 106, 110–111, 114–116, 307

public officials—110, 111, 114–116, 307

public records—102

Rachel Weeping—63, 65–66

RDR Books—28, 50

recipes—24, 25, 26, 45, 52

Red Hat Club, The—94

registration (business)—185–187, 225–226, 238, 239, 307

registration (copyright)—19, 29–31, 68, 77, 222, 232, 237, 261, 307

registration (trademark)—208, 226, 239, 259, 261, 307

Rent—32

representation by an agent—156–159, 235–236, 307

representations (warranties)—147–148, 159, 165, 224, 234, 237, 307

reprint rights (magazines)—168–169, 237

reserve against returns—132–133, 233, 307

reverse passing off—215–216, 307

reversion clauses—151–153, 307

revision clauses— 146, 234

Reyher, Rebecca— 47–48

right of publicity—106–107, 231–232, 308

right to privacy—99–107, 231–232, 308

Rivera, Geraldo—87–88

Rogers, Ginger—213–214, 217

"Rosa Parks"—214

Rowling, J.K.—49–50

royalties—32, 123, 129–133, 146, 148, 152, 158, 161–162, 164, 191, 196–201, 220–221, 233, 235, 239–240, 308

Rushdie, Salman—16

sales taxes—186–187, 191, 225, 239, 308

Salinger, J.D.—48–49, 56, 62, 64, 257

satire—62, 211–213 , 308

satisfactory manuscript clauses—135–139, 233

scènes à faire—22, 47, 308

Scrabble—51, 124–125

second rights (magazines)—168–169

second serialization rights (books)—134

Seinfeld, Jessica—52

Seinfeld—44, 49, 51

self-employment taxes—185–186, 191, 239, 308

self-publishing—183–184, 219–227, 237–238, 239, 308

Sellers, Eschol—21, 96

service marks—205–206, 308

Sidis, William—102, 105, 253

Simpson, O.J.—62

simultaneous rights (magazines)—169, 237

slogans—20, 21, 229

Smith, Haywood—94

Sneaky Chef, The—45, 52

www.ingramcontent.com/pod-product-compliance
Lightning Source LLC
Chambersburg PA
CBHW031145270326
41931CB00006B/149